# W O M E N
# IN MODERN
# AMERICA:
## A Brief History

Third Edition

# W O M E N
# IN MODERN
# AMERICA:
## A BRIEF HISTORY
### Third Edition

## Lois W. Banner

University of Southern California

**Harcourt Brace College Publishers**

Fort Worth  Philadelphia  San Diego  New York  Orlando  Austin  San Antonio
Toronto  Montreal  London  Sydney  Tokyo

| | |
|---|---|
| **Publisher** | Ted Buchholz |
| **Senior Acquisitions Editor** | Drake Bush |
| **Assistant Editor** | Kristie Kelly |
| **Project Editor** | Jeff Beckham |
| **Production Manager** | Tom Urquhart |
| **Art Director** | Sue Hart |
| **Picture Development Editor** | Sandra Lord |

COVER IMAGE: © Susan Lapides 1980/Design Conceptions

FRONTISPIECE: Culver Pictures

Requests for permission to make copies of any part of the work should be mailed to: Permissions Department, Harcourt Brace & Company, 6277 Sea Harbor Drive, Orlando, Florida 32887-6777.

Address for Editorial Correspondence: Harcourt Brace College Publishers, 301 Commerce Street, Suite 3700, Fort Worth, TX 76102.

Address for Orders: Harcourt Brace & Company, 6277 Sea Harbor Drive, Orlando, Florida 32887. 1-800-782-4479, or 1-800-433-0001 (in Florida).

Acknowledgments and permissions appear on page 295, which constitutes a continuation of this copyright page.

Printed in the United States of America

ISBN: 0-15-500948-6

Library of Congress Catalog Card Number: 93-80821

4 5 6 7 8 9 0 1 2 3   039   9 8 7 6 5 4 3 2 1

# PREFACE

Until the mid-1960s, the history of women was neglected by historians. A few general works were written from time to time, but most authors assumed that the women's suffrage movement was all there was to it. Increasing concern with social history on the part of historians and the advent of a new feminist movement coincided to stimulate studies about women. The result has been to create a field of historical investigation that seeks to rescue both major figures and the ordinary woman from obscurity and provide a corrective to the traditional histories from which women are absent.

This book examines the history of women in America from 1890 to the present. Three periods, each characterized by distinctive qualities, seem to stand out. The first, from 1890 to 1920, was one of energy and innovation. Many of the traditional discriminations against women came to an end, and an impressive number of feminist and women's reform groups were organized. The second period, from 1920 to 1960, was one of greater complacency about women's problems. The nation struggled with economic depression and war, and feminist groups declined in vitality. The third period, from 1960 to the present, witnessed the emergence of a feminism more radical than any of its predecessors.

In my study of this era, I have had three aims: to explore the reasons why feminism rose and fell and rose again; to examine the history of various groups of women, including the working class, women of color, immigrants, farm women, and the middle class, each of which responded to the pressures and opportunities of the times in a different way; and, finally, to focus on the dramatic and continuing struggle waged by determined, innovative women to achieve their rights.

I have attempted to examine and correlate the complex factors that have affected women's lives. Common strains run through every period. One has been the influence of a society undergoing rapid changes. These changes have included the progress of industrialization and the move to the cities; changing attitudes toward sex and marriage; the growing power of the mass media; the expansion of the economy and certain occupations within it, such as secretarial work; two world wars that opened up new jobs for women; a depression and a war that made the family seem a haven of stability and security; and technological advances that offered women more leisure time.

A second factor influencing women in America throughout these years has been the overriding discrimination against women in every area of their lives, whether they have been seeking education, jobs, justice under the law, or simply the freedom to lead their lives as they see fit.

A third factor has been the dichotomized and abiding images of woman as either "good" or "bad." Women have predominantly been portrayed either as a wife, mother, homemaker, and repository of human virtue on the one hand (the "Virgin Mary" image of Christian belief) or on the other as the "evil" temptress (the Pandora of classical mythology and the Eve of Judeo-Christian belief). These two stereotypes have dominated thinking about women throughout the history of western culture, and they continue to exist today. They have also existed in both similar and different forms as applied to women of other races and ethnicities. Thus within the white mind, Indian women were either "Pocahontas," descendants of the noble Native American woman who rescued John Smith from death in colonial Virginia; or they have been seen as "squaws," sexual, stupid women who too easily cohabited with white men.

When it came to black women, the stereotyping, if anything, was even more vicious, for whites held no strong image of African-American women as virtuous. Instead, black women were seen either as mammies, broad of both body and grin, simple and happy, willing to devote their lives to domesticity on behalf of white families; or they were "Sapphira," again an overly sexual woman always ready for sexual intercourse.

Finally, in the figures of the Virgin of Guadeloupe and La Malinche, Mexican Americans have expressed their own sense of victimization through conquest. The Virgin of Guadeloupe, revered by the Mexican Catholic church, the country's dominant religion, is the mother protector, woman as total virtue. La Malinche was an

Aztec noblewoman who was given to Cortés as a slave when he landed in Mexico and who became his translator and lover. She is seen as an evil goddess, the mother-whore who created a new mixed Spanish-Indian race. This history of women is also a history of feminism, a term that is difficult to define precisely. Generally, "feminism" has meant the advocacy of the rights of women. But the view of what constitutes those rights has changed since the mid-nineteenth century, especially since the term "feminism," first coined in France, was introduced in this country in about 1910. Subsequently, "feminism" came to replace the standard nineteenth-century term "woman's rights." To solve the problem of definition, different terms are used to distinguish the various kinds of feminism. I use the term *feminist* broadly to apply to those men and women who have consciously worked to end discriminations against women and to gain gender equality. *Radical feminist* refers to those who envision a fundamental reordering of society and/or gender relationships as necessary to achieve equality. For those feminists whose position is uncompromisingly hostile to patterns or institutions of discrimination, I use the term *militant*. *Social feminist* (a term first coined by historian William O'Neill) applies to activists for whom working for social reforms (generally involving women) takes priority over such strictly women's causes as suffrage or the Equal Rights Amendment. Finally, *domestic feminists* are those who argue that a fundamental solution to women's problems lies in raising the status of homemaking and ending the common deprecation of domesticity and motherhood within American culture.

To help the reader who wishes to pursue any particular aspect of this history more fully, I have provided a critical bibliography at the end of each chapter.

I would like to acknowledge Phyllis Palmer of George Washington University, who reviewed the second edition and provided suggestions for this edition. I would also like to acknowledge the editorial assistance of Drake Bush and Kristie Kelly, and the production assistance of Jeff Beckham, Sue Hart, Tom Urquhart, and Sandra Lord, all of Harcourt Brace College Publishers.

Lois W. Banner

# TABLE OF CONTENTS

Chapter 1   THE EMERGENCE OF THE MODERN AMERICAN
            WOMAN: THE 1890s
**WOMEN'S STATUS IN 1890**   1
   Legal Codes   1
   Educational Opportunities   2
   Occupations   5
   Medicine and Sexuality   10
   A "Strange New Note"   13
   Aging Women; Menopause 15
   Women's Organizations   15
   Public Image—The "Gibson Girl"   19
**ROOTS OF CHANGE**   21
   Dress Reform   23
   Expansion of the Women's Labor Force   26
   New Inroads   26
      Women in College   26
      Women in Medicine and Law   28
      Women in Journalism   30
      Conservative Arguments Produce Progressive Results   30
   Men—A Help and a Hindrance   31
   Technology and Housekeeping   35
   Women's Separate Culture   35
   **NOTES**   36
   **BIBLIOGRAPHY**   38

Chapter 2   THE AMERICAN WOMAN FROM 1900 TO
            THE FIRST WORLD WAR: A PROFILE
**THE MAIN PROSPECT—MARRIAGE AND
MOTHERHOOD**   45
   The Middle-Class Wife   46
   Rural Women: Midwestern, Southern, Southwestern   48
**THE WORKING-CLASS WOMEN**   53
   Immigration and Ethnicity   53
      Asian Immigration   57
      African-American Women   60
      Working Conditions   62
      Strikes and Unions   64

Married Life and the Working-Class Community   69
Native Americans   71
**THE OTHER WAY—PROSTITUTION**   73
The Practitioners   75
**THE NEW SENSUALITY**   76
The World of the Waitress   78
**NOTES**   79
**BIBLIOGRAPHY**   80

Chapter 3   **WOMEN AS ORGANIZERS AND INNOVATORS:
SUFFRAGE, REFORM, AND FEMINISM,
1890-1920**
**SUFFRAGISM ON THE WANE**   87
**FEMINISM AND PROGRESSIVISM: A CASE OF GIVE AND
TAKE**   91
The Organizations: Growth and Changing Goals   92
Ethnic and Black Women's Organization   97
Progressive Reform and Settlement Houses   99
A Measure of Success   100
**THE RADICALS**   102
A Ferment of New Ideas   102
A New Breed of Scholars   104
Feminist Action Groups: A Faint Voice   105
**SHAKY GROUNDS FOR ARGUMENT**   108
Women's Frailty and Special Legislation   108
Housekeepers in Government—and Out   109
Suffrage as a Cure-All   110
Sex versus Soul   111
**TWO GENERATIONS**   114
**SUFFRAGE ACHIEVED**   115
A United Front   115
Tactics and Techniques   117
The Aftermath of Victory   120
**NOTES**   122
**BIBLIOGRAPHY**   124

Chapter 4   **THE 1920S: FREEDOM OR DISILLUSIONMENT?**
**WOMEN'S ORGANIZATIONS IN TRANSITION**   130
The Sheppard-Towner Act: Successes and Failures   134
**ANTIFEMINIST UNDERCURRENTS AND FEMINIST
CONSERVATISM**   136
**"FLAMING YOUTH"—NEW LIBERTIES,
OLD ATTITUDES**   143
**WOMEN AT WORK: PROGRESS AND SETBACKS**   148
Professional Women   148

**LATINA IMMIGRATION: WOMEN, WORK, AND ACCULTURATION**   153
**WORKING-CLASS WORKING WOMEN**   156
**THE NEW HEROINES**   158
  **NOTES**   164
  **BIBLIOGRAPHY**   165

**Chapter 5   WOMEN IN DEPRESSION AND WAR**
**FEMINISM AND WOMEN'S ORGANIZATIONS**   171
  Southern Women and the Antilynching Movement   172
**ELEANOR ROOSEVELT: EXEMPLAR OF HER ERA**   174
**THE WOMEN'S NETWORK AND NEW DEAL PROGRAMS**   179
  The NRA: Benefits and Drawbacks   182
**CHANGES FOR THE WORKING WOMAN**   185
**LATIN- AND AFRICAN-AMERICAN WOMEN**   187
**UNIONS IN AN AGE OF DEPRESSION**   189
**THE SECURITIES OF MARRIAGE IN AN INSECURE AGE**   193
**FASHIONS AND MOVIES:  OLD AND NEW IMAGES**   199
**AFRICAN-AMERICAN WOMEN AND POPULAR CULTURE**   203
**WOMEN AS PART OF THE WAR EFFORT**   205
  **NOTES** 210
  **BIBLIOGRAPHY**   212

**Chapter 6   FEMINISM COMES OF AGE: 1945-1970**
**A GENERAL CONSENSUS ON WOMAN'S ROLE**   217
  Women Under Attack   217
  Expert Opinion: Freud and Functionalism   219
  The Evidence from Popular Culture   220
  The Back-to-the-Home Movement   222
    Sex and Childrearing   227
  Feminism in the 1950s   227
  The Reemergence of Domestic Feminism   229
**EVIDENCE TO THE CONTRARY**   230
  New Economic, Demographic, and Medical Factors   230
  The New Trends—Revolutionary or Not?   232
**THE SHIFT TO MILITANCY**   233
  A New Reform Climate   233
  New Faces and the Formation of NOW   239
  Minority Protest   244
  Women of Color Organize   248
  Lesbians, Gays, and the Stonewall Riot   249

**NOTES**    250

**BIBLIOGRAPHY**    251

**Chapter 7    PROGRESS AND BACKLASH: 1970-1993**

**THE FEMINIST POSITION IN THE 1970s**

Marriage and the Family: "Equality" versus "Difference"
Feminists    260

**FEMINIST ACHIEVEMENTS AND THE HOUSTON
NATIONAL WOMEN'S CONFERENCE**    263

**BACKLASH**    265

The New Right    266

Prolife and Prochoice    268

Backlash in the Media, in Appearance, in the Movies    270

The Men's Movement    273

Robert Bly in the Context of Feminist Spirituality    274

**THE FEMINIST MOVEMENT: UNITED AND DIVIDED**    275

Lesbians    275

Women of Color    277

**RECENT IMMIGRATION**    280

**THE RECENT SITUATION**    281

**WOMEN AND AGING IN CONTEMPORARY TIMES**    286

**THE PRESENT—REVOLUTIONARY OR NOT?**    287

**NOTES**    290

**BIBLIOGRAPHY**    290

**PHOTO CREDITS**    295

**INDEX**    296

# 1

# THE EMERGENCE OF THE MODERN AMERICAN WOMAN: THE 1890s

" **A** T THE OPENING of the twentieth century," wrote suffragist Ida Husted Harper, women's status "had been completely transformed in most respects."[1] Her judgment was only partially correct. Much had been gained for women by 1900, but much remained to be achieved. During the 1890s, the advances for women began to add up to significant progress, and women's organizations entered a period of rapid growth. But discrimination still existed in every area of women's experience.

## WOMEN'S STATUS IN 1890

### Legal Codes

By 1890, states had come a long way in amending discriminatory laws against women. Many states had modified the common law doctrine of *femme couverte*, under which wives had been chattels of their husbands, with no direct control over their earnings, children, or property, unless a premarital agreement had been negotiated and their property placed in trust. (Such restrictions did not apply to single women, *femme sole* under the common law.) New laws in many states gave wives control over their inherited property and their earnings, although in 14 states, earnings still belonged to husbands. In 37 states, married women were still denied rights over their children, although in the case of divorce the practice increasingly was to award children to mothers, in line with the Victorian conviction that women by nature were best able to raise children.

In every state voting laws still discriminated against women. In some states, women could vote in local school-board and municipal elections, but only four states allowed women to vote in state and federal elections. These states were Wyoming, Utah, Colorado, and Idaho. In 1874, the Supreme Court ruled unanimously in *Minor v. Happersett* that voting was not coextensive with citizenship (as

*The suffragist executive committee, including foreign delegates, that arranged the first International Council in 1888. In the front row are Susan B. Anthony (second from left) and Elizabeth Cady Stanton (fourth from left).*

feminists argued); thus, the states could withhold the vote from women. In some states, women could not enter into business partnerships without the consent of their husbands; in most states, husbands had the right to determine where the family would live.

Such discriminatory laws varied from state to state. It has taken a century of feminist agitation to abolish them; some are still on the books. As late as 1930, for example, one-fourth of the states did not allow wives to make contracts, and married women's property rights over real estate were not equal to their husbands' in 17 states.

### Educational Opportunities

In education, women had made more promising gains. At the beginning of the nineteenth century, it was difficult for women to secure any education. No colleges accepted them. In many areas

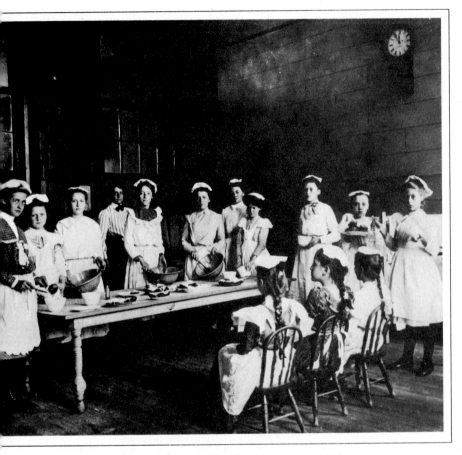

*A domestic science class in a public school in the early 1900s.*

of the country, public grammar schools as well as private academies restricted their pupils to boys or allowed girls to attend only in the summer, when sons worked on family farms and classrooms were vacant. It was considered sufficient that girls learn to read and write, and they could acquire these skills from their mothers or at local "dame" schools established for that purpose. The educated woman was regarded with suspicion for leaving the domestic sphere. Mockingly, women with education or woman's rights inclinations were called "bluestockings." This term derived from the

*Vassar College advertises for students in The American Agriculturist, April 1877.*

# Vassar College,

## For the Higher Education of Women,

### POUGHKEEPSIE, NEW YORK.

#### J. H. RAYMOND, LL.D., President.

### ADMISSION.

Applicants for admission to the College must be at least sixteen years of age, and must present satisfactory testimonials of character. None are received for a shorter period than till the close of the current collegiate year.

### REGULAR STUDIES.

Mental and Moral Philosophy, The Greek, Latin, French, German and English Languages and their Literatures. Rhetoric, Mathematics, Astronomy, Physics, Natural History, Chemistry, Physiology, and Hygiene.

### ART STUDIES.

Vocal, Piano and Organ Music, Painting and Drawing.
Every department of instruction is under the direction of an able Professor, assisted by competent Teachers.

### THE COLLEGE HOME.

The College is situated two miles east of Poughkeepsie. Street-cars run regularly to and from the city. The Western Union Telegraph Company has an office in the College.

The College buildings are warmed by steam, lighted with gas, and supplied with an abundance of pure water. Bathing-rooms and other needful conveniences are amply provided.

All the students are members of the College family, and are subject to its regulations. The domestic and social life is under the supervision of the Lady Principal.

The grounds, embracing two hundred acres, with several miles of gravel walks, a flower-garden, lake, and the well-furnished Gymnasium, afford ample scope for healthful recreation.

A regular physician, residing in the College, devotes her entire time to the care of its health.

There are daily prayers in the Chapel, and a religious service and Bible classes every Sunday.

### EXPENSES.

The uniform price of Board and Tuition for all students, whether regular, special, or preparatory, is $400 for the College year; of which $300 is payable in advance, and the balance on the first day of March following.

No extra charge is made, except for private lessons in art studies; for which the additional charges are as follows, payable three quarters in advance:

Pianoforte, two lessons a week and one
practice period daily.................. $100 per annum.
Organ, two lessons a week and one prac-
tice period daily.... ................. 100     "
Solo Singing, two lessons a week and
one practice period daily............ 100     "
Thorough-Bass and Composition, two
lessons a week........................ 80      "
Drawing, Painting, or Modelling, two
lessons a week........................ 80      "

A nominal charge is made for medical attendance.

### ENTRANCE EXAMINATIONS.

The entrance examinations for the year 1877-78 commence on Wednesday, September 19, 1877, and continue three days, from 9 a. m. until 5 p. m., with an intermission of one hour and a half for dinner.

### CORRESPONDENCE.

Letters respecting departments of instruction, admission or dismission of students, etc., should be addressed to the President; Letters respecting Finances to Matthew Vassar, Jr., Treasurer; other business letters to William F. Forby, General Superintendent.

☞ CATALOGUES containing full particulars may be obtained by addressing WILLARD L. DEAN, Registrar, Poughkeepsie, N. Y.

blue stockings worn by some members of women's intellectual groups in England in the 1750s. By the end of the century, however, elementary and secondary education was available to women. In fact, because boys more often than girls dropped out of high school to seek gainful employment, by 1890 more girls than boys were graduating from high school. Higher education, too, was open to women by then. Before the Civil War, enterprising men and women had founded private academies for women, and a number of states had established teacher-training schools, known as "normal schools," which attracted mostly women students. A few colleges, too, had opened their doors to women during the antebellum period—notably Oberlin in 1837 and Antioch in 1853. In the years after the Civil War, numerous colleges for women were established, particularly in the Northeast, where the elite male colleges were especially opposed to coeducation. The women's colleges included Vassar (1865), Wellesley (1875), Smith (1875), and Bryn Mawr (1885). In 1893, Mount Holyoke Seminary, founded in 1837 as a high school, gained collegiate status. In these same years, many state institutions, particularly in the Midwest and the West, ended their restrictions against women, and new private coeducational colleges appeared. By 1900, 80 percent of the colleges, universities, and professional schools in the nation admitted women.

This significant educational gain was crucial to the expansion of women's roles in the 1890s and 1900s. Women were now able to enter such statused professions as law and medicine, while their newfound education gave them the self-confidence and critical perception to question their position in American society. Most college-trained women became elementary-school teachers, and most professional schools admitted only a few women. Still, that women were going to school and gaining knowledge and self-confidence was fundamental to the growth of the women's movement in the late nineteenth and early twentieth centuries.

## Occupations

The employment situation for women was more ambiguous. True, more women had jobs: in 1870, about 15 percent of all women over 16 years of age were regularly employed away from home for wages; by 1900, the figure had risen to 20 percent. Women were being taught new employment skills, including typing

*Women harvesting hops on an upstate New York farm in the 1880s.*

and stenography, and they were beginning to dominate such professions as nursing and teaching. Women had even forced their way into the professions of ministry, law, and medicine over the course of the century. In the theater, prima donnas such as Lillian Russell and Lily Langtry commanded huge salaries and avid newspaper publicity. In 1840 Harriet Martineau, prominent English feminist and author, contended that only seven occupations in the United States were open to women: teaching, needlework, keeping boarders, setting type, working as servants, or laboring in bookbinding and cotton factories. But by 1890 women were represented in all but nine of the 369 occupations listed in the federal census.

From the census of 1910, we can discern what kinds of work women did. Over 50 percent of working women were employed as farm workers or as domestic servants: 18 percent in the former occu-

*Woman employed in a shoe factory, circa 1905.*

pation and 37 percent in the latter. Nearly 30 percent of working women were employed in manufacturing; 8 percent, in professions (mostly as teachers and nurses); 5 percent, in clerical occupations; and about 4 percent, in trade (mostly as saleswomen). A small number of women were classified in transportation and in public service, primarily as telephone and telegraph operators.

Yet there was still significant discrimination against working women. In almost every category of work, skills were divided into men's and women's jobs. This division resulted partly from women's propensity to seek employment related to their traditional work in the home. In the field of manufacturing, which employed a sizable minority of working women by 1900, most women worked in clothesmaking, textile, and millinery factories; in commercial food production; and in the cigar, tobacco, and shoemaking industries, for which women had previously done piecework in their homes.

In all these industries, women performed the less prestigious and lower-paid tasks. For example, in the women's garment industry, which by the early twentieth century was one of the largest

*A typical office scene, when men still dominated the clerical labor force.*

employers of factory women, men were the cutters and pressers (positions of higher authority and pay) and women were the sewers and finishers. This situation existed partly because most factory women were young and unmarried and therefore transient members of the work force. In general, however, women had little chance for advancement. They were the assemblers, not the skilled operatives. At best, a long-term female employee might be promoted to forewoman over a group of female workers. But even in this position, she could expect to be paid less than male foremen, just as women workers across the board were paid less than male workers, even when their jobs were similar.

This division between men's work and women's work was also characteristic of the professions. Women who became doctors and

*As the need for clerical work increased in the early 1900s, women replaced men because they could be paid lower wages.*

lawyers typically undertook tasks related to female roles. They could expect less remuneration for their services than men, although dedicated woman's rights advocates might seek them out. Most women lawyers performed quasi-office work, collecting claims or preparing probate papers. One woman doctor in general practice, who found attracting patients almost impossible, recounted a tale she thought characteristic. Finally sought out by a mother with a sick child, she discovered that her new client presumed that the rates of a "lady" doctor would be less than those of a "real" doctor.[2]

The majority of women who entered the professions became teachers and nurses, in line with women's traditional family roles of instructing the young and nursing the ailing. And as women moved into teaching and nursing in large numbers, men either left these fields to pursue other careers or moved up to more elite positions. Subsequently pay and status decreased. "Feminization" is the term sociologists have coined for this pattern of lessened pay and status as women become the majority in a profession. By 1910, 77 percent of all teachers were women. Like women factory workers, women teachers were predominantly young and single, and many school systems prohibited them from continuing to teach if they married. They clustered in elementary-school positions, while men dominated university teaching and administrative positions in elementary and secondary schools.

Such a pattern was evident in librarianship and also in clerical labor, which more than any other occupation has come to characterize women's work in the twentieth century. The field first opened to women when typewriter manufacturers discovered that attractive women demonstrators sold more machines than male demonstrators. Then, as clerical work underwent a rapid expansion during this period of business growth, it became apparent that women could be paid less then men. Once women became typists and stenographers, men left the clerical field, which they had previously dominated. Some moved up to sales and managerial positions, where they earned higher salaries and more prestige. Office work, with higher status and pay for women than factory work, had its problems. For several decades, typists were known as "typewriters," and this confusion between women and their machines was the subject of jokes in offices and in popular journalism alike.

### Medicine and Sexuality

The 1890s were also a time of advance in the medical treatment of women and in the medical and popular views of female sexuality. From 1850 to 1900, life expectancy for women rose from 40 to 51 years. This increase was partly due to improved sanitation as well as to improvements in medical care. New vaccines for diseases such as yellow fever headed the list of these advances, while developments in gynecological surgery made curable such debilitating female disorders as a prolapsed, or herniated, uterus—a condition not uncommon among women who have borne a number of children. The introduction of antiseptic techniques in delivering babies lessened the danger of puerperal fever, an infection of childbirth that had killed women and their newborns for centuries. The "hysterical" or neurotic woman who was unmarried might still be advised to marry to relieve her difficulty, while the surgical excision of the uterus, a procedure first attempted in 1881, was called a "hysterectomy." This term referenced the ancient belief that the uterus controlled female emotional functioning.

But women were being viewed more as human beings and less as fragile creatures prone to illness. After years of debate, reformers who advocated simple dress for women and attention to diet and exercise were gaining authority. For decades educators and doctors debated whether a woman's constitution could withstand the rigors of a college education. In 1873, Dr. Edward H. Clarke, in his influential *Sex in Education*, even contended that intensive studying would make a woman infertile. But by 1900, studies were showing that college women maintained good levels of health. Moreover, ministers no longer preached sermons, as they had earlier in the century, identifying women's presumed inferior physiology as part of the "curse" of Eve, whom God had more severely punished than Adam in the Garden of Eden because she had first taken the apple from the serpent. Women, however, commonly called menstruation "the curse."[3]

In addition, menstruation and childbirth were beginning to be considered natural functions, rather than illnesses during which women went to bed. And some progressive doctors such as Edward Bliss Foote, author of numerous editions from the 1880s through the 1900s of *Plain Home Talk on Love, Marriage, and Parentage*, challenged the Victorian notion that sexual intercourse was not pleasurable for women. Indeed, Foote even counseled in the 1904 edition that it was physiologically damaging for women to engage in intercourse if they did not enjoy it.

Yet many individuals were not open about sexual matters. Masturbation was commonly regarded as immoral and bound to result in bodily ailments and insanity. Sex was often a taboo subject between parents and children. Journalist Rheta Childe Dorr remembered that when a girl turned 14, scores of new rules were introduced, "and when you asked for an explanation, you met only embarrassed silence."[4] For many girls, the onset of menstruation was a shock because, given Victorian prudery, they had not been told about it. The bride who married knowing nothing about sex was not uncommon. Such was the experience of novelist Frances Parkinson Keyes, who married in 1904. In her middle-class circle, the mother of the bride was supposed to have "a little talk" with her daughter shortly before the wedding ceremony. But, explained Keyes, mothers were often so embarrassed during this conversation that they said nothing enlightening. Besides, continued Keyes,

"many mothers felt very strongly that prenuptial revelations about the marriage relationship would sully a young girl's innocence and make her less desirable. . . ."[5]
Nor had attitudes about childbirth changed everywhere. In the 1890s, Elizabeth Peabody, daughter of the wealthy Peabody family of Boston, was shocked when a schoolmate referred to one of her mother's yearly pregnancies. Frances Parkinson Keyes remained in bed for weeks before and after the birth of her first child, and she was stunned to discover that one of the maids, for whom there had been no hiatus in household labor, had given birth secretly and on her own to an illegitimate child shortly after Keyes' own carefully attended pregnancy and childbirth. The middle class could afford the fiction of the fragile female; for the working class, it was a different matter.[6]

In the latter part of the nineteenth century, restrictions on sex became even more strict as most states outlawed the sale of contraceptives and the dissemination of birth-control information. "Social purity" was an objective of many late nineteenth-century Victorians and even of many otherwise liberal reformers. Social-purity advocates comprised a heterogeneous group, including organizations like the Woman's Christian Temperance Union (WCTU) and the Young Women's Christian Association (YWCA). While many of these organizations worked to eliminate prostitution and venereal disease, epidemic in the early twentieth century, social-purity reformers were also an important group working for the open discussion of sexual issues. However, even many reformers held the view that birth control was a means, not of liberating women, but of freeing men to pursue their supposedly greater sexual urges outside of marriage.

In 1873, opposition to birth control gained momentum when Congress passed the so-called Comstock Law, named after its chief proponent—the single-minded anti-vice crusader, Anthony Comstock. This law banned the dissemination of pornography, abortion devices, and "any drug, medicine, article, or thing designed, adapted, or intended for preventing conception." Most states passed their own laws modeled after the Comstock statute. Birth control was thus cataloged with pornography as immoral, and there were overtones that birth control, like masturbation, sapped bodily energy and produced physical decay.

In the post-Civil War years, state laws also prohibited abortion. Under the common law, abortion had been permitted until "quickening," or the first felt movements of the fetus in the womb, occurring at about the fifth month of pregnancy. Once nineteenth-century scientists discovered that the sperm fertilized the egg soon after intercourse, some doctors became uneasy about defining life as beginning at the fifth month of gestation. They were also critical of poorly trained abortionists who used crude techniques. But many medical prohibitionists were also engaged in a drive to professionalize and thus control medical practice. Abortion prohibitions would help drive out of business alternatively trained physicians operating outside the medical establishment who had flourished in the early nineteenth century, employing homeopathic and other natural techniques.

Moreover, antiabortionists were concerned about evidence of the rising rate of abortions among white, middle-class women. By 1870, as many as one in five pregnancies among such women was being medically terminated. Conservative and nativist, the antiabortion doctors began to advance the kinds of "race suicide" arguments that Theodore Roosevelt would later popularize. Women of the middle class, they argued, were destroying the nation's fabric by reducing the number of their offspring in comparison with that of immigrant and working-class women. Even more, they were threatening the structure of the traditional family by taking measures to control its basic reproductive function.

Doctors were also assuming greater control over women's bodies by taking over the delivering of babies, formerly the task of female midwives, and by inventing the lucrative specialties of obstetrics and gynecology. Still, until the 1930s more babies would be delivered by midwives at home than by doctors in hospitals.

## A "Strange New Note"

Despite the prohibition on birth control and abortion, family size continued to decrease in the late nineteenth century, as it had since 1800. In 1804 the birth rate stood at about seven children per family; in 1880, at 4.24; and in 1900, at 3.56. Some historians consider this "demographic transition" to be the single most important factor in the history of modern women. It freed women from constant childbirth and allowed them flexibility in life choices. And the high rate of abortion among women indicates

*Lillian Russell, idol of theater audiences around the turn of the century.*

that women themselves supported reproductive control. What nineteenth-century woman's rights advocates called "voluntary motherhood" seemed to be widely popular. Whether couples employed continence, coitus interruptus, douching, or condoms (and historians disagree over what method was most popular), women were asserting control over their lives.

Writing about the frontier Illinois of her youth, Mary Austin dated women's decision to practice birth control there from about 1870. "The pioneer stress was over," she wrote, and with it had ended "the day of large families, families of from a dozen to fifteen." According to Austin, "a strange new note had come into the thinking of the granddaughters of the women who had borne their dozen or so cheerfully and with the conviction of the will of God strong in them." And this "strange new note," as Austin described it, grew out of women's yearning for a world outside the home.[7]

## Aging Women; Menopause

In addition to women's increased life expectancy and improved health care, new opportunities in the workforce and in voluntarism brought a more positive valuation of their aging. And, numbers of eminent women who remained vigorous into their older years ratified the new perception. Actresses such as Lily Langtry and Lillian Russell remained active on the stage into their 60s and 70s. Reformers such as Jane Addams and Lillian Wald launched new reform initiatives in their 50s and 60s, while older women dominated women's reform organizations. One commentator identified a "renaissance of the middle aged" in this era.[8]

Old medical notions of the dangers of menopause also began eroding, and some doctors even accepted folk beliefs that menopause was a positive, rather than a negative, experience. Others pointed to research showing that men as well as women experienced a midlife climacteric. Grandmothers were still viewed as doubly domestic beings, doting on grandchildren, but an alternative image portrayed them, with children gone, as individuals who could contribute to social betterment. And, an emerging beauty culture of beauty parlors and cosmetic companies began to cast them as consumers who could use commercial services and products to remain youthful.

For the most part, families cared for debilitated and indigent aging relatives in their own homes; while in ethnic and black cultures, in particular, aging women were accorded special authority, often serving as folk doctors and midwives. Yet ageism and attendant economic despair were major problems for older Americans, especially in eras without pension plans, Social Security payments, or old-age homes. State poorhouses and workhouses, established to deal with poverty through incarceration, were on the way out by the 1890s, but they still contained many old people who had no place else to go. Before the 1930s, however, aging was only of minimal concern to those formulating government social welfare policies.

## Women's Organizations

Women were beginning to view themselves differently, and their new consciousness led them increasingly to organize—not only to gain the vote, but also to achieve a variety of professional and

*A meeting of the Daughters of the American Revolution, 1898.*

reform goals. Women were active in the major farmer and labor organizations of the 1890s: the Knights of Labor, the Farmers' Alliances, and the Populist Party. As many as one-fourth of the members of the Southern Alliance were women, and Populist Party women were active as public speakers. Mary Elizabeth Lease, renowned as the orator who told farmers "to raise less corn and more hell," was replicated by others who crisscrossed the Midwest and the South.

The appearance of women doctors, lawyers, and college graduates resulted in the formation of professional women's associations, while women flocked into local women's clubs seeking education, culture, and involvement in civic concerns. In 1873, the WCTU was formed; in 1890, the national General Federation of Women's Clubs was organized. In that same year, the two branches of the women's suffrage movement, which had split in

1869, were reunited in the National American Woman Suffrage Association (NAWSA). Among the women's groups that appeared during the 1880s and 1890s were the YWCA, the Daughters of the American Revolution (DAR), the National Council of Women, the Association of Collegiate Alumnae (later to become the American Association of University Women), and the Congress of Mothers (later to become the National Parent-Teachers Association).

Even the Protestant churches experienced women organizing. Early in the century, women's auxiliaries to their missionary societies had been women's main form of church organization. These groups had served as precursors to women's antebellum temperance and abolitionist societies and women's service organizations during the Civil War. After 1865, denominational women's missionary boards came to dominate the religious missionary movement. Especially in the South, where traditionalism remained strong, women's organizations had a religious base. According to historian Anne Firor Scott, the public life of every Southern woman leader in this period began in a church society.[9] The largest of these societies was the Methodist Board of Foreign Missions. This group contributed to women's clubs and suffrage organizations and also initiated the social settlement movement in the South.

In 1893, women captured public attention by participating in the Chicago Columbian Exposition, a "world's fair" celebrating Columbus's discovery of America. A special woman's building at the fair housed a yearlong display of arts and handicrafts by women and provided a forum for speeches and conferences; it was designed by architect Julia Morgan. The participation of women in the exposition was a brilliant publicity stroke. Early in the nineteenth century, it had been considered a disgrace for a woman's name to appear in print. Now, as one observer noted, women were constantly "in the glare of publicity."[10]

Yet there were ominous overtones at this exposition of an overriding racism, even among woman's rights leaders. Among the many exhibitors at the woman's building, African-American women were not allowed to participate. Black leaders Fannie Barrier Williams and Julia Cooper gave speeches at the exposition identifying white women's racism. But it was not their message that predominated. Rather, the Betty Crocker baking company

*The "mammy" stereotype pre-dominated the black woman's public image at the turn of the century.*

hired a black woman of smiling demeanor and ample girth to make pancakes from their new pancake mix and to serve them at a booth on the fair's midway. She proved to be so popular that, dubbed "Aunt Jemima," she became a Betty Crocker trademark. The racist "mammy" stereotype was thereby brought into the modern world.

*The "New Woman" of the 1890s: the Gibson Girl.*

## Public Image—The "Gibson Girl"

The advances for women brought into being a new and laudatory term for women: the "New Woman." For the most part, this "New Woman" worked only until marriage, although she might choose a career instead of marriage. She could be identified by her new style of dress. Instead of trailing petticoats and beribboned gowns, she wore a tailored suit or a dark skirt and a simple blouse, or "shirtwaist," modeled after men's attire. Her skirts might not rise above her ankles, but she might loosen her corset—that torture instrument of Victorian dress that gave women 18-inch waistlines and damaged internal organs.

The "New Woman" of the 1890s was typified by the popular "Gibson Girl" of the period. The creation of artist Charles Dana Gibson in a series of drawings in *Life* magazine in the 1890s, this healthy and athletic maiden, simply dressed, became a national favorite. Prints of Gibson drawings appeared in countless American homes. The Gibson Girl was not designed to be a sex object, as were the "vamp" of the 1920s and the "siren" of the 1950s.

*A 1900 corset, made of steel and bone, that pushed the bust up, the stomach in, and the bottom out.*

Although she might be permitted some décolletage for evening, her regular attire was maidenly. Often, she wore a shirtwaist and a simple skirt. She was, however, rarely pictured in employment outside the home. Gibson's pictures centered on the traditional themes of courtship and marriage, but the "Gibson Girl" was also depicted playing tennis and golf, bicycling, and even driving an automobile. She was the American virgin-woman, but around her was a refreshing aura of health and rebellion.

*The "Bloomer Dress."*

Amelia Bloomer

## ROOTS OF CHANGE

Why were women, who in the 1820s had little legal, professional, or educational standing, seemingly on the road to achieving equality with men by the 1890s? Most often, change was brought about by the interaction of two factors: new social forces and the efforts of individuals. In case after case, reformers agitated for change and their arguments gained force as altered conditions in an industrializing nation made new life-styles for women imperative.

*WCTU leader Frances Willard receiving her first cycling lesson.*

*Photograph taken by Alice Austen in 1896 for Maria Ward's book Bicycling for Ladies, showing a woman dismounting.*

### Dress Reform

In the 1840s, health reformers had begun to rail against middle-class women's dress, particularly the corset. Few Americans had listened to them. In 1850, feminists Susan B. Anthony and Elizabeth Cady Stanton, among others, had adopted a modified version of Victorian dress in a long-sleeved, mid-calf dress worn over a pair of baggy trousers. The reform costume was called the "Bloomer Dress," after Stanton's reform associate, Amelia Bloomer. But public ridicule soon made them give it up. By the 1890s, however, attitudes were changing. One reporter at the Columbian

Exposition found that audiences responded enthusiastically to fashion shows of simplified dress at the woman's building. By her account, she heard many women express "their great desire to be free from the bondage of skirts—women, too, who would, one would suppose, rather die in long skirts than let the world know they had legs."[11]

By the 1890s, women, with their new freedoms, were bolder than before. Besides, Victorian fashions no longer were the only status style to differentiate middle-class women from poor or rural women, whose shapeless figures and simple clothes mirrored lives of hard work. By late century, simplicity in dress had become associated with exciting models—actresses, professional women, sportswomen.

Women began to appreciate the ease of simple clothing as they began to participate in sports. In the early years of the nineteenth century, genteel women rarely exercised because of their presumed physical delicacy. But as ice-skating became popular in the 1850s and croquet in the 1860s, women were not barred from these activities. Bicycling first appeared in the 1880s and soon became a national craze. To pedal their bicycles, women had to wear simpler and shorter garments. In the 1890s tennis and golf became popular.

New styles did not appear overnight. Novelist Edna Ferber recalled that in the 1890s neighbors in her hometown of Appleton, Wisconsin, were shocked when her mother, who managed the family store, began to wear shirtwaist blouses and skirts that did not reach the ground. But who could resist the tide of change when even the *Ladies' Home Journal*, the venerable organ of middle-class opinion, in 1893 endorsed the right of women to choose their own clothes on the basis of comfort?[12] Thus, dress reform gained authority because of the preaching of health reformers, because of the rise of sports, because women at work needed simpler clothes, and because women and men found the emancipated woman appealing.

*Suffragists Elizabeth Cady Stanton and Susan B. Anthony.*

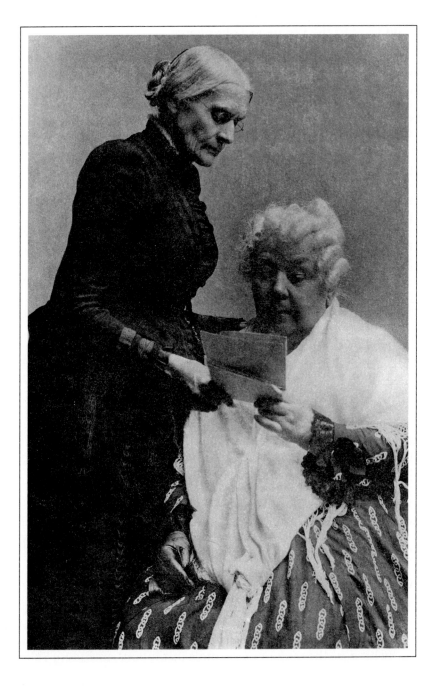

## Expansion of the Women's Labor Force

In employment, changing demographic and industrial patterns were probably more important than individual actions in opening up new jobs for women. Even before the Civil War, migration patterns had created sex imbalances in many areas of the country; particularly in older settlement areas, women outnumbered men. Work had to be found for these women, since there simply were not enough men for them to marry. Moreover, the average age of first marriage for women by the late nineteenth century was about 22. Thus for a number of years between maturity and marriage, many women were able to contribute to family support or to save money for their own marriage.

Within the burgeoning American economy existed a demand for this supply of workers. Owners of the earliest factories in the nation—the textile mills in Lowell and in Waltham, Massachusetts—turned to young women as a labor source in the 1820s. Later in the century, even after immigration produced more male workers, industrialists continued to employ women, especially because piecework that women had done at home moved into factory production and also because women could be paid less than men. Similarly, the rapid growth of public-school systems created a need for teachers, while local communities found persuasive the arguments that women were suited to elementary-school teaching and that, as in manufacturing, they could be paid lower salaries than men. Moreover, the Civil War, like most modern wars, extended women's employment. With men in the Army, more women were needed in teaching and manufacturing, and some new job areas, including the federal civil service, began to open up to women.

For the most part, the expansion of women's employment outside the elite professions occurred without pressure from woman's rights advocates. Yet a number of women leaders began their careers as schoolteachers, including suffragist Susan B. Anthony and temperance leader Frances Willard.

## New Inroads

*Women in College*   Women's entry into higher education was to a large extent the result of actions of individual women and men. Eastern women's colleges like Vassar and Smith were founded partly because the major private male institutions, including Yale,

Harvard, and Princeton, refused to admit women. In 1889, Barnard College was opened as a coordinate branch of Columbia University after 15 years of pressure by women seeking admission and by prominent civic and women's groups. Radcliffe College began under similar circumstances as an annex to Harvard.

Some Western colleges were caught in an overexpansion of institutions of higher education and admitted women to remain solvent, particularly after Civil War casualties decimated the number of college-age men. But state colleges in the Midwest and West became coeducational also because women pressured authorities to admit them. The example of the University of Indiana and Sarah Parke Morrison is not atypical. An 1857 graduate of Mount Holyoke Seminary, Morrison determined to integrate the public college of her home state. Her father, a trustee of the university, was sympathetic to her cause. The administration and the faculty, however, were against her. Even the undergraduates, who did not want women competing in their classes or fraternizing in their clubs, opposed her admission. It took her nine years to achieve her goal.

According to the historian of the University of Indiana, Morrison was equal to the task. She "remembered Lucy Stone and Susan B. Anthony and asserted her rights." Indeed, two years after her admission in 1866, 12 other women were admitted to the university. But Victorian prejudices did not die easily. Like many women pioneers in education, Morrison was subjected to petty annoyances throughout her college years. Commencement, for example, was a difficult experience, for she feared, with good reason, that the audience would subject her to "curious" and "hostile" stares as she walked across the stage to receive her diploma and that her ankles might be exposed to "immodest views."[13]

Sarah Morrison is a minor figure in American history. Yet her determination to advance the cause of women was an important ingredient in the mixture of forces that brought coeducation to state colleges in the Midwest and the West. Colleges in states that had more recently passed through a frontier stage, it is true, seemed more easily integrated than colleges in older, more settled states. But it is incorrect to conclude that a democratic "frontier" spirit alone brought about coeducation in the West. Outspoken women—and male allies—put pressure on faculties, administrations, and state legislatures.

*New York World reporter
Nellie Bly.*

***Women in Medicine and Law***    Individual women were responsible for gaining admission to the elite professions, often against great odds. In the case of medicine, Harriot Hunt, a self-trained doctor with a private practice in Boston, was repeatedly refused admission to Harvard Medical School because of her sex and never received a medical degree. Elizabeth Blackwell, the first licensed doctor in the United States, was turned down by medical schools throughout the nation and was admitted in 1847 to the Geneva

Medical College in Geneva, New York (now part of Hobart College), only because the male students thought it would be "amusing" to have a woman there. Although Blackwell boarded with a family in Geneva, the townspeople avoided her because they thought that only a woman of loose morals would attend medical school. This was a charge not infrequently leveled against women in professional training as well as against working women in general. And, although Blackwell graduated at the head of her class, like Sarah Morrison she feared the graduation ceremonies and did not appear on the stage to receive her diploma.

Once women were admitted to professional schools, not only were higher standards demanded of them, but they were also subjected in and out of class to hostile jokes and embarrassing off-color stories. Mary Putnam-Jacobi, one of the first medical-school graduates after Blackwell, reported that women students in several Eastern hospitals were able to observe operations only after forcing their way through cordons of male students determined to keep them out of operating rooms.[14] County and state medical associations, too, were loathe to certify women doctors: Only after a 24-year battle did the Massachusetts Medical Society admit women to its membership in 1879.

Women found it even more difficult to become lawyers than doctors. Because English common law prohibited women from being called to the bar, the law had to be changed in each state before application could be made to state licensing boards. And, although practicing medicine could be seen as an extension of women's nurturing role, practicing law intruded on men's public sphere. Arabella Mansfield, the nation's first woman lawyer, gained her training by studying with her brother and was licensed by the Iowa bar in 1869 with no difficulty. Other women, however, encountered problems. Like many law schools, particularly in the Northeast, the Columbian College of Law (now George Washington University's law school) in 1869 and 1887 refused to admit women on the grounds that coeducational classes would be an "injurious diversion of the attention of the students" and that "women had not the mentality to study law."[15]

In California, the law schools and the state bar admitted women only after a long judicial contest produced a ruling in their favor. In Illinois and Wisconsin, aspiring women lawyers had to secure special legislation to overturn adverse rulings of state bar associations and courts. As late as 1910, there were only 1,500 women lawyers in the nation, compared to almost 9,000 women doctors.

**Women in Journalism**    The profession of journalism offers an impressive example of women's persistence in the face of hostility. Since mid-century, women had been employed on newspapers as gossip columnists and editors of women's pages. But rarely had a woman been hired as a regular reporter. It took a succession of determined women to overcome this barrier. Elizabeth Seaman, employed by the New York *World*, was the most famous of them. Like most women journalists of her time, Seaman assumed a pseudonym, and hers, Nellie Bly, came from the title of a popular Stephen Foster song. Her persistence in hounding editors brought her initial assignments, and the stories she submitted were so compelling that editors could not reject them.

Flamboyant exposés of exploitation were her specialty. She worked in a paper-box factory to see how workers were treated; she had herself arrested to investigate conditions in the city jail; and she posed as a high-class prostitute to expose the city's roués. In 1889, Bly accomplished her most famous exploit: She traveled around the world in 72 days to prove that a woman could complete the trip in less than the 80 days it had taken the fictional Phileas Fogg in Jules Verne's famous story.

**Conservative Arguments Produce Progressive Results**    It is incorrect to assume that the activism of Nellie Bly and other women professionals implied that they were woman's rights advocates. Women pioneers in the professions and in education were often moderates, and their moderate rhetoric created a sympathetic climate for them. A standard argument for medical and legal training for women, for example, was not that women had the right to it, but that women clients had the right to consult professionals of their sex to protect their womanly modesty. How could any woman, the argument went, undergo a gynecological examination by a male doctor and preserve her sense of honor? When conservatives contended that only women of dubious virtue would want to know about legal cases of rape and adultery, supporters of women lawyers argued that many of the defendants in these cases were women who had the right to female counsel because they could not be expected to discuss their sexual situation openly with a male lawyer.

Many of the arguments advanced in favor of women's education were also moderate. Henry Durant, who founded Wellesley College, wanted to educate women so that they could take a role in shaping society. But L. Clark Seelye, the first president of Smith College, proposed that "it is to preserve her womanliness that this College has been founded; it is to give her the best opportunities for mental culture, and at the same time, the most favorable conditions for developing those innate capacities which have ever been the glory and charm of true womanhood."[16]

The most compelling conservative argument for the education of women was one advanced early in the century by Catharine Beecher, sister of author Harriet Beecher Stowe and founder of one of the nation's first secondary schools for women. Beecher wanted to educate women, in the first instance, for their own intellectual profit. But she was more concerned that they become the intellectual equals of their husbands as well as better housewives and mothers. Aside from teaching, she did not envision a future of remunerative employment for women. She wanted mainly to upgrade the status of housekeeping and to teach women effective domestic techniques. In this quest, Beecher was a forerunner of the leaders of the domestic science movement of the 1910s and the home economics movement of the 1920s. In terms of the debate over women's roles, she might be classified as a "domestic feminist"; in terms of women's education, her arguments spoke powerfully to a nation which glorified the institution of the family.

Even though the higher education of women might be viewed in terms of women's traditional roles, such education easily produced different results. Students at Eastern women's colleges were often expected to equal or excel male students and to take on a special mission to society. M. Carey Thomas, president of Bryn Mawr, captured the spirit of this belief when she wrote in 1901 of her expectation that Bryn Mawr graduates would chart new paths in the professions, that they would be social innovators, and that they would form marriages based on equality and shared roles rather than on the traditional division of duties.[17]

### Men—A Help and a Hindrance

Men were not always antagonistic to competition from women. The head of the Bucks County Medical Association led the fight in Pennsylvania for the certification of women doctors. Another male doctor donated the funds to build the Women's Medical College in Philadelphia because he wanted his sister, who had supported him through school, to have the medical education she had deferred on his behalf. The original endowments for several private women's colleges in the Northeast, including Vassar and Bryn Mawr, were provided by wealthy men. In both medicine and law, many early women careerists, like Mary Putnam-Jacobi, were married to men in the same field who supported their wives' endeavors. Indeed, a study of 31 of the approximately 200 women lawyers in the nation in 1896 revealed that a number of them became interested in the law after they married lawyers and worked as clerks in their husbands' offices.[18]

Many men also agitated for the opening of elementary and secondary education to women. Fathers as well as mothers wanted their daughters to be educated. Men, too, took an active part in modifying the common law statutes regarding married women. Given the volatile nature of the American economy in the nineteenth century, fathers of means could not help but be concerned about the legal and economic security of their daughters. After all, the financial ruin of a son-in-law might also include the money his wife had brought to the marriage.

Men's aid was not so disinterested in other instances. Women were permitted to become foreign missionaries because many non-Western cultures did not allow contact between male missionaries and native women. And, it was not easy for nineteenth-century men to allow wives and daughters independence. Anna Howard Shaw was a minister, a physician, and an eventual president of the NAWSA. Yet, she was afraid to tell her family of her invitation to preach her first sermon because "to them it would mean nothing short of personal disgrace."[19] Rheta Childe Dorr's husband wanted her to become a novelist in the tradition of

*Housekeeping was still hard work and the woman's responsibility.*

*"A Clarion Call for World Prohibition"*—the WCTU presents the Great Temperance Petition to the state legislature in Albany, New York.

George Eliot, who reflected on public events from a distance, but he opposed her becoming a journalist in the center of public controversy. Novelist Mary Austin thought that male arrogance toward women turned them toward the woman's movement. According to Austin, when women at suffrage conferences discussed what made them suffragists they invariably cited the way men treated women in their families. "'Well, it was seeing what my mother had to go through that started me'; or 'It was being sacrificed to the boys in the family that set me going.'" Austin remembered how "women of high intelligence and education went white and black telling how, in their own families, the mere whim of the dominant male member had been allowed to assume the whole weight of moral significance."[20]

## Technology and Housekeeping

Some historians of women have proposed that the growth in women's organizations in the late nineteenth century resulted from the appearance of labor-saving appliances, which gave housewives the leisure time for volunteer activities. This thesis, however, is only partially correct. The advent of canned goods, the sewing machine, and new kitchen appliances, as well as improved sanitation and water supplies in the cities, did lessen the burdens of housekeeping by the 1890s. But as Helen and Robert Lynd reported in *Middletown*, their study of Muncie, Indiana, many women in the 1890s were still baking their own bread and canning their own fruits and preserves—partly to economize, partly out of habit, and partly because society expected that an able wife should demonstrate extensive housekeeping abilities.[21] Even wealthy Maude Nathan of New York City felt so guilty about leaving her home to do volunteer work that she did all the marketing for the family and, once a year, canned a year's supply of pickles, preserves, and corned beef.

By late century, many women were using sewing machines, but they still made their own and their children's clothes. Indeed, the only mechanical aids in most homes in 1890 were the sewing machine, the egg beater, and the nonelectric carpet sweeper. But the crucial timesaver for the housewife was electrical equipment such as the vacuum cleaner and the washing machine. Although a fully electric kitchen was displayed at the Columbian Exposition in 1893, electrical equipment was not widely available until the 1920s.

## Women's Separate Culture

Women's increased education and leisure time sparked an organizational explosion among women in the late nineteenth century. Moreover, their activism was a logical outgrowth of a central theme of their lives—their intense involvement with other women. At the core of nineteenth century gender-role definitions was the belief that men and women had different natures and should occupy different social spheres. The public world of affairs belonged to men; the private sphere of the home to women. Undergirding such ideas was the culture's devotion to the nuclear family and the fear, generated by rapid modernization, that if women moved into the male public sphere, the traditional family might be destroyed. In a culture with rigid gender-role differentiations and prohibitions on sexuality, intense friendships among women flourished. WCTU leader Frances Willard wrote: "The loves of women for each other grow more numerous each day. . . . That so little should be said about them surprises me, for they are everywhere."[22] Something approaching a separate culture of women came into being. It was evident in the female bonding surrounding marriage, childbirth, and death, in the passionate letters women wrote to one another, and in the pairing of women that contemporaries called "Boston marriages." These relationships, monogamous and lifelong, in some instances probably were sexual, although the term lesbian, coined in France in the late nineteenth century, was not yet in widespread use in the United States. And, homosexuality was so hidden in this period that there was virtually no public discussion of it.

Women's gender solidarity in the nineteenth century was partly responsible for women's organizational drive. On occasion, anger against men prompted women's movement from friendship networks to social organizations. The WCTU was the largest nineteenth-century women's organization. It emerged from women's rage against men's drinking and their violence in the family. The politicizing of women also proceeded out of the belief that women were innately morally superior to men.

This belief in the moral superiority of women provided support for women's separate sphere as well as for women leaving the private world of home and family for the public one of reform. For when feminists argued that morally superior women should be allowed to reshape society, it was difficult for conservatives to disagree, despite their desire to restrain women's morality to the home. And as we will see, the argument for women's moral superiority became a leitmotif of women's organizational activity in the early twentieth century, both furthering and restraining the effectiveness of women's appeals for social reform and gender equality.

## NOTES

[1] Elizabeth Cady Stanton et al., *History of Woman Suffrage*, 6 vols. (New York: Fowler & Wells, 1881–1922), V, xvii.

[2] Mabel S. Ulrich, "A Doctor's Diary, 1904–1932," *Scribner's* (June 1944). Reprinted in *Ms.*, 1 (July 1972): 11–14.

[3] Cf. Margaret Mead, *Blackberry Winter: My Earlier Years* (New York: William Morrow, 1972), p. 76.

[4] Rheta Childe Dorr, *A Woman of Fifty* (New York: Funk & Wagnalls, 1924), p. 50.

[5] Frances Parkinson Keyes, *All Flags Flying: Reminiscences of Frances Parkinson Keyes* (New York: McGraw Hill, 1972), p.5.

[6] Marian Lawrence Peabody, *To Be Young Was Very Heaven* (Boston: Houghton Mifflin, 1967), p. 169.

[7] Mary Austin, *Earth Horizon: Autobiography* (New York: Literary Guild of America, 1932), p. 31.

[8] Anne H. Wharton, "The Prolongation of Youthfulness in Modern Women," *Chataqua Collection*, Elizabeth Bancroft Schlesinger Library, Radcliffe College, p. 85.

[9] Anne Firor Scott, *The Southern Lady: From Pedestal to Politics, 1830–1930* (Chicago: University of Chicago Press, 1970), p. 141.

[10] Lydia Commander, *The American Idea* (1907; reprint ed., New York: Arno Press, 1972), p. 144.

[11] *Arena*, IX (1893): 305.

[12] Edna Ferber, *A Peculiar Treasure* (Garden City, NY: Doubleday, 1938), p. 33.

[13] Thomas D. Clark, *Indiana University: Midwestern Pioneer*, 2 vols. (Bloomington: University of Indiana Press, 1925), I:125.

[14] Mary Putnam-Jacobi, "Women in Medicine," in Annie Nathan Meyer (ed.), *Woman's Work in America* (New York: Henry Holt, 1891), pp. 139–205.

[15] Karen Meyer Willcox, "Women Lawyers in the United States, 1870–1900," unpublished senior honors thesis, Douglass College, New Brunswick, NJ, 1973, p. 28.

[16] L. Clark Seelye, *The Early History of Smith College, 1871–1910* (Boston: Houghton Mifflin, 1923), p. 29.

[17] M. Carey Thomas, "Notes for the Opening Address at Bryn Mawr College, 1901," quoted in Barbara M. Cross (ed.), *The Educated Woman in America: Selected Writings of Catharine Beecher, Margaret Fuller, and M. Carey Thomas* (New York: Columbia Teachers College Press, 1965), p. 41.

[18] Willcox, "Women Lawyers," p. 28.

[19] Anna Howard Shaw, *Story of a Pioneer* (New York: Harper & Row, 1915), p. 60.

[20] Austin, *Earth Horizon*, p. 128.

[21] Helen Merrell Lynd and Robert S. Lynd, *Middletown: A Study in Contemporary American Culture* (New York: Harcourt Brace Jovanovich, 1929), pp. 156–68.

[22] Frances Willard, *Glimpses of Fifty Years: The Autobiography of an American Woman* (Chicago: Woman's Temperance Publication Association, 1889), pp. 641–42.

## BIBLIOGRAPHY

The details of women's changing status in the late nineteenth century, especially in the area of legal rights, have not yet been systematically explored. On the law, see Joan Hoff, *Law, Gender, and Injustice: A Legal History of United States Women* (New York: New York University Press, 1991). On general educational change, Thomas Woody, *A History of Women's Education in the United States*, 2 vols. (New York: Science Press, 1929), although outdated, is still the definitive work.

On primary and secondary education, Redding Sugg, *Motherteacher: The Feminization of American Education* (Charlottesville: University Press of Virginia, 1978), provides some information. More work is available on women and higher education. The major source is Barbara Miller Solomon, *In the Company of Educated Women: A History of Women and Higher Education in America* (New Haven, CT: Yale University Press, 1985). See also Roberta Frankfort, *Collegiate Women: Domesticity and Career in Turn of the Century America* (New York: New York University Press, 1977); Lynn D. Gordon, *Gender and Higher Education in the Progressive Era* (New Haven, CT: Yale University Press, 1990); Helen Horowitz, *Alma Mater: Design and Experience in Women's Colleges from Their Nineteenth Century Beginnings to the 1930s* (New York: Alfred A. Knopf, 1984); and Ellen Condliffe Lagemann, *A Generation of Women: Education in the Lives of Progressive Reformers* (Cambridge, MA: Harvard University Press, 1979). In *Frontier Women: The Trans-Mississippi West, 1840–1880* (New York: Hill & Wang, 1979), Julie Roy Jeffrey provides information on Western coeducation as well as on the life of Western women. For an interesting study of women at Cornell University, which in 1872 was the first major Eastern institution to admit women, see Charlotte Williams Conable, *Women at Cornell: The Myth of Equal Education* (Ithaca, NY: Cornell University Press, 1977).

On the entry of women into the professions, Barbara Harris, *Beyond Her Sphere: Women and the Professions in American History* (Westport, CT: Greenwood Press, 1978), and Pernina Migdal Glazer and Miriam Slater, *Unusual Colleagues: The Entrance of Women into the Professions, 1890–1940* (New Brunswick, NJ: Rutgers University Press, 1987), contain information. Numerous studies of women in specific professions and occupations have appeared. Among these are Cindy Slonik Aron, *Ladies and Gentlemen of the Civil Service: Middle-Class Workers in Victorian America* (New York: Oxford University Press, 1987); Susan Porter Benson, *Countercultures: Saleswomen, Managers, and Customers in American Department Stores, 1890–1940* (Urbana: University of Illinois Press, 1986); Margery W. Davies, *Woman's Place Is at the Typewriter: Office Work and Office Workers, 1870–1930* (Philadelphia: Temple University Press, 1982); L. Dee Garrison, *Apostles of Culture: The Public Librarian and American Society, 1876–1920* (New York: Free Press, 1979);

Marion Marzolf, *Up From the Footnote: A History of Women Journalists* (New York: Hastings House, 1977); Barbara Melosh, *"The Physicians's Hand": Nurses and Nursing in the Twentieth Century* (Philadelphia: Temple University Press, 1982); Susan Reverby, *Ordered to Care: The Dilemma of American Nursing, 1850–1945* (New York: Cambridge University Press, 1987); and Margaret W. Rossiter, *Women Scientists in America* (Baltimore: Johns Hopkins University Press, 1983). Sharon Hartman Strom, *Beyond the Typewriter: Gender, Class, and the Origins of Modern American Office Work* (Urbana: University of Illinois Press, 1992), deals with a variety of office occupations, such as bookkeeping and office management.

For the medical profession, see Mary Roth Walsh, *Doctors Wanted—No Women Need Apply: Sexual Barriers in the Medical Profession, 1835–1975* (New Haven, CT: Yale University Press, 1977), and Regina Markell Morantz-Sanchez, *Sympathy and Science: Women Physicians in American Medicine* (New York: Oxford University Press, 1985). An interesting study of women's role as philanthropists for art museums and the like is Kathleen D. McCarthy, *Women's Culture: American Philanthropy and Art, 1830–1930* (Chicago: University of Chicago Press, 1991).

Women's general participation in the work force has received much attention. In particular, see Ava Baron, *Work Engendered: Toward a New History of American Labor* (Ithaca, NY: Cornell University Press, 1990); Milton Cantor and Bruce Laurie (eds.), *Class, Sex and the Woman Worker* (Westport, CT: Greenwood Press, 1977); Susan Easterbrook Kennedy, *If All We Did Was to Weep at Home: A History of White Working Women in America* (Bloomington: Indiana University Press, 1979); Alice Kessler-Harris, *Out to Work: A History of Wage-Earning Women in the United States* (New York: Oxford University Press, 1982); and Barbara Mayer Wertheimer, *We Were There: The Story of Working Women in America* (New York: Pantheon Books, 1977). For women in specific industries, see the bibliography for Chapter 2.

A large literature has developed on female sexuality and the medical treatment of women in the nineteenth century. A summary is provided in Carl N. Degler, *At Odds: Women and the Family in America From the Revolution to the Present* (New York: Oxford University Press, 1980), although his conclusions have occasioned debate. See also John D'Emilio and Estelle Freedman, *Intimate Matters: A History of Sexuality in America* (New York: Harper & Row, 1988), John S. Haller, Jr., and Robin M. Haller, *The Physician and Sexuality in Victorian America* (Urbana: University of Illinois Press, 1974), and Diane Price Herndl, *Invalid Women: Figuring Feminine Illness in American Fiction and Culture, 1840–1940* (Chapel Hill: University of North Carolina Press, 1993). In *Searching the Heart: Women, Men, and Romantic Love in Victorian America* (New York: Oxford University Press, 1990), Karen Lystra proposes that married couples in the nineteenth century enjoyed full and free sexual relations, a position challenged by Carol Z. Stearns and Peter N. Stearns, in "Victorian Sexuality: Can Historians Do It Better?" *Journal of Social History*, 18 (Summer 1985): 625–34, and by Steven Seidman, in "The Power of Desire and the

Pleasure of Danger: Victorian Sexuality Reconsidered," *Journal of Social History*, 24 (Fall 1990): 47–60.

For rousing attacks on nineteenth-century medical treatment of women, see C. J. Barker-Benfield, *The Horrors of the Half-Known Life: Male Attitudes Toward Women and Sexuality in Nineteenth-Century America* (New York: Harper & Row, 1976), and Ann Douglas Wood, "'The Fashionable Diseases': Women's Complaints and Their Treatment in Nineteenth-Century America," in Mary S. Hartman and Lois W. Banner (eds.), *Clio's Consciousness Raised: New Perspectives on the History of Women* (New York: Harper & Row, 1974), pp. 1–22. See also Regina Morantz's rejoinder to Wood and Barker-Benfield in the same volume.

For scientific views of women, see Cynthia Eagle Russett, *Sexual Science: The Victorian Construction of Womanhood* (Cambridge, MA: Harvard University Press, 1989). For the feminist response to male views, see Rosalind Rosenberg, *Beyond Separate Spheres: The Intellectual Roots of Modern Feminism* (New Haven, CT: Yale University Press, 1982). Childbirth and midwifery are covered in Judy Barrett Litoff, *American Midwives: 1860 to the Present* (Westport, CT: Greenwood Press, 1978), and Richard W. Wertz and Dorothy C. Wertz, *Lying-In: A History of Childbirth in America* (New York: Free Press, 1977). On child rearing, see Rima D. Apple, *Mothers and Medicine: A Social History of Infant Feeding, 1890–1950* (Madison, WI: University of Wisconsin Press, 1987).

On abortion, see James C. Mohr, *Abortion in America: The Origins and Evolution of National Policy* (New York: Oxford University Press, 1978). On birth control, see Linda Gordon, *Woman's Body, Woman's Right: A Social History of Birth Control in America* (New York: Grossman, 1976), and James Reed, *From Private Vice to Public Virtue: The Birth Control Movement and American Society Since 1830* (New York: Basic Books, 1978). The most recent study of the anti-vice reformers of Victorian America is David J. Pivar, *Purity Crusade: Sexual Morality and Social Control, 1868–1900* (Westport, CT: Greenwood Press, 1973). In *Female Complaints: Lydia Pinkham and the Business of Women's Medicine* (New York: W.W. Norton, 1981), Sarah J. Stage has written an interesting study of a successful businesswoman and of women's health.

On changes in domestic technology, both in this period and later, see Ruth Schwartz Cowan, *More Work for Mother: The Ironies of Household Technology from the Open Hearth to the Microwave* (New York: Basic Books, 1983); Glenna Mathews, *'Just a Housewife:' The Rise and Fall of Domesticity in America* (New York: Oxford University Press, 1987); and Susan Strasser, *Never Done: A History of American Housework* (New York: Pantheon Books, 1982). On the dress-reform movement, the relationship between female fashions and social change, and the influence of actresses on women's self-perception, see Lois W. Banner, *American Beauty* (New York: Alfred A. Knopf, 1983). On images of women, see Martha Banta, *Imaging American Women: Ideas and Ideals in Cultural History* (New York: Columbia University Press, 1987).

For demographic analysis, Robert V. Wells, "Women's Lives Transformed: Demographic and Family Patterns in America, 1600–1970," in Carol Ruth Berkin and Mary Beth Norton (eds.), *Women of America: A History* (Boston: Houghton Mifflin, 1979), pp. 17–33, is useful. Anne Firor Scott, *The Southern Lady: From Pedestal to Politics* (Chicago: University of Chicago Press, 1970), is a good introduction to the subject of Southern women, as is Janet James (ed.), *Women in American Religion* (Philadelphia: University of Pennsylvania Press, 1980), to the subject of women and religion. See also Margaret Bendroth, *Fundamentalism and Gender, 1875 to the Present* (New Haven, CT: Yale University Press, 1993). For an interesting narrative of women in the 1893 Columbian Exposition, see Jeanne Madeline Weimann, *The Fair Women* (Chicago: Academy, 1981). On women and aging, see Lois W. Banner, *In Full Flower: Aging Women, Power, and Sexuality* (New York: Alfred A. Knopf, 1992).

The most important exploration of the "separate culture of women" argument is Carroll Smith-Rosenberg, "The Female World of Love and Ritual: Relations Between Women in Nineteenth-Century America," *Signs: Journal of Women in Culture and Society*, 1 (Autumn 1975): 1–25. On lesbianism in this era, as well as earlier and later, see Lillian Faderman's two works: *Surpassing the Love of Men: Romantic Friendship and Love Between Women, From the Renaissance to the Present* (New York: Morrow, 1981), and *Odd Girls and Twilight Lovers: A History of Lesbian Life in Twentieth-Century America* (New York: Columbia University Press, 1991). Linda Kerber has critiqued the "separate sphere" idea in "Separate Spheres, Female Worlds, Woman's Place: The Rhetoric of Women's History," *Journal of American History*, 75 (June 1988): 9–39.

For every period of the history of American women, numerous biographies and autobiographies are available. Useful for the late nineteenth and early twentieth centuries are Mary Austin, *Earth Horizon: Autobiography* (New York: Literary Guild, 1932); Lois W. Banner, *Elizabeth Cady Stanton: A Radical for Woman's Rights* (Boston: Little, Brown, 1979); Elizabeth Blackwell, *Pioneer Work in Opening Up the Medical Profession to Women* (London: Longmans, Green, 1895); Edna Ferber, *A Peculiar Treasure* (Garden City, NY: Doubleday, 1938); Helen Thomas Flexner, *A Quaker Girlhood* (New Haven, CT: Yale University Press, 1940); Margaret Mead, *Blackberry Winter: My Earlier Years* (New York: William Morrow, 1972); Maude Nathan, *Once Upon a Time and Today* (New York: G.P. Putnam's Sons, 1933); Kathryn Kish Sklar, *Catharine Beecher: A Study in American Domesticity* (New Haven, CT: Yale University Press, 1973); Jean Strouse, *Alice James: A Biography* (Boston: Houghton Mifflin, 1980); and the revealing autobiographies of Agnes de Mille, *Where the Wings Grow* (Garden City, NY: Doubleday, 1978); Rheta Childe Dorr, *A Woman of Fifty* (New York: Funk & Wagnalls, 1924); and Frances Parkinson Keyes, *All Flags Flying: Reminiscences of Frances Parkinson Keyes* (New York: McGraw Hill, 1972).

Acclaimed contemporary novels about gender include Willa Cather, *My Antonia* (1918); Kate Chopin, *The Awakening* (1890); Theodore Dreiser,

*Sister Carrie* (1900); Charlotte Perkins Gilman, *The Yellow Wallpaper* (1892); and Edith Wharton, *The House of Mirth* (1905). For discussions of the methodology of women's history, see Nancy F. Cott, "What's in a Name? The Limits of 'Social Feminism': Or, Expanding the Vocabulary of Women's History," *Journal of American History*, 76 (Dec., 1989): 809–29; Ellen Carol DuBois, et al., "Politics and Culture in Women's History: A Symposium," *Feminist Studies*, 6 (Spring 1980): 26–84; and Joan Wallach Scott, *Gender and the Politics of History* (New York: Columbia University Press, 1988). On cultural images for ethnic women, mentioned in the preface, see Norma Alarcón, "Chicana's Feminist Literature: A Revision Through Malintzin / or Malintzin: Putting Flesh Back on the Object," in Cherríe Moraga and Gloria Anzaldúa, (eds.), *This Bridge Called My Back: Writings by Radical Women of Color* (New York: Kitchen Table, 1981), pp. 182–190; King-Kok Cheung, "The Woman Warrior versus The Chinaman Pacific: Must a Chinese American Critic Choose Between Feminism and Heroism?" in Marianne Hirsch and Evelyn Fox Keller, (eds.), *Conflicts in Feminism* (New York: Routledge, 1990), pp. 234–51; and Rayna Green, "The Pocahontas Perplex: The Image of Indian Women in American Culture," in Ellen Carol DuBois and Vicki L. Ruiz, (eds.), *Unequal Sisters: A Multicultural Reader in U.S. Women's History* (New York: Routledge, 1990), pp. 15–21.

Several analyses of the history of women in the twentieth century have informed my narrative. They include William H. Chafe, *Women and Equality: Changing Patterns in American Culture* (New York: Oxford University Press, 1977); Robert L. Daniel, *American Women in the 20th Century: A Festival of Light* (San Diego, CA: Harcourt Brace Jovanovich, 1987); Rosalind Rosenberg, *Divided Lives: American Women in the Twentieth Century* (New York: Hill and Wang, 1992); Sheila M. Rothman, *Woman's Proper Place: A History of Changing Ideals and Practices, 1970 to the Present* (New York: Basic Books, 1978); and especially William Chafe, *The American Woman: Her Changing Social, Economic, and Political Roles, 1920–1970* (New York: Oxford University Press, 1972).

A number of useful compilations of primary source documents and secondary articles have been published, including Rosalyn Baxandall, Linda Gordon, and Susan Reverby (eds.), *America's Working Women: A Documentary History—1600 to the Present* (New York: Random House, 1976); W. Elliott Brownlee and Mary M. Brownlee (eds.), *Women in the American Economy: A Documentary History, 1675–1929* (New Haven, CT: Yale University Press, 1976); Nancy F. Cott and Elizabeth Pleck (eds.), *A Heritage of Her Own: Toward a New Social History of American Women* (New York: Simon & Schuster, 1979); John C. Fout and Maura Shaw Tantillo, (eds.), *American Sexual Politics: Sex, Gender, and Race Since the Civil War* (Chicago: University of Chicago Press, 1993); Mary S. Hartman and Lois W. Banner (eds.), *Clio's Consciousness Raised: New Perspectives on the History of Women* (New York: Harper & Row, 1974); Nancy Hewitt and Suzanne Lebsock, (eds.), *Visible Women: New Essays in American History* (Urbana: University of Illinois Press, 1993); Kathy Peiss and Christina

Simmons (eds.), *Passion and Power: Sexuality and History* (Philadelphia: Temple University Press, 1989); and Louise A. Tilly and Patricia Gurin (eds.), *Women, Politics, and Change* (New York: Russell Sage, 1990). Indispensable to any research on women's history is Edward T. James, Janet Wilson James, and Paul S. Boyer (eds.), *Notable American Women, 1607–1950,* 3 vols. (Cambridge, MA: Harvard University Press, 1970), a collection of brief biographies; and its continuation by Barbara Sicherman and Carol Hurd Green (eds.), *Notable American Women: The Modern Period* (Cambridge, MA: Harvard University Press, 1980). Valuable also is Andrea Hinding, Ames Sheldon Bowers, and Clarke A. Chambers, *Women's History Sources: A Guide to Archives and Manuscript Collections in the United States* (New York: R.R. Bowker, 1979).

In recent years, the dynamic interest in the history of women has sparked an interest in the history of male roles and behavior. On this subject, see Peter Filene, *Him/Her/Self: Sex Roles in Modern America,* 2nd. ed. (Baltimore: Johns Hopkins University Press, 1986); Elliott Gorn, *The Manly Art: Bare-Knuckle Prizefighting in America* (Ithaca, NY: Cornell University Press, 1986); Robert Griswold, *Fatherhood in America* (New York: Basic Books, 1993); E. Anthony Rotundo, *American Manhood: Transformations in Masculinity From the Revolution to the Modern Era* (New York: Basic Books, 1993); and Kevin White, *The First Heterosexual Revolution: The Emergence of Male Heterosexuality in Modern America* (New York: New York University Press, 1993). In *Suburban Lives* (New Brunswick, NJ: Rutgers University Press, 1990), Margaret S. Marsh challenges the standard view that men left the private sphere of domesticity and child rearing up to women.

# 2

## THE AMERICAN WOMAN FROM 1900 TO THE FIRST WORLD WAR: A PROFILE

IN THE YEARS before World War I (1914–1918), the lives of women of every class, ethnic group, and region were governed by the fact that the overwhelming majority would marry. Throughout the twentieth century, about 90 percent of American women have married at some time during their lives. Most women who worked prior to marriage in the early part of the century left their jobs once they married. In 1900, only 5 percent of the nation's married women were gainfully employed outside the home. By 1910, this statistic had increased to 11 percent. Yet these statistics mask an underlying reality of remunerative employment for many married women, especially women of the working class.

## THE MAIN PROSPECT—MARRIAGE AND MOTHERHOOD

Marriage was a life goal for women, and many women were undoubtedly content with this role. The image of the happy housewife portrayed by the media from early women's magazines to contemporary television serials has always been based on a real type. And for the unmarried working woman enduring the drudgery of factory or domestic work, becoming a housewife and mother offered release.

Yet married women were not invariably contented. Sociologists assert that modernization produced a decline in family functions. Schools took over education; doctors took over health care; family income production shifted from home-centered farms to factories or offices. New rights for women expanded women's expectations of marital happiness. Increased life expectancy brought an increase in marital life span; death less often provided a release from marital discontent. Divorce, with its attendant anxieties, was on the rise; in 1905, one out of twelve marriages ended in divorce.

## The Middle-Class Wife

During these years, the middle class experienced a vast expansion and regrouping. The managerial needs of a complex industrial society created not only new business magnates and a new clerical occupation for women but also scores of new middle-level plant executives, insurance underwriters, and traveling salesmen. Between 1870 and 1910, their number increased eight times. In 1910, they numbered almost five million. Often socially upwardly mobile, they adopted the "white collar" on their shirts as the symbol of emancipation from "blue collar" manual labor.

The search for middle-class status placed pressure on the wives of this group. In many ways, the position of middle-class wives had improved. Social convention no longer dictated that they appear subservient to their husbands; by 1909, civil marriage vows, and many church ones, no longer included the word obey. Observers commented that companionship was the new standard in marriage. But companionship was difficult in an American culture that expected men to achieve material success no matter the cost. In pursuit of success, according to many accounts, men were rarely at home. "The habit and fury of work," wrote one critic, "is a masculine disease in this country."[1]

Left to their own devices, many middle-class wives were drawn to shopping. Among them, noted one observer, bargain hunting was a "mania."[2] Or they turned to social climbing. According to sociologists Helen and Robert Lynd: "The coinage in this social market is much more subtle than that with which their husbands deal."[3] Like women throughout history, some turned inward on families to become the shrews and matriarchs long stock characters of fiction. Middle-class women resorted to divorce with increasing frequency. To display neurotic symptoms was not uncommon among them; physicians reported that most of their emotionally disturbed patients were women.[4]

The confusion of middle-class women in this modernizing era is evident in the way they treated their servants. Given status considerations and the still-demanding nature of housework, middle-class employment of domestics remained common. An outpouring of writings on a so-called "servant problem" focused on the shortage of women willing to work as domestics. This literature revealed that the demands of female employers, and not just working conditions,

*Women in Black Falls, Wisconsin, get together for tea, gossip, and sewing.*

drove servants away. Servants were expected to work long hours and were paid poorly, but they were also subject to the whims and status anxieties of their mistresses. So empty were the lives of many of these well-to-do women, wrote one observer, that the "3 D's" occupied their time—"dress, disease, and domestics."[5]

Some middle-class women found fulfillment by joining voluntary associations. Many found contentment in home and family; one could contend that as the older functions of the family eroded, women found new ones. As families grew smaller, children became increasingly important and child rearing more complex. The growth of publishing and the development of the domestic-science movement produced no end of books advising wives on home management, thereby reinforcing women's traditional roles. Magazines like the *Ladies' Home Journal*, first published in 1889, glorified home and motherhood. Women joined a host of new organizations for the study of child rearing. By 1912, these groups joined together into the Federation for Child Study. In 1914, Congress declared the second Sunday in May the nation's official "Mother's Day." Barbara Ehrenreich and Dierdre English conclude that, in fact, the ideal role for women in the early twentieth century was neither the career woman nor the reformer but the homemaker.[6]

In this era the majority of middle-class women probably held traditional views about woman's nature. Novelist Frances Parkinson Keyes wrote that marriage and motherhood were a woman's destiny and that love was a woman's "whole existence." In the sex act, according to Keyes, the woman "surrendered" to the man, and the birth of a child produced a sense of "blinding glory."[7] Yet Keyes herself was both a wife and a professional writer, although she took up writing mainly because her husband's salary as governor of Vermont provided insufficient family support. Other middle-class women, too, combined marriages and careers. Among them were the women lawyers and doctors married to men in the same profession. For many women, however, such balancing was not easy. Charlotte Perkins Gilman, the day's leading feminist writer, suffered a nervous breakdown because she felt trapped in a traditional marriage. She had to leave her husband and embark on a career before she recovered. Carrie Chapman Catt, a NAWSA president, drew up a contract with her fiancé guaranteeing freedom from marital responsibilities for three months each year to fulfill her duties as president.

In the early decades of the twentieth century, women who tried to combine marriage and a career faced problems. Governor Keyes opposed his wife's career because he thought it degraded his position as head of the household. One woman doctor married to a colleague catalogued further difficulties. Intellectually, her husband accepted her career, but emotionally, he wanted her to stay home. The problem was that he idealized his domesticated mother and in subtle ways undermined his wife's career. Yet, she concluded, "it can't be so easy being the husband of a 'modern' woman. She is everything his mother wasn't—and nothing she was."[8]

### Rural Women: Midwestern, Southern, Southwestern

By 1900, the frontier era had ended in the West. One observer in 1910 found families in Montana and Colorado still living in isolation in log cabins, but this frontier situation was unusual.[9] Yet throughout the West, women bore heavy responsibility for farm maintenance, typically a family enterprise. In addition to housekeeping chores, farm wives cared for the family's vegetable plot and for poultry and livestock for family use. During harvest time, they cooked around-the-clock for family and farm hands. Among the

*A middle-class family and servants—the Drummonds on the back porch of their home on West 22nd Street in New York City, circa 1910.*

*Magazines like The Ladies' Home Journal glorified home and motherhood for the average middle-class woman.*

*Maintaining the farm: a family enterprise.*

majority of non-wealthy farm families, daughters often worked as teachers or as domestic servants in other households to supplement the family income.

Farm life could be volatile. Farm income was dependent on variable crop production, and the fluctuations caused uncertainty, as did the movement of farmers to the cities, and sometimes back again. Divorce rates were higher in the West than in the East, although this difference partly reflected the less stringent divorce laws in many Western states. Surveys of Midwestern farm wives were filled with complaints of hard work and isolation. Yet by the 1890s, small towns dotted the rural landscape. Churches provided social life, revolving around sewing circles and community dinners. Women on farms and in small towns dominated the WCTU.

Not all adult farm women were married. The sizable percentages of working women classified as farm workers in the censuses of this period included single women who hired themselves out, like men, to pick crops and do farm chores. Most women in this group were African-American women in the South. The census of 1900 also counted 300,000 women—predominantly native-born whites—who were farmers, planters, and overseers. Most of these women were probably widows working land they had inherited, but some single women owned and worked farm land. Single women, for example, could acquire free land under the 1865 Homestead Act. In Colorado and Wyoming, women filed about 12 percent of such land claims.

In the South, the prolonged post-Civil War agricultural depression forced white as well as black women to join husbands and fathers in the fields, while many daughters of the less well-to-do found employment in rural textile mills. The situation for black farmers was particularly difficult, since the ending of slavery in the South did not bring African Americans the anticipated emancipation. Rather, social and legal discrimination continued through laws enforcing segregation and a second-class status for them, while an agricultural peonage developed which resembled their situation under slavery. "Sharecropping" was the name given to this system of farming. Under it, blacks farmed land owned by white planters who allotted them a yearly share of the crops. At the same time, the sharecroppers were beholden to white merchants, to whom they accumulated long-term and virtually unpayable debts for seeds and supplies.

A variant situation emerged in the Southwest, including Texas, New Mexico, Arizona, and California. Here the appearance of intensive agriculture in the form of "factory" farms owned by Anglo-Americans undermined the position of the Hispanic-Americans who had previously worked the land in small-scale, subsistence farms, often in communal settings. These Hispanic-Americans were a mixture of Native Americans, Mexicans, and the Spanish who had conquered the Southwest in the seventeenth century. (The U.S. penetration of this region dated from the late 1840s.)

In Texas, Anglos enclosed common grazing land and reduced Hispanics to field hands and tenant farmers working on large cotton farms. They also recruited cheap laborers among Mexican families emigrating northward, especially after the Mexican Revolution of 1910 created havoc in Mexico. In New Mexico,

*A North Carolina sharecropper's homestead in 1919.*

Anglo professionals in the cities used a combination of money and graft to buy out Hispanic owners and to combine their subsistence farms into cattle ranches. The Hispanic owners were able to hold onto their land for a time by leaving farms in the charge of their wives while the men found day labor elsewhere. In California, as agribusiness took over farming, Hispanics were reduced to seasonal laborers picking crops such as grapes and lettuce.

This Anglo takeover of land produced widespread poverty among those they displaced. Historian Jacqueline Jones has described the typical living situation among Southern sharecroppers: Families lived in one- or two-room cabins of 15 to 20 square feet, lacking glass windows, screens, running water, sanitary conditions, and adequate insulation.[10] These difficult living arrangements were not untypical of what poor people endured throughout the nation—whether in urban tenements, or Mexican-American barrios in Texas and California, or the overcrowded living conditions of early Chinatowns. Such living conditions bred disease, low life expectancy, and high rates of infant mortality.

# THE WORKING-CLASS WOMEN

## Immigration and Ethnicity

Immigrants fleeing economic upheaval and political tyranny in Europe, and drawn by economic opportunity in the United States, began to flood American shores in the 1880s. Without funds and thrust on an industrial, urban society, they and their families became prey to industry's demand for cheap labor. They jammed tenement flats in decaying city districts and crowded company towns associated with the New England mills and the Pennsylvania mining fields. Earlier German immigrants had had sufficient funds to make their way to Midwestern farm lands, but the Italians, Slavs, Greeks, and Jews, who were the majority of turn-of-century immigrants, did not have such resources. Entering the United States through Ellis Island, they remained in Eastern cities and worked in factories and mines. Mexicans migrating to the United States during those years entered primarily through Texas, and they found employment as seasonal farm laborers and as workers in Southwestern mines and on the railroads then being built.

Among working-class women, unmarried daughters were the primary group who worked for remuneration outside the home. For immigrant women, the percentage was high. In 1900, approximately 25 percent of unmarried immigrant women worked, compared with 15 percent of native-born Anglo women. Immigrant women entering the work force encountered a gender hierarchy that reflected their own culture's values as well as the nativism rampant during the period. White native-born women monopolized clerical work, sales work, and semiskilled factory labor. Immigrant Slavic women found employment in unskilled factory labor and in domestic work. Many Jewish women entered the garment industry, which even employed them in skilled positions—largely because they had often done skilled work in the Eastern European towns from which they had fled anti-Semitic persecution. The work patterns of Italian and Mexican-American women were influenced by strong patriarchal cultures in which male family members guarded the virtue of unmarried women. For the most part, young women of these groups rarely sought employment in sales or as domestics, because in these positions they might find themselves alone with men to whom they were not related.

*Immigrants arriving in the United States, circa 1910.*

In addition to ethnic values and mainstream racism, important variables determining the patterns of women's industrial employment included the types of industrial employment available and the location of factories and fields in relation to the location of ethnic neighborhoods. Women in cities such as New York and Philadelphia with a variety of light industries were more likely to work in factories than women in heavy-industry cities, such as Buffalo and Cincinnati, or in single-industry towns, such as Homestead, Pennsylvania, which was devoted exclusively to steel production. The assumption was that women were not strong enough for the strenuous physical labor heavy industry required. In Pittsburgh, however, Italian women were employed in a variety of industries whose proximity to Italian neighborhoods allowed male family members to provide oversight. And in textile towns like Lawrence, Massachusetts, the mills employed entire families, including women and children.

*Cotton mill workers, circa 1900.*

Even though immigrant women bore primary responsibility for home and children, it is incorrect to assume, no matter how patriarchal their culture, that they made no financial contribution to the family economy. Italian and Polish wives, for example, often had lived and worked independently in their countries of origin while husbands and fathers went back and forth to the United States as part of a seasonal work migration. In Buffalo, New York,

*An immigrant woman and her children do piecework at home.*

Italian married women picked crops in the summers on nearby farms; they had done similar work in Italy. Married Jewish women in New York City pushed vending carts and tended family stores, as they had in Eastern European *shtetls*. In Los Angeles, Mexican-American women were sometimes the first family members to take up new sorts of jobs. Like New York City Jewish women, they became street vendors selling, in their case, homemade tamales.

Married immigrant women who did not work outside the home often found remunerative employment within it. Much of this work went unrecorded by census takers, since women from patriarchal cultures often did not want to reveal work that might demean their husband's sense of masculinity. Married immigrant women ironed and did laundry for middle-class women. These were substantial tasks in an age with neither electric washing machines nor wash-and-wear fabrics. Or they took in piecework from garment factories. They housed boarders, accommodating the large numbers of single men among certain migrant groups, especially Slavs, Italians, and Mexican Americans. In Homestead, Pennsylvania, where there was little employment for women outside their homes, more than 40 percent of families housed at least one paying boarder.

***Asian Immigration***    Chinese and Japanese individuals also migrated to the United States in the late nineteenth century. Settling primarily on the West Coast, Chinese immigration was composed almost entirely of single men who worked in the mines and on the transcontinental railroad. Often these men provided support for families on the verge of starvation in the overpopulated and economically depressed Chinese province of Canton from which most of them came. Expecting to return to China, many of them married before they left their homeland. But their intention to return often did not work out. In 1900, there were 1,887 Chinese men in the United States for every 100 women, or a ratio of almost 19 to 1. Immigrant Chinese women in this period were mostly prostitutes, kidnapped or purchased from their families by the Tong associations which controlled many Chinatowns. They were brought to the United States to insure that Chinese men would not become involved with American women and would remain loyal to their families of origin.

West Coast nativism against the Chinese was virulent, and in 1882, Congress prohibited any further Chinese immigration. The predominantly male character of Chinese communities was thus continued for many decades. In 1910, about one married Chinese man in ten had his wife with him in the United States. As with Italians and Mexican Americans, Chinese family structure was especially patriarchal, and this trait was furthered by the Chinese veneration of ancestors. In China, male sons, as carriers of the family lineage, were prized, and daughters were considered of little value. Although polygamy did not develop, concubinage was not unknown. In China, married couples lived with the patrilineal family, which was extended rather than nuclear in composition, and young wives served their husbands and their mothers-in-law.

This structure broke down somewhat in the United States, where financial need often necessitated that wives work alongside husbands in stores and laundries, and limited immigration often produced a nuclear family structure. Small business ownership attracted the Chinese because the immigration laws allowed "merchants" to bring their wives to the United States. (The Chinese association with the laundry business began during the California gold

*A Chinese woman who was believed to be a prostitute.*

rush days of the late 1840s, when few women were present to do men's washing, and Anglo men scorned what they considered women's work.) Still, Chinese women usually did not leave their homes to work as domestics or factory employees.

Moreover, traditionalism could control their lives in unique ways. For centuries the Chinese had considered beauty in women to be associated with small feet; hence affluent families in China bound girls' feet so that they would not grow, in a painful and dangerous process which produced what were often little more than deformed stumps. (The European Cinderella folk tale, with its emphasis on small feet, may have originated in China.) One Chinese woman, living with her family in Butte, Montana, almost never left her home. On hearing of the Chinese Revolution in 1911, she unbound her feet. It was a "symbolic act of personal emancipation." She subsequently discarded her Chinese clothes for American dress.[11]

Japanese migrants first came to the United States as workers on Hawaiian sugar plantations. Subsequently, some of them came from Hawaii to California because Chinese exclusion opened up jobs. However, they soon encountered a strong nativist reaction from Anglos. Given Japan's military strength, President Theodore Roosevelt was reluctant to offend the Japanese government through direct exclusion. Thus in 1907, he signed a "Gentlemen's Agreement" with the Japanese rulers, under which they agreed to restrict Japanese migration to the United States. Because by the terms of this treaty wives in Japan were allowed to join their husbands in the United States, the Japanese did not have the same problem with family formation as the Chinese, for whom the policy was to exclude all women, even wives.

The notion of romantic love as a condition for marriage did not exist in these Asian cultures. Thus the Japanese solved the problem of finding wives through a system known as "picture bride" exchange. Under this system marriage brokers circulated pictures of eligible women living in Japan among Japanese men in the United States wanting wives. Married in Japan by proxy, and as wives eligible to emigrate to the United States, many Japanese women met their husbands for the first time at the San Francisco boat dock. In 1907, the small Japanese-American community was located primarily in California, and it numbered about 50,000. Males outnumbered females four to one. By 1920, however, as a result of the "picture bride" exchange, the gender imbalance among Japanese Americans had been ended. The Cable Act of 1922, which forbade citizenship to foreign-born wives, ended the practice.

In contrast to the Chinese, the Japanese tended to locate in farm areas rather than in cities. There many became specialists in fruits and vegetables being introduced into the United States. For example, they pioneered in growing cantaloupes in California's Imperial Valley. They marketed these specialties in stands and shops in urban areas. Many grew prosperous as a result of this industry. As was standard among farm families, wives worked alongside husbands in these enterprises. They also maintained the traditional Japanese family, in which their role, like that of Chinese women, was one of service.

The experience of the tiny group of Korean migrants to the United States in these years was similar to that of the Japanese. About 7,000 Koreans came to the United States between 1902 and

1905. They were imported to work on Hawaiian sugar plantations because the Japanese laborers there were engaging in work stoppages and strikes. About 1,000 of the original number migrated to California, where they worked as migrant crop laborers. Like the Japanese, they began to engage in truck farming outside the cities. Korea had become a possession of Japan in 1905; thus they were subject to the 1907 "Gentlemen's Agreement." They, too, imported "picture brides" as wives, and these women found adjustment to life in the United States especially difficult, since traditionalism was so strong in Korea that families of any means confined their women to "inner rooms" and forbade them to go out during the day. In the United States, however, many worked alongside their husbands in the fields and took in boarders to make ends meet.

In Korea, American missionaries had converted many Korean women and their families to Christianity, which offered women less confining gender arrangements than the traditional culture. In the United States, Korean women were known for their support of the movement for Korean independence from Japan. Picture brides, many of whom were educated, were especially involved in the work of public education and fund-raising for this cause.

With the 1907 restriction of Japanese and Korean immigration, Hawaiian planters imported workers from the Philippines, a U.S. colony after 1898. By 1932 they comprised 70 percent of plantation workers.

***African-American Women***    Among American women, black women have born the double burden of gender and race discrimination, the latter magnified by attitudes stemming from centuries of slavery. In 1900, 43 percent of African-American women were employed outside the home, compared with 15 percent of white native women and 25 percent of immigrant women. One-fourth of black married women were in the work force, compared with less than 4 percent of white wives. Almost all African-American women were employed as farm workers or domestics. Sales and clerical work, in addition to factory labor, were almost completely denied them.

In the years before World War I, American racism reached the heights of virulence. Schools and public facilities in the South were openly segregated; in the North the segregation was more subtle, since it was often the result of blacks living in areas separate from whites. Yet it was nonetheless real. In the South, where the vast majority of blacks lived, lynchings of black males and riots against black communities were not uncommon. Black women were stereotyped as "mammies" or as oversexed, willing sexual partners. In Southern black schools, female students were taught to dress and to behave formally when off campus to discourage the attentions of white men. Some states forbade black women to use the titles "Miss" or "Mrs." or to try on clothing before purchasing it. The penalty for raping a black woman was less stringent than when a white woman was the victim. Separate washrooms were provided for white women and men in public places, but black women and men often had to share the same facilities.

Faced with such difficulties, black women were not nourished on any myth of female fragility. Nor was the gender traditionalism that was found in Asian, Mexican, and Italian cultures typical of their experience. American blacks came from African societies which were matrilineal (descent traced through the mother), and female independence had been furthered under slavery, which undermined family ties. African-American women expected to assume as much responsibility for family support as husbands and fathers. Often, black women could secure work more easily as domestics than their husbands could as laborers. Surveying conditions for blacks nationwide, muckraker Ray Stannard Baker concluded that "a Negro woman of the lower class rarely expects her husband to support her."[12]

Such strength also underlay the success of African-American women who entered the professions. In medicine and law, the percentages were higher for African-American women than for Anglo women. In 1910, about 3 percent of all black lawyers were women (5 percent for whites) and 13 percent of all black doctors were women (6 percent for whites). At the same time, African-American women's professional advancement may have represented an adaptation to economic realities. Upwardly mobile black women could not enter clerical work and therefore had to secure professional training. Most would become schoolteachers; many were more educated than their husbands.

Nursing, like schoolteaching, was a non-elite profession open to African-American women. But white training hospitals and schools excluded them: they were denied admission in the South, while Northern institutions enforced quotas. As a result, African

*Working conditions show little improvement as women make Army uniforms in 1917.*

Americans established a national network of 200 training hospitals and schools. Most of them were initially supported by funds from black women's clubs, although some white foundations, like the Rockefeller Foundation, provided support.

Discrimination and poverty, in addition to migration to Southern cities and to the North, placed great stress on the African-American family structure, leaving many women as heads of households. Yet such family patterns did not necessarily reflect disorganization or result from male desertion. The death rate among black men was higher than among black women, and many African-American women were widows. And, the northward migration of blacks contained a disproportionate number of women, for whom there were simply not enough men to marry. Moreover, most African Americans continued to live in nuclear families, as they had attempted to under slavery and ever since.

***Working Conditions***    In all occupations, conditions were difficult for women workers. Without strong unions to represent workers' interests, employers paid low wages and violated state safety laws with impunity. Waitresses often worked under unsanitary conditions and depended on tips for a living. Even department-store

saleswomen—who occupied positions of higher status—often had
no vacations, no rest breaks, and no chairs on which to sit. (Store
owners wanted saleswomen to appear busy even when they were
not serving customers.)

Similar exploitative conditions characterized factory labor for
women. The women's garment industry, a major industrial
employer of women in the early twentieth century, was representative. Centered in cities, the industry was organized around both
factory and home labor. Major firms often sent finishing work to
individual subcontractors, who set up small workshops in tenement
apartments where rents were low and where they could hire women
who lived nearby for a pittance. This cheap method of production
became a national scandal because of the unsafe and unsanitary
conditions of the so-called "sweatshops."

Women employees in garment factories worked 10 hours a day
during the week, and a half day on Saturday. They were required
to buy their own equipment. They were relegated to tasks less
prestigious and lower-paid than those that male workers performed. They suffered other indignities. The Triangle Shirtwaist
Company in New York City in 1911 became notorious as the
scene of a major industrial fire. Many lives were lost in the fire
because, to discourage pilferage, the only exit from the building
was locked during working hours.

Under such conditions, why did working-class women work?
Many Americans at the time believed that they did so to accu-
mulate a dowry and to buy clothes and other frivolities. Some
native Anglo women may have worked for this reason. Yet studies
by both private foundations and government agencies concluded
that the "pin-money theory" was a myth. Daughters of the working class worked because limited family incomes required their
contribution. The many working women who lived with their families did so, not to save money to spend on themselves, but
because there was insufficient housing in American cities for
unmarried working women; because many immigrant cultures
considered it disgraceful for unmarried daughters to live alone;
and, most important, because many working women were not
paid sufficient wages to afford a private residence. A 1910
Women's Trade Union League survey of Chicago department-
store saleswomen showed that as many as 30 percent of these
workers earned little more than a subsistence wage.

Mary "Mother" Jones, labor organizer, 1916.

**Strikes and Unions**    Why, then, did working women not rebel against their lot? They often did. Leaders of the labor movement included women as well as men. The nonagenarian Mary "Mother" Jones devoted her long life to organizing laborers in the most oppressive industries in the nation—coal, Western mining, and Southern cotton mills. Elizabeth Gurley Flynn's fiery oratory brought her to public prominence at the age of 17. Women also participated in strikes and labor organizations. Layoffs or wage cuts could rouse the anger of women workers as well as of men. In 1898, women glovemakers in Chicago went on strike when new assembly-line techniques were introduced. They had tolerated piecework wages, tyrannical male foremen, and having to buy their own equipment. But the threat of a wage cut was more than they could bear. In 1905, in Troy, New York, 8,000 women working in commercial laundries went on strike because of the introduction of fines for talking and lateness, irregular work assignments, and a new machine—all of which had the effect of cutting wages.

Between 1909 and 1913, such episodes became common, particularly in the garment industry. In 1909, 20,000 shirtwaist workers in New York City and Philadelphia took to the streets in the most famous women's strike of the early twentieth century. In 1910 in New York City, 60,000 workers in the cloak and suit business struck; 10 percent of these workers were women. Strike activity that year spread to garment workers in Chicago, Cleveland, and Milwaukee.

*Shirtwaist workers on strike.*

In 1911, protesting the conditions that produced the Triangle fire, 80,000 workers marched up Fifth Avenue for four hours. In 1912, the determination of striking women textile workers in Lawrence, Massachusetts, was central to the success of one of the decade's most violent confrontations between industry and labor.

These strikes demonstrate that working women in the early twentieth century had the capacity for labor militancy and organization. The International Ladies' Garment Workers Union (ILGWU), founded in 1900 as an American Federation of Labor (AFL) affiliate, greatly increased its membership as a result of these strikes. By 1913, it was the third largest AFL affiliate. Some

*The bodies of workers killed in the 1911 Triangle Shirtwaist Company fire.*

observers at the time contended that women made better strikers than men. One analyst judged that women possessed a "characteristic feminine tenacity" and that, without husbands and children dependent on them, unmarried women workers felt freer to challenge their employers.[13]

For strikes to succeed was difficult. To break up strikes, employers had behind them the power of the courts and the police, who did not always hesitate to use brutality against women strikers. The 1909 shirtwaist worker's strike succeeded in part because a number of well-to-do philanthropists joined the picket lines. Their participation brought public sympathy to the strikers and forced the owners to settle. But even in this strike, not all the workers were successful. Women at the Triangle Shirtwaist Company, among the organizers of the strike, gained no concessions from their employer. Instead, a number of them were killed in the devastating 1911 Triangle fire.

Moreover, despite the growth of the ILGWU, to unionize women workers was not easy. In 1900, about 3 percent of factory women were unionized; in 1913, after the garment strikes, the statistic stood at only 6 percent. To discourage organizing, employers often hired women from different immigrant backgrounds, with different languages and social customs. The female labor force was unstable. Many women did seasonal work and were laid off during slack periods. Young women, who made up the majority of female workers, often looked on work as a temporary occupation before marriage. Raised to be dependent, many women workers hesitated to assert their individuality by joining a union and challenging parental authority.

And the workplace itself could be intimidating, reinforcing the sense of powerlessness inculcated by families and the environing culture. Many male supervisors were aggressive, reprimanding the workers under them in line with the prejudice that unskilled laborers were naturally lazy. To ensure productivity, women were not permitted to sit down in many factories. Moreover, sexual harassment was not uncommon. Faced with such difficulties, it was easier for some young women to repress complaints against the rigors of their jobs and to focus on the rites of courtship and the opportunities to socialize with their friends in the workroom.

Finally, women failed to unionize because existing labor unions were hesitant to organize them. The Knights of Labor, which flourished in the 1880s, had supported women's strikes and recruited women as members. But violence and economic depression destroyed the Knights of Labor in the 1890s. The AFL, founded in 1886 and composed mainly of skilled craftsmen, came to dominate organized labor. Given the difficulties of unionization, skilled workers had little interest in taking on the problems of unskilled laborers. (The craft-organized AFL also excluded African Americans and most immigrant males.) Nor did AFL members want job competition from women, always a cheap source of labor. The AFL was devoted to the idea of the "family wage," under which men made the income for their families, while women stayed at home.

The AFL constitution officially outlawed sex discrimination among member unions, and most unions nominally complied. But because women and men performed different tasks in many industries, union leaders simply excluded women's work when defining the crafts included in their union, even when this work might be considered skilled labor. One official of the International Association of Machinists told a labor investigator that "a machinist is born and not made. One must have a feeling for machines, and women haven't got that."[14] Such beliefs about women dominated many skilled crafts. Even in those few AFL

unions like the ILGWU, where women members were the majority, the officers were invariably men—with the exception of the
secretary, frequently a woman. There were other reasons for the exclusion of women. For men,
the union was often a club, a refuge from the family, a place of
male bonding, and an escape from everyday life. Unions generally
met in saloons, traditional sites of male camaraderie. Moreover,
many wives of working men were probably suspicious of allowing
their husbands to socialize with other women. And many women
workers viewed unions as "male" institutions.

The gender discrimination of the AFL was not so true of the more
radical unions. Like the Knights of Labor, the Industrial Workers of
the World (IWW) did not exclude women. The IWW initially
focused on unskilled, mass production industries in the West and
the South, and its picket lines often included the nonworking wives
of copper and coal miners, who battled the police with brooms and
buckets. When the IWW moved East, the union concentrated on the
textile mills, which employed entire families.

Similarly, the militant activism of socialist women was central
to the garment strikes of 1910. Led by a strong Woman's National
Committee, socialist women's neighborhood locals gave them community access to garment workers, many of whom were young
Jewish women whose Eastern European backgrounds included radicalism. Still, both the IWW and the socialists emphasized class
struggle above gender concerns, while male members exhibited
gender chauvinism. Such attitudes were particularly true of the
IWW, which never outgrew the masculine culture of Western mining in which it had first taken root.

The sexism of male unions, in addition to middle-class
reformism, resulted in cross-class alliances of women to improve
conditions for working women. Two major Progressive organizations grew from this alliance. The first, the Consumers' League,
emerged in 1890 in New York and then in 1899 on the national
level. It was formed to improve working conditions for department-
store saleswomen through consumer boycotts. The second, the
Women's Trade Union League (WTUL), was founded in 1903 at a
convention of the AFL. Its goal was to educate and organize both
middle-class and working-class women to support the cause of
women's labor, especially factory labor. The WTUL remained an
amalgam of workers and well-to-do women. Among its early state

and national presidents were Ellen Henrotin, a former president of the General Federation of Women's Clubs; Margaret Dreier Robins, a wealthy New York philanthropist; and Mary Anderson, a daughter of Swedish immigrants. Anderson began her career working in a shoe factory and later became director of the Women's Bureau in the Department of Labor between 1920 and 1944. In addition to other efforts, the WTUL led the garment strikes in 1910.

Yet even with some funding from the AFL, the WTUL was always short of money, and its successes were limited. In local chapters, middle-class members, called "allies," often stressed cultural uplift above union organization. Although the WTUL constitution stipulated that working-class women constitute a majority of its board of directors, workers often felt patronized by the "allies". Socialist members of the WTUL also felt alienated. By 1913, these differences, plus the WTUL's difficulty in organizing women outside the garment trades, led the League to downplay union campaigns to work for legislation on behalf of working women. Still, for a decade and more it brought women of varying economic statuses together. The WTUL has been one of the few women's organizations in the twentieth century in which women have crossed class lines in support of a common cause.

***Married Life and the Working-Class Community***   The paramount goal of most young working women was probably not improved working conditions, but marriage. Films, plays, and novels hammered the theme home. The message of popular culture supported both the traditional goals of parents intent on good matches for their daughters and the rebelliousness of those daughters for whom marriage seemed the way to end their status as dependents supplementing family income. Yet marriage among the working class produced its own stresses. Particular conditions varied among different cultures, regions, income levels, and age groups. Still, some general conclusions can be drawn.

Life was not easy for working-class women. Men left the responsibility for contraception to their wives, who were expected to be sexually available to their husbands. But information about birth control was not easy to come by. Margaret Sanger contended that she began her crusade for birth control because, as a visiting nurse in New York City's Lower East Side, she was horrified by the numbers of botched abortions she observed. When she opened her first

*Margaret Sanger, crusader for birth control availability and information.*

birth control clinic in the Brownsville section of Brooklyn, over 400 women came there as clients the first day.

Many sociologists contend that the rigid patriarchal family remained the model in the working class longer than in the middle class. One observer at the time wrote that "the conventions of the working class are more rigid than any other class. They are the last to be affected by changing psychology or institutions."[15] Given the financial pressures on the working class, the father-dominant model underlay harsh treatment of wives by husbands, and children by parents. Under these circumstances, marriages could become strained, with husbands and wives living, according to one observer, with "little affection."[16] Husbands generally gave wages to wives to distribute, but each then retreated to their own territory—the men to saloons or sporting events; the women to homes or children. For the working class, divorce was difficult. It was expensive; it required a lawyer and, among Catholics, it was a disgrace. Estranged couples did not, however, always remain together. Desertion was not uncommon among the working class, and by the 1920s, their divorce rate equalled that of the middle class.

Variations existed in all these patterns of behavior. Within African-American rural communities in the South, for example, families banded together around kin and community, helping one another to celebrate weddings and to bury their dead. Women formed mutual aid societies to help each other's families pay for life insurance and medical care. These black women in the South, according to Jacqueline Jones, had a more equal relationship with husbands than did middle-class white women because their rural folk culture was based on group cooperation rather than on male competition and the accumulation of goods.[17]

Such cooperation also characterized the original Hispanic communities in the Southwest. In this society daughters inherited equally with sons, and the whole family participated in child rearing. In both these societies—blacks in the rural South and Hispanics in the Southwest—aging women were held in great respect. They were the Southern midwives and the Southwestern *curanderas* who delivered babies and practiced herbal medicine. In the Hispanic communities, godmothers and godfathers were "comadres" and "copadres," who helped parent children.

Some historians contend that many immigrant communities developed similar arrangements, especially since migration had to it a "chain" character, with new migrants locating where kin and friends already lived. When living quarters were tight, people gathered on stoops and in streets. And, when destitution was an ever present threat, the boundaries between family and neighbors could blur, with the shared community providing support.

**Native Americans**  Such patterns of cooperation were especially evident in Native-American communities. By the late nineteenth century, invading United States settlers and the nation's army had conquered these original inhabitants and had forced them onto reservations, which usually consisted of the areas of a tribe's original

*Indian children were sent to boarding school where they were taught Anglo values rather than those of their Indian heritage.*

territory that were the least desirable to whites. The federal government was uncomprehending of Indian culture, which bore little similarity to that of a modernizing capitalist society. Under the Dawes Severalty Act (1887), individual land ownership was imposed on many Indian tribes, replacing their traditional communal ownership. Concurrently, Indian children were removed from their families and placed in boarding schools, where they were taught Anglo values rather than those of their Indian heritage.

Native-American societies were many, reflecting their origin in separate tribal groups, with differing languages and customs. Some, like the Pueblos, were settled agriculturalists; others, like the Utes, were nomadic hunters and gatherers. In 1900, more than 100 languages were still in use among Native Americans. Some Native-

American societies practiced patrilineal descent; others were matrilineal. Most, however, lived in extended families, with demarcations among clans. Like the Hispanics of the Southwest, whom they probably influenced, most Native Americans lived in small, tightly knit communities. They revered the land and had no concept of private ownership. According to Paula Gunn Allen, an important contemporary Native-American writer: "They believe that the human and the nonhuman world are linked in one vast, living sphere; that the linkage is not material but spiritual."[18]

In many Native-American tribes, women held great authority. Among the Cherokees, women voted with men in selecting leaders. Moreover, women in each Cherokee village elected delegates to a Women's Council, which was presided over by a "Beloved Woman." Among the Hopi, the leader of the village was assisted in his duties by a female relative called the "keeper of the fire," while every clan in a Hopi village was headed by a matriarch, or clan mother. In this society, houses were owned by the women and inherited through the youngest daughter. This system is known as ultimogeniture. Most Native-American societies held a rite to honor girls at the onset of menstruation; in all of them, aging people were respected for their wisdom; in some, women were shamans and healers.

In many Native-American societies, male homosexuals, revered as "berdaches," took on the roles of tricksters and shamans. Lesbian women, called "amazons" by anthropologist Walter Williams, married individuals of their own gender. In some tribes, they joined men in hunting expeditions. In many Native American religions a female figure heads the pantheon. Among the Iroquois, the genatrix spirit is Sky Woman; among the Hopi, Hard Beings Woman. Others honor Spider Woman, or Corn Woman, or Serpent Woman. Among the Lakota, the belief is that woman was created first, and that man was then fashioned out of a drop of the original woman's menstrual blood.

## THE OTHER WAY—PROSTITUTION

Not all nonnative women in the early twentieth century assumed the roles of wife and mother or of volunteer worker or paid employee. Some turned to prostitution. In the late nineteenth

*Prostitution—innate depravity
or just another kind of work?*

century, prostitution was on the increase due to the explosive growth of cities. With a characteristic Victorian attitude, many public officials regarded prostitution as a "necessary evil" to protect the virtue of respectable women. In many cities the police drove prostitution into so-called "red-light districts," away from middle-class areas.

In the nineteenth century, officials in many cities tried to introduce the European system of licensing, under which prostitution was not illegal but rather prostitutes were required to register with

*"Crib girls"—prostitutes at a drinking "bee" at White Chapel in the mining town of Dawson, Alaska at the turn of the century.*

municipal authorities and to have periodic examinations for venereal disease. In every instance, however, coalitions of woman's-rights and social-purity reformers defeated these attempts. After 1900, cities and states appointed vice commissions to study ways of ending prostitution. As a result of their reports, by the 1920s red-light districts were mostly closed down. But clever madams reopened their houses under the guise of dance studios and massage parlors. They also invented "call-girl systems," keeping lists of women whom they telephoned to arrange meetings with clients. Prostitution seems to have declined in the 1920s, but the freer morality of that era may have been more important than the work of the vice commissions in this decline.

### The Practitioners

Many prostitutes worked in brothels, where madams—often resourceful businesswomen—arranged solicitation and protection. Others were connected with male pimps, then called "cadets," to whom they gave their earnings in return for protection. Many prostitutes worked on their own, making assignations in dance halls and saloons or on the streets and then using hotels that catered to prostitutes and clients.

Why did women become prostitutes? The widespread belief was that male procurers employed by large syndicates forced women into a "life of vice." For a time around 1910, concern about the "white-slave trade" escalated to a national hysteria, with rumors that men with hypodermic needles sought victims to drug and abduct. But with the exception of Chinese prostitution in the West, there was little evidence of control by large syndicates.

Most surveys of prostitution played down the white-slave theory and found the explanation in economic need. Women became prostitutes because they could not find employment or because they could earn more money as a prostitute than as a seamstress or a salesclerk. "Poverty causes prostitution," concluded the Illinois vice commission in 1916.[19] This argument was satisfying to a society still ambivalent about female sexuality. Yet it provided only a partial explanation. Many prostitutes disclosed that they had entered the occupation due to "personal inclination." What this statement indicated was their participation in a society where sexuality was open and where prostitution was simply another form of work.

## THE NEW SENSUALITY

By the 1890s, a new civilization was emerging in America. This society was more secular, more commercial, more modern. Department-store owners constructed lavish buildings with large stocks of consumption items. Beauty parlors for curling hair and massaging skin appeared. New forms of entertainment celebrated sensuality. Sensational daily newspapers (so-called "yellow journals"), which focused on celebrities and scandal, were successfully launched by publishers like Joseph Pulitzer and William Randolph Hearst. There were dance halls, amusement parks at the end of trolley lines, such as New York's Coney Island, and the movies, which initially played in working-class neighborhoods.

By and large, these institutions of pleasure were designed for young, urban, working-class men and women. They were an expanding group of consumers eager to establish their autonomy,

*The lavish dance hall of the Biltmore Hotel.*

and they had limited space at home for courtship. The women of this group expected to go to dance halls and amusement parks and to meet men. For some, sex was the next step. Investigators for the Massachusetts Vice Commission reported in 1914 that in every Massachusetts city, young women loitered around dance halls, waiting to be picked up by men. "To the total stranger," the investigators reported, "they talk [about] their desire to 'see life,' to 'get out of this dead hole,' to go to Boston or to New York." Many of these women, the investigators found, were willing to have sexual relations with them.[20] This may have been sexual license, but it was not prostitution, as the Massachusetts investigators pointed out. For most of these women were incensed by an offer of payment. Payment meant prostitution, and they did not consider themselves prostitutes.

The attitude of these women reflected the freer morality that was emerging in the United States in the 1900s and that appeared first among young, working-class women. By 1912, it was evident among their middle-class peers. In that year occurred the so-called "dance craze." All over America, it seemed, dance halls were thronged with people dancing the bunny hug, the turkey trot, and the tango—dances previously identified with the working class. The new vogue of sensual dances signaled the emergence into the mainstream of a new sensuality among women—a sensuality which would be both freeing and yet confining.

### The World of the Waitress

For several months in 1920, reporter Frances Donovan worked as a waitress to study that occupation. Donovan's action was not unique. In the Progressive reform era a number of educated young women eager to advance themselves and the cause of women entered the working-class world and recorded their experiences. Few, however, were so challenged by their findings as was Donovan.

At first Donovan was shocked. In their spare time, her new acquaintances boasted of their affairs and openly discussed their abortions. Her sheltered upbringing had not prepared her for this or for the women's use of obscenities and their retelling off-color jokes heard from patrons. But slowly Donovan came to respect these women. She began to believe that their way of life represented a critique of middle-class values. Many of them had left their husbands; they were economically independent and thus free from male dominance. "The waitress has achieved a man's independence in her relations with men; she doesn't have to get married, and she doesn't have to stay married. . . . She is a free soul," wrote Donovan.[21]

Undoubtedly, Donovan romanticized waitressing, which was characterized by long hours and hard work. Yet there was truth in what she had to say. Were not these women more honest about life than their middle-class peers? "Here," Donovan concluded, "we have the feminist movement and ideals embodied in a class."[22] But was sexual and economic liberation enough? Should marriage so easily be condemned as oppressive? And if women left the home, who would raise their children? (Children are absent from Donovan's narrative.) These were some of the questions facing American women of all classes in the early years of this century.

## NOTES

[1] Katherine G. Busbey, *Home Life in America* (New York: MacMillan, 1910), p. 149.

[2] Busbey, *Home Life in America,* p. 149.

[3] Helen Merrell Lynd and Robert S. Lynd, *Middletown in Transition: A Study in Cultural Conflicts* (New York: Harcourt Brace Jovanovich, 1937), p. 95.

[4] American Sociological Society, *Papers and Proceedings of the Third Annual Meeting of the American Sociological Society: The Family* (Chicago: University of Chicago Press, 1908), p. 132.

[5] Lucy Maynard Salmon, *Progress in the Household* (Boston: Houghton Mifflin, 1906), p. 95.

[6] Barbara Ehrenreich and Dierdre English, *For Their Own Good: 150 Years of the Experts' Advice to Women* (Garden City, NY: Doubleday, 1978), p. 128.

[7] Frances Parkinson Keyes, *All Flags Flying: Reminiscences of Frances Parkinson Keyes* (New York: McGraw Hill, 1972), pp. 13, 31.

[8] Mabel S. Ulrich, "A Doctor's Diary, 1904–1932," *Scribner's,* June, 1933. Reprinted in *Ms.,* I (July 1972): 11–14.

[9] Busbey, *Home Life in America,* p. 283.

[10] Jacqueline Jones, *Labor of Love, Labor of Sorrow: Black Women, Work, and the Family from Slavery to the Present* (New York: Basic Books, 1985), p. 86.

[11] Rose Hum Lee, *The Chinese in the United States of America* (Hong Kong: Hong Kong University Press, 1960), pp. 192–93.

[12] Ray Stannard Baker, *Following the Color Line: American Negro Citizenship in the Progressive Era* (Garden City, NY: Doubleday, Page, 1908), p. 141.

[13] Helen Marot, *American Labor Unions, by a Member* (New York: Henry Holt, 1914), p. 74.

[14] Theresa Wolfson, *The Woman Worker and the Trade Unions* (New York: International, 1926), p. 110.

[15] Wolfson, *Woman Worker and the Trade Unions*, p. 43.

[16] Streightoff, *Standard of Living*, pp. 138–64.

[17] Jones, *Labor of Love*, p. 99.

[18] Paula Gunn Allen, *The Sacred Hoop: Recovering the Feminine in American Indian Traditions* (Boston: Beacon Press, 1986), p. 22.

[19] State of Illinois, *Report of the Senate Vice Committee* (Chicago, 1911), p. 203.

[20] Massachusetts Commission for the Investigation of the White Slave Traffic, *Report of the Commission for the Investigation of the White Slave Traffic, so-called* (Boston, 1914), p. 43.

[21] Donovan, *Woman Who Waits*, p. 224.

[22] *Ibid.*, p. 226.


## BIBLIOGRAPHY

A wealth of material is available to reconstruct a profile of the middle-class woman during any period of her history. For the early twentieth century, one can consult newspapers and journals, diaries and biographies, contemporary analyses and novels. On the history of the family, see Carl Degler, *At Odds: Women and the Family In America From the Revolution to the Present* (New York: Oxford University Press, 1980); Michael Gordon (ed.), *The American Family in Social-Historical Perspective*, 3rd. ed. (New York: St. Martin's Press, 1983); Steven Mintz and Susan Kellogg, *Domestic Revolutions: A Social History of American Family Life* (New York: Free Press, 1988), and Linda W. Rosenzweig, *The Anchor of My Life: Middle Class American Mothers and Daughters, 1880–1920* (New York: New York University Press, 1993). Arthur Calhoun, *Social History of the American Family*, 3 vols. (Cleveland: Arthur Clark, 1918), remains interesting.

Studies by contemporary writers and later sociologists are also useful. These include Sophonisba P. Breckinridge, *The Family and the State: Select Documents* (1934; reprint ed., New York: Arno Press, 1972); Hugh Carter and Paul Glick, *Marriage and Divorce: A Social and Economic Study* (Cambridge, MA: Harvard University Press, 1970); Ruth Shonle Cavan, *The American Family* (New York: Crowell, 1969); Lydia Commander, *The American Idea* (1907; reprint ed., New York: Arno Press, 1972); Ernest Mowrer, *Family Disorganization: An Introduction to a Sociological Analysis* (Chicago: University of Chicago Press, 1927); Anna A. Rogers, *Why American Marriages Fail and Other Papers* (Boston: Houghton Mifflin, 1909); John Sirjamaki, *The American Family in the Twentieth Century* (Cambridge, MA: Harvard University Press, 1953); and American Sociological Society,

*Papers and Proceedings of the Third Annual Meeting of the American Sociological Society: The Family* (Chicago: University of Chicago Press, 1908). For an interesting analysis of an important artifact of girls' socialization, see Miriam Formanek-Brunnell, *Made to Play House: Dolls and the Commercialization of American Girlhood, 1830–1930* (New Haven, CT: Yale University Press, 1993).

For divorce in general, see Glenda Riley, *Divorce: An American Tradition* (New York: Oxford University Press, 1991). More detailed studies include Robert L. Griswold, *Family and Divorce in California, 1850–1890: Victorian Illusions and Everyday Reality* (Albany: State University of New York Press, 1982); Elaine Tyler May, *Great Expectations: Marriage and Divorce in Post-Victorian America* (Chicago: University of Chicago Press, 1980); and William L. O'Neill, *Divorce in the Progressive Era* (New Haven, CT: Yale University Press, 1967), on the ideas of divorce reformers.

For rural women, Joan M. Jensen has written a number of works, including *With These Hands: Women Working on the Land* (Old Westbury, NY: Feminist Press, 1981). *Pacific Historical Review*, 61 (Nov., 1992), contains a series of essays reviewing the latest work and suggesting new directions. See also Deborah Fink, *Open Country, Iowa: Rural Women, Work, and Change* (Albany: State University of New York, 1986), and her *Agrarian Women: Wives and Mothers in Rural Nebraska, 1880–1940* (Chapel Hill: University of North Carolina Press, 1992). Paula Baker, *The Moral Frameworks of Public Life: Gender, Politics, and the State in Rural New York, 1870–1930* (New York: Oxford University Press, 1991), discusses reform in the context of farmer's concerns.

The interaction of concerns relating to a specific category of women, namely, widows, and the Southwest region of the United States are addressed in Arlene Scadron (ed.), *On Their Own: Widows and Widowhood in the American Southwest, 1848–1939* (Urbana: University of Illinois Press, 1988). On the Pacific Northwest, see Karen J. Blair (ed.), *Women in Pacific Northwest History: An Anthology* (Seattle: University of Washington Press, 1988).

On working-class women, the autobiographical material is more limited than for middle-class women. There are, however, many studies of ethnic cultures, and recently some of them have begun to pay specific attention to women. In particular, see Charlotte Baum, Paula Hyman, and Sonya Michel, *The Jewish Woman in America* (New York: Dial Press, 1976); Elizabeth Ewen, *Immigrant Women in the Land of Dollars* (New York: Monthly Review Press, 1985); Deborah Dash More, *At Home in America: Second-Generation New York Jews* (New York: Columbia University Press, 1981); Cecyle S. Neidle, *America's Immigrant Women* (Boston: Twayne, 1975); Maxine S. Seller (ed.), *Immigrant Women* (Philadelphia: Temple University Press, 1980); Judith Smith, *Family Connections: A History of Italian and Jewish Immigrant Lives in Providence, Rhode Island, 1909–1914* (Albany: State University of New York Press, 1985); Virginia Yans-McLaughlin, *Family and Community: Italian Immigrants in Buffalo, 1880–1930* (Ithaca, NY: Cornell University Press, 1977); and the powerful contemporary novels by

Agnes Smedley, *Daughter of Earth* (New York: Feminist Press, 1973), and by Anzia Yerzierska, *Bread Givers* (New York: Braziller, 1925). The movie, *Hester Street*, is a moving story of immigrant acculturation, family conflict, and the nature of gender in the Jewish community. It is available from Cinema 5, 595 Madison Avenue, New York, NY, 10022.

Any study of gender and race in United States history should begin with Ellen Carol DuBois and Vicki L. Ruiz, *Unequal Sisters: A Multicultural Reader in U.S. Women's History* (New York: Routledge, 1990, 2nd. ed., 1994), an excellent compilation of articles in a field that is still underdeveloped, and Teresa L. Amott and Julie A. Matthaei, *Race, Gender, and Work: A Multicultural Economic History of Women in the United States* (Boston: South End Press, 1991). On black women, the major work is Jacqueline Jones, *Labor of Love, Labor of Sorrow: Black Women, Work and the Family, from Slavery to the Present* (New York: Vintage, 1986). A useful compilation of primary source material is Gerda Lerner (ed.), *Black Women in White America* (New York: Pantheon Books, 1972). See also Paula Giddings, *When and Where I Enter: The Impact of Black Women on Race and Sex in America* (New York: William Morrow, 1984); Sharon Harley and Rosalyn Terborg-Penn (eds.), *The Afro-American Woman: Struggles and Images* (Washington, DC: National University Publications, 1978); Darlene Clark Hine, *Black Women in America: An Historical Encyclopedia*, 2 vols. (Brooklyn, NY: Carlson, 1993), and Phyllis Palmer, *Domesticity and Dirt: Housewives and Domestic Servants in the United States, 1920–1945* (Philadelphia: Temple University Press, 1991). On African-American women and nursing, see Darlene Clark Hine, *Black Women in White: Racial Cooperation and Conflict in the Nursing Profession, 1890–1950* (Bloomington: Indiana University Press, 1989).

There is no general history of either Chicana or Asian-American women. Useful works for the former include Rodolfo Acuña, *Occupied America: A History of Chicanos* (New York: Harper & Row, 1988); Albert Camarillo, *Chicanos in California: A History of Mexican Americans in California* (Sacramento, CA: Boyd & Fraser, 1984); Richard Griswold Del Castillo, *La Familia: Chicano Families in the Urban Southwest, 1848 to the Present* (Notre Dame, IND: University of Notre Dame Press, 1984); Adelaida R. Del Castillo, *Between Borders: Essays on Mexicana\Chicana History* (Encino, CA: Floricanto Press, 1990); and Alfredo Mirandé and Evangelina Enríquez, *La Chicana: The Mexican-American Woman* (Chicago: University of Chicago Press, 1979). For the early twentieth century, see Mario T. García, *Desert Immigrants: The Mexicans of El Paso: 1880–1920* (New Haven, CT: Yale University Press, 1981), Ramón Saldívar, *Chicano Narratives: The Dialectics of Difference* (Madison, WI: University of Wisconsin Press, 1990); and Sarah Deutsch's superb *No Separate Refuge: Culture, Class, and Gender on an Anglo-Hispanic Frontier in the American Southwest, 1880–1940* (New York: Oxford University Press, 1987). See also George J. Sanchez, *Becoming Mexican American: Ethnicity, Culture and Identity in Chicano Los Angeles, 1900–1945* (New York: Oxford University Press, 1993). For Puerto Ricans, see Virginia Sánchez Korrol, *From Colonia to Community: The History of Puerto Ricans in New York City, 1917–1948* (Westport, CT: Greenwood Press, 1983).

On Asian-American women, useful general works include Asian Women United of California, *Making Waves: An Anthology of Writings By and About Asian Women* (Boston: Beacon Press, 1989); Suchen Chan, *Asian Americans: An Interpretive History* (Boston: Twayne, 1991); Lucie Cheng Hirata, "Chinese Immigrant Women in Nineteenth-Century California," in Carol Ruth Berkin and Mary Beth Norton (eds.), *Women of America: A History* (Boston: Houghton Mifflin, 1979), pp. 223–44; Yuji Ichioka, "Amerika Nadeshiko: Japanese Immigrant Women in the United States, 1900–1924," *Pacific Historical Review*, 44 (1980): 339–57; Valerie Matsumoto, *Farming the Home Place: A Japanese American Community in California, 1919–1982* (Ithaca, NY: Cornell University Press, 1993); John Modell, The Japanese American Family: A Perspective for Future Investigations," *Pacific Historical Review*, 37 (1968): 67–81; and Ronald Takaki, *Strangers From a Different Shore: A History of Asian Americans* (Boston: Little, Brown, 1989). Akemi Kikumura, *Through Harsh Winters: The Life of a Japanese Immigrant Woman* (Novato, CA: Chandler & Suep, 1981), offers an interesting biographical perspective, as do Ruthanne McCunn, *A Thousand Pieces of Gold: A Biographical Novel* (New York: Dell, 1983), Jade Snow Wong, *Fifth Chinese Daughter* (New York: Harper & Row, 1950), and Monica Sone, *Niesei Daughter* (Boston: Little, Brown, 1953). On Korean women, the autobiography by Mary Paik Lee, *Quiet Odyssey: A Pioneer Korean Woman in America* (Seattle: University of Washington Press, 1990), is interesting, and the introduction by Suchen Chang provides a detailed history of Korean women in the United States.

On Native-American women, see Patricia Albers and Beatrice Medicine, *The Hidden Half: Studies of Plains Indian Women* (New York: Lanham, 1983); Paula Gunn Allen, *The Sacred Hoop: Recovering the Feminine in American Indian Traditions* (Boston: Beacon Press, 1986); Clara Sue Kidwell, "The Power of Women in Three American Indian Societies," *Journal of Ethnic Studies* 6 (Fall 1978): 113–21; Diane Lebow, "Rethinking Matriliny Among the Hopis," in Ruby Rohrlich and Elaine Hoffman Baruch (eds.), *Women in Search of Utopia: Mavericks and Mythmakers* (New York: Schocken Books, 1984); Carolyn Niethammer, *Daughters of the Earth: The Lives and Legends of American Indian Women* (New York: Collier Books, 1977); and James Olson and Raymond Wilson, *Native Americans in the Twentieth Century* (Provo, UT: Brigham Young University Press, 1984). On the berdache and "Amazons," see Walter Williams, *The Spirit and the Flesh: Sexual Diversity in American Indian Culture*, 2nd. ed., (Boston: Beacon Press, 1992).

For recent autobiographies and novels pertaining to these various minority groups, see the bibliography to Chapter 7.

On working-class women generally, consult the works cited in the bibliography to Chapter I. For specific subjects and industries, see Mary H. Blewett, *Men, Women, and Work: Class, Gender, and Protest in the New England Shoe Industry, 1780–1910* (Urbana: University of Illinois Press, 1988); Eileen Boris, *Home to Work: Motherhood and the Politics of Industrial Homework in the U.S.* (New York: Cambridge University Press, 1994); Patricia A. Cooper, *Once A Cigar Maker: Men, Women, and Work Culture in American Cigar Factories,*

*1900–1919* (Urbana: University of Illinois Press, 1987); S. J. Kleinberg, *The Shadow of the Mills: Working-Class Families in Pittsburgh, 1870–1907* (Pittsburgh: University of Pittsburgh Press, 1989); Joanne J. Meyerowitz, *Women Adrift: Independent Wage Earners in Chicago, 1880–1930* (Chicago: University of Chicago Press, 1988); Kathy Peiss, *Cheap Amusements: Working Women and Leisure in Turn of the Century New York* (Philadelphia: Temple University Press, 1986); and Leslie Woodcock Tentler, *Wage-Earning Women: Industrial Work and Family Life in the United States, 1900–1930* (New York: Oxford University Press, 1979).

Studies of individual industries and labor unions can be used with profit. These include Leon Stein, *The Triangle Fire* (Philadelphia: Lippincott, 1962), and Benjamin Stolberg, *Tailor's Progress: The Story of a Famous Union and the Men who Made It* (Garden City, NY: Doubleday, 1944). The most extensive contemporary survey of working conditions is U.S. Bureau of Labor, *Report on the Conditions of Woman and Child Wage-Earners in the United States,* 19 vols. (Washington, DC: Government Printing Office, 1910). On women in the labor movement, see Philip S. Foner, *Women and the American Labor Movement: From Colonial Times to the Eve of World War One* (New York: Free Press, 1979); and Meredith Tax, *The Rising of the Women* (New York: Monthly Review Press, 1980). On the Women's Trade Union League, see Nancy Schrom Dye, *As Equals and as Sisters: Feminism, the Labor Movement and the Women's Trade Union League of New York* (Columbia, MO: University of Missouri Press, 1980), and Elizabeth Anne Payne, *Reform, Labor, and Feminism: Margaret Dreier Robins and the Women's Trade Union League* (Urbana: University of Illinois Press, 1988).

Several older works are still useful. These include Alice Henry, *The Trade Union Woman* (New York: Appleton-Century-Crofts, 1915); Helen Marot, *American Labor Unions, by a Member* (New York: Henry Holt, 1914); and Theresa Wolfson, *The Woman Worker and the Trade Unions* (New York: International, 1926).

Progressive reformers conducted numerous surveys and exposés of working conditions for women. Among the most revealing are Elizabeth Butler, *Women and the Trades: Pittsburgh, 1907–1908* (New York: Charities Publication Committee, 1909); Helen Campbell, *Prisoners of Poverty: Women Wage-Workers, Their Trades and Their Lives* (Boston: Roberts Brothers, 1890); and Mrs. John Van Vorst and Marie Van Vorst, *The Woman Who Toils: Being the Experiences of Two Gentlewomen as Factory Girls* (Garden City, NY: Doubleday, Page, 1904). Several interesting autobiographies include Agnes Nestor, *Woman's Labor Leader: Autobiography of Agnes Nestor* (Rockford, IL: Bellevue Books, 1954); Dorothy Richardson, *The Long Day: The Story of a New York Working Girl as Told by Herself* (New York: Century, 1905); and Rose Schneiderman (with Lucy Goldthwaite), *All for One* (New York: Paul S. Erikson, 1967).

Several scholars have investigated the Progressive anti-vice movement and the culture of prostitution in the early twentieth century, including Mark Thomas Connolly, *The Response to Prostitution in the Progressive Era* (Chapel Hill: University of North Carolina Press, 1980); Timothy J. Gilfoyle,

*City of Eros: New York City, Prostitution, and the Commercialization of Sex, 1790–1920* (New York: W. W. Norton, 1992); and Ruth Rosen, *The Lost Sisterhood: Prostitution in America, 1900–1918* (Baltimore: Johns Hopkins University Press, 1982). Ruth Rosen (ed.), *The Mamie Papers* (Old Westbury, NY: Feminist Press, 1977), has assembled a fascinating selection of letters between a prostitute and a middle-class reformer.

On the breakdown in Victorian culture during this period, see Lois W. Banner, *American Beauty* (New York: Alfred A. Knopf, 1983); Lewis A. Erenberg, *New York Nightlife and the Transformation of American Culture, 1890–1930* (Westport, CT: Greenwood Press, 1981); John P. Kasson, *Amusing the Million: Coney Island at the Turn of the Century* (New York: Hill & Wang, 1978); and Albert F. MacClean, Jr., *American Vaudeville as Ritual* (Lexington: University of Kentucky Press, 1965).

# 3

# WOMEN AS ORGANIZERS AND INNOVATORS: SUFFRAGE, REFORM, AND FEMINISM, 1890–1920

Between 1890 and the First World War, organized women were vigorous and active. Historians have sometimes interpreted these years as monopolized by the drive for woman suffrage. In fact, a range of innovative activities appeared, and women's organizations proliferated. Never before had so many women belonged to so many women's organizations; not until the 1960s was feminism again so vigorous. Most organized women were social feminists. But there were radical women, too. Some concentrated their efforts on political causes; others, on women's causes. By 1914, most segments of the women's movement had joined together behind suffrage. But before then, feminism looked in many directions.

## SUFFRAGISM ON THE WANE

In the first decade of the twentieth century, the suffrage movement fell on hard times. The suffrage crusade had followed a difficult path since Reconstruction (1867–1877), when Congress enfranchised black males but not women. Although suffrage leaders had drafted a woman suffrage amendment which was introduced into Congress in 1869, no vote was taken on it then or in subsequent years. Despite suffragist lobbying, Congress paid little attention to the amendment. Campaigns for passage in the states were also not especially successful. Between 1896 and 1910, referenda on the suffrage amendment were held in only six states and the amendment was defeated in all six. In 1910, women had equal suffrage in only four states: Wyoming, Utah, Colorado, and Idaho.

These failures were partly due to vigorous antisuffrage opposition. Local antisuffrage groups, often headed by socially prominent women, appeared in the late nineteenth century. In 1911, they united to form the National Association Opposed to the Further Extension of Suffrage to Women. This group claimed a membership larger than that of the NAWSA, and it drew support from three powerful groups: the liquor industry, fearful that

*A turn-of-the-century post card pokes fun at suffragists.*

**SUFFRAGETTE VOTE-GETTING**
THE EASIEST WAY.

suffrage for women would bring prohibition; the political bosses, afraid that women with suffrage would vote for reform politicians; and the Catholic Church, with its dogma that women's place was in the home.

The arguments of the antisuffragists spoke powerfully to traditionalists. Politics, they believed, was no place for a woman. It was a male preserve, central to the male public sphere. It drew on underhanded practices and barroom deals, especially since most polling places in this period were set up in saloons and barbershops. (They were moved to schools, churches, and firehouses after women could vote.) Politics was, as suffrage leader Abigail Scott Duniway put it, "sacred to the aristocracy of the [male] sex."[1] Antisuffrage arguments played on conservative fears: If women held office, they

*Anna Howard Shaw: minister, physician, and president of the National American Woman Suffrage Association.*

would leave the home, destroy the family, and take power away from men. "Woman," wrote one antisuffragist,

> has not incorporated in her nature those qualities as mystical and as holy as the life which she transmits to the world; she has not become an inspiration and the very savior of our life, in order that she may turn traitor to herself and her ideal for a paltry bit of paper and the boast that, from being a man's superior, she has now become his equal.[2]

Yet the antisuffragists were not always conservative on issues other than women voting. Many of them were social feminists, active in reform organizations. Their reform involvement provided them with a further argument against woman suffrage. For they reasoned that without the vote and party affiliation, women could more effectively influence legislators because their motives could not be questioned. However naive this view of politics, the argument had an impact on women's organizations such as the

General Federation of Women's Clubs, which did not endorse suffrage until 1914.

The appeal of the antisuffrage argument, however, does not entirely explain the failure of the suffrage movement in the first decade of the twentieth century. Indeed, there were problems with the movement's leadership. By the turn of the century, a generation of moderate women had taken control as the original leaders—Elizabeth Cady Stanton, Susan B. Anthony, and Lucy Stone—either died or retired. Among the moderates, Anna Howard Shaw became president of the NAWSA in 1904. She held the post until 1915. She was an unfortunate choice. Although a brilliant orator, Shaw had limited administrative skill. She was dictatorial as president, and backbiting began to emerge among the NAWSA leadership.

Rather than encouraging new directions, Shaw and her associates followed traditional paths. They held conventions each year; they circulated petitions; they issued instructions to state organizations. They avoided any militancy that might associate them with radicals, and they made no attempt to form alliances with working-class groups, which might have aided them in counteracting the opposition of political bosses and the Catholic Church. Harriot Stanton Blatch, daughter of Elizabeth Cady Stanton and a suffrage leader in New York, judged that "the old order of suffragists had kept youngsters 'in their place,'" [and] "had left working women alone."[3]

Yet the moderation of these turn-of-century suffragists helped to defuse fears over giving women the vote. Stanton and Anthony had argued that women deserved the vote because, like men, they had a "natural right" to it. The leaders who followed them contended that women, as mothers, needed the vote to protect the home and that the nation needed the votes of Anglo women to counteract the supposedly pernicious effects of immigrant and black males' voting. The argument of "natural right" challenged conventional gender roles. The new "argument from expediency," as historian Aileen Kraditor has called it, posed no direct threat. M. Carey Thomas, president of Bryn Mawr College, wrote that the subject of suffrage was so inflammatory in 1906, when she was instrumental in founding the National College Equal Suffrage League, that college students hesitated to discuss it, while the Association of Collegiate Alumnae barred the subject from its convention agendas. Within a few years, these reservations vanished, and suffrage became respectable in the academic community. Thomas suggested that the change occurred because the old arguments based on women's right to the vote were replaced by the argument that women needed the vote to protect the home and to become effective reformers.[4]

In any case, between 1890 and the First World War the suffrage movement was one women's cause among many, and the majority of organized women probably did not support it. Before 1912, wrote Rheta Childe Dorr, the suffrage movement was dead. "No newspaper or magazine editor would have printed an article on the subject. No politician gave it a thought."[5] Dorr may have exaggerated, but her comment indicates that issues other than suffrage held the attention of organized women in the early years of this century.

## FEMINISM AND PROGRESSIVISM: A CASE OF GIVE AND TAKE

Central among these concerns was a renewed interest in social justice for women and the disadvantaged, as Americans widely questioned the benefits of unregulated industrialism and urbanization. The debate over the viability of capitalism and democracy was vigorous. Membership in voluntary associations for social welfare flourished. Muckraking journals, too, were willing to print feminist exposés of the lives of working women as well as articles about the general oppression of women. The subjects were fresh and a stimulus to the reform impulse.

As much as Progressivism sparked feminism, feminism was important in the Progressive movement. In the past, historians viewed Progressivism as a movement of male reformers attempting to wrest power from political bosses or to reform the political process through legislation. Alternatively, they saw it as a movement of status-conscious professionals attempting to re-create an older, simpler society or of certain business interests attempting to gain favorable legislation. But more recently a new interpretation of the period has emerged. This interpretation stresses social reform aspects like conservation, child-welfare legislation, and educational innovation. It finds a main source of the reform impulse in women's interest in expanding their role outside the home and in providing viable lives for their families in an industrial and urban America.

## The Organizations: Growth and Changing Goals

Since the early nineteenth century and especially after the Civil War, women organized social-welfare associations. The Woman's Christian Temperance Union, for example, put social reform at the forefront of its program. The charismatic Frances Willard headed the WCTU between 1879 and 1898, and she articulated a campaign of "Do Everything." Under her leadership the organization worked not only for the prohibition of alcohol, but also for such reforms as kindergartens in the public schools, police matrons for women prisoners, and child-labor laws. Willard secured WCTU support for the Knights of Labor and for the peace movement. In 1896, Willard's conservative opponents gained control of the WCTU and made temperance its main concern. But during Willard's leadership, the WCTU educated many rural and small-town women to a sense of social responsibility. Women often joined the WCTU and then became involved in the woman suffrage movement and Progressive reform causes. As Willard herself put it, their "consciousness" of themselves and of their society was raised.[6]

Similarly, the women's clubs that flourished in these eras often drew up reform platforms. The widely read journalist Jane Croly, who wrote under the pseudonym Jennie June, founded the first women's club, Sorosis, in New York City in 1868, after organizers of a banquet in honor of visiting English author Charles Dickens excluded women journalists. Many of the subsequent women's clubs were established as lecture and discussion groups with an emphasis on art and literature, and they often adopted social welfare causes in response to local conditions. Lectures on art and beauty stimulated drives to beautify cities by planting flowers and grass; these drives, in turn, generated an interest in public parks and playgrounds and, ultimately, in a variety of municipal functions bearing on family welfare.

One mother's concerns over her children's schooling might lead to an investigation of the local school system or to the introduction of kindergartens—the German innovation that promised better education for young children and more free time for their

*A kindergarten class, 1914.*

mothers. Or, as one observer, explaining women's advocacy of improved street cleaning, commented, "It is their dresses which must sweep up the debris."[7] In 1890, Jane Croly, among others, organized the General Federation of Women's Clubs, and the national organization increased the pressure on local clubs to undertake reform causes.

Women's clubs made headway in many areas of reform between the 1890s and World War I. When a hurricane in Galveston, Texas, wiped out portions of the city in 1901, women organized a Women's Health Protective Association. This organization persuaded the city government to adopt ordinances covering health and sanitation issues ranging from milk inspection to tuberculosis clinics. The Chicago Civic Club and the Boston Women's Municipal League led drives in their cities to raise investment capital to buy and improve tenement housing to show that landlords could improve slum conditions and still make a profit. Federations of women's clubs in Iowa, Ohio, Pennsylvania, and Michigan were responsible for the creation of juvenile court systems in those states. Many observers credited the passage of the federal Pure Food and Drug Act of 1906 to a letter-writing campaign coordinated by women's organizations.

*A meeting of the National Board of the Young Women's Christian Association, 1914.*

The spectrum of women's groups in the Progressive period included organizations with a variety of programs. The YWCA focused on recreation and housing for working women. The Association of Collegiate Alumnae worked for municipal reform and supported the efforts of settlement-house workers. Even the Daughters of the American Revolution undertook letter-writing campaigns on behalf of conservation and child-labor reform. Voluntarism was characteristic of America's years of unsettling urbanization, immigration, and industrialization. But the commitment of so many women's organizations to social reform was unique. According to one observer in 1906, this interest in the public welfare was not characteristic of men's clubs.[8]

Women's participation in social reform took many forms. An interest in cooperative housing had been a subtheme of women's reform thought since the days of Frances Wright's Nashoba and other utopian communities of the nineteenth century. Architects and urban planners designed ideal urban cooperative communities, although few were actually built. In many ways the settlement houses, communities of middle-class reformers located in areas of urban poverty, represented the most successful achievement of the cooperationists.

*Henry Street Settlement House nurses on their way to the homes of the poor and needy in New York.*

Women not only supported the Progressive movement through joining organizations, but they also took on individual leadership roles. Albion Fellows Bacon of Evansville, Indiana, was married and the mother of four children. She began her reform career as a volunteer member of the sanitation committee of Evansville's Civic Improvement Society. She then worked as a "friendly visitor" for Evansville's associated charities. ("Friendly visitors" were the predecessors of the modern social worker.) Like many Progressives, Bacon decided that inadequate housing lay at the heart of poverty.

She launched a statewide campaign in Indiana for the regulation of housing—a goal she achieved in 1913. Katherine Bement Davis, a Vassar graduate with a doctorate in sociology, headed a Philadelphia settlement house for some years before she became superintendent of a new women's reformatory in Bedford Hills, New York, in 1901. Under her headship, the Bedford Hills institution was, according to one historian, "the most active penal experiment station in America."[9] In 1914, Davis became commissioner of corrections for New York City. Three years later she took the job of general secretary of the Bureau of Social Hygiene of the Rockefeller Foundation. In this position, she authored studies of prostitution, narcotics addiction, and sexual behavior.

That women like Bacon and Davis were able to pursue careers in reform should not seem surprising. With the era's expansion in reform activity, many women were able to move from voluntary to paid employment because of the expertise they had acquired in voluntarism. In North Carolina, for example, women achieved law establishing welfare departments in every county of the state. Subsequently, women who had worked for the reform were appointed county welfare directors. Dr. Alice Hamilton was a pioneer in the field of industrial medicine, which identified environmental pollution as a major cause of worker illness. She contended that her gender was an advantage in her work, because most Americans believed that women naturally would judge workers' health more important than owners' profits. Such impulses in a man, she contended, would be regarded as unmanly sentimentalism or radicalism.[10]

Women also began to assume leadership roles in male-dominated Progressive organizations. At first, men did not accept women easily into their midst. Lillian Wald was prominent among women Progressives for founding the Henry Street Settlement in New York City and for her efforts to improve the status of the nursing profession. She reported that in 1894 her name had been dropped from the list of potential members of a New York mayoral commission on industrial safety because of the objections of male members. They feared that if a woman were present, proper etiquette would not permit them to take off their coats and roll up their shirt sleeves.[11] Such attitudes subsequently weakened, and, according to historian Anne Firor Scott, men and women eventually worked together in national organizations like the Consumers' League, the National

Child Labor Committee, and the National Association for the Advancement of Colored People (NAACP). However, the grass-roots support for major legislation like state minimum wage laws, workmen's compensation, and antilynching laws was generated by women's organizations, with their connections to kin and community networks.

## Ethnic and Black Women's Organizations

The mainline Progressive organizations, composed primarily of white Anglo women, did not usually include members of other racial and ethnic groups. But these Anglo women were not the only ones to organize for community improvement and humanitarian ends. Within the Jewish community, the National Council of Jewish Women, founded in 1893, encouraged the adoption of social service as a goal of American Jewish organizations. By the 1890s, Zionism, the movement to establish a separate Jewish state, was strong among American Jews. Hadassah, the women's Zionist organization, was formed in 1912 to provide funds for medical services for the Jewish community in Palestine.

After the Civil War, African-American women, too, founded local clubs, and in 1895 these clubs federated into the National Association of Colored Women. The primary purpose of the black organization was social welfare, and the association was the nation's first social-service agency for African Americans. It was founded nearly 15 years before the better-known, male-dominated black rights and service organizations—the NAACP and the Urban League.

Because African-American women often played key roles in black churches and other voluntary organizations, their assumption of leadership roles in social welfare was natural. Local black women's clubs established day nurseries, playgrounds, old people's homes, and homes for female juvenile delinquents, while they worked for better housing, schools, and employment opportunities for African-American women. They attempted to challenge Southern sexual mores, including the view that black women were naturally promiscuous. Still, Southern repression of African Americans through segregation laws—the so-called "Jim Crow" system—dictated that black organizations follow Booker T. Washington's accommodationist position. (Booker T. Washington,

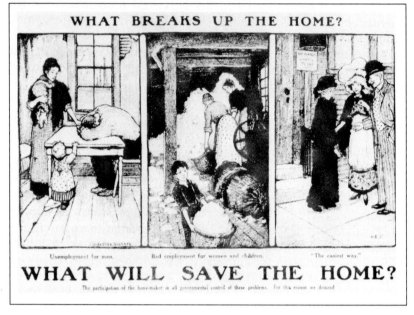

*A poster issued by the NAWSA to gain working-class women's support for suffrage.*

founding president of Tuskegee Institute in Alabama, was a national spokesperson who advocated a self-help strategy for African Americans and accommodation to racial segregation, which was on the increase in the 1890s.) When journalist Ida Wells-Barnett violated this mandate to write a series of articles in her Memphis newspaper attacking the lynching of black men for sexual crimes they did not commit, her office was bombed. Fearing for her life, she fled to Chicago, where she became involved in social-welfare work in the African-American community. In 1909, she participated in the founding of the NAACP. Eventually the black women's clubs undertook much of the grass-roots organizing for the NAACP and the National Urban League.

Mexican-American women also organized behind community betterment. But, given their strong family and kin networks and their dedication to the Catholic Church, their involvement in social welfare characteristically took the form of aid through family and church associations. For example, they participated in *cofradias* (lay brotherhoods), sponsored by the Catholic Church, which took care of church members in times of crisis. At the same time, a number of Mexican-American women, radicalized by the Mexican War for Independence in 1910, worked both in Mexico and in the United States to organize workers, protest legal abuses, and establish mutual aid societies. They were the forerunners of the Chicana women who would emerge as labor organizers in the 1930s and after.

## Progressive Reform and Settlement Houses

Within the Progressive movement, women were often innovators. Nowhere was this more apparent than in the settlement houses. Jane Addams at Hull House and Lillian Wald at Henry Street were the two most famous women settlement residents, but there were many more. For the most part, they were first-generation college graduates, fired with dedication to women and to humanity and determined to prove to a skeptical world that educating women was not wasteful, that women could be as forceful and as innovative as men. Faced after college with the choices of marrying, training for professions which still discriminated against women, or taking low-status jobs as schoolteachers or nurses, they responded with typical American ingenuity. They invented their own profession by founding houses in the midst of urban slums where they could live and provide social services to the poor and the new immigrants who were streaming into American cities. Settlement-house work fit women's traditional role of service—and men did not control it.

For many young women and men, settlement work was an interlude between college and marriage. Like the Peace Corps of the 1960s, it was for some a brief experiment in idealism. Some women married male coworkers and adopted more conventional life-styles. Others became social workers or entered a profession. A few, such as Jane Addams and Lillian Wald, remained throughout their lives at the institutions they had founded. From these bases they reached out to influence mayors, legislators, and the general public. A few were appointed to government positions. Jane Addams' Hull House in Chicago held the record for such appointments. Julia Lathrop became the first woman member of the Illinois State Board of Charities and the first director of the Children's Bureau of the federal government, established in 1912. Grace Abbott followed her

*Jane Addams, who founded Hull House (a settlement house in the slums of Chicago), working with neighborhood children.*

in this position. Sophonisba Breckinridge became dean of the pioneer School of Civics and Philanthropy, later taken over by the University of Chicago as the School of Social Service Administration. Mary McDowall became the first president of the Chicago Women's Trade Union League, and Florence Kelley became head of the National Consumers' League. All of these women began their careers at Hull House.

### A Measure of Success

Women settlement-house workers and social feminists focused on women, children, and the home. The settlements in particular provided assistance for women, including visiting-nurse services and day care for children of working mothers. Settlement workers, social workers, and women's club members investigated employment agencies, assisted newly arrived immigrants, and established legal agencies to help women enforce payment of wages, prevent violations of contracts, and obtain divorces. They worked with vice commissions to investigate prostitution and campaigned for the open discussion of sex as a way of ending prostitution and venereal disease. According to historian Robyn Muncy, their activities on behalf of women and children were sufficiently organized on the national level through the Children's Bureau to constitute a "female dominion." Women who staffed this bureau, according to Muncy, established similar agencies in the states. These state agencies joined women's local and national voluntary associations as the "dominion's" lower echelons. Educational institutions like the University of Chicago's School of Social Service Administration trained women to staff these agencies. As a result of their efforts, many states by 1920 had passed laws extending special legislation to women in the area of maximum hours and minimum wages, as well as laws providing for "pensions" to needy mothers raising children without husbands present.

Yet to what extent social feminists succeeded in the overall area of social reform is debatable. A study of Progressivism in Wisconsin leaves the impression that women revolutionized the social services of the state. However, a 1909 study of services for working women in Pittsburgh, where there were numerous women's clubs, settlements, and YWCA facilities, concluded that only about 2 percent of working women were being reached.[12] A study of kindergartens in Massachusetts contends that relatively few were actually opened and that they offered little more than preparation for the rigid discipline of the elementary grades.[13]

Historian Nancy Hewitt has found a situation in Tampa, Florida, that she implies was replicated elsewhere. In Tampa, wives of the city's industrial leaders dominated the major women's organizations. Their reforms for working women, including maximum hours legislation for women, as well as compulsory school attendance laws for children, had the effect of controlling immigrant women and families at the same time that the reformers' husbands were organizing vigilante action against strikers to maximize industrial profits at the expense of workers. And, sociologist Theda Skocpol is critical of the successful movement for mothers' pensions. These pensions, which formed the basis of the modern welfare system in the United States, implied that the state bore little responsibility for the general relief of poverty, which was stigmatized as an issue different from unemployment and disability. These insurance programs were guaranteed as the right of workers and not considered charity. Indeed, according to Skocpol, the "maternalist" thrust of Progressive women reformers, their concentration on women and children and not poverty in general, contributed to the conservatism of later welfare legislation in the United States.

## THE RADICALS

Social feminists attempted to achieve reform within existing institutions. Radical feminists, although advocating many of the same causes, were more militant in their ideas and their actions. Their outspoken style contributed to the flavor of the age.

### A Ferment of New Ideas

Crusaders like Margaret Sanger, who fought for birth control, and Charlotte Perkins Gilman, who called for the building of large apartment complexes with general kitchens, cleaning services, and nurseries staffed by professionals, were continually in the public eye. Their demands were supported by lesser-known but no less vocal men and women who argued for the opening of every occupation to women, for the equalization of men's and women's wages, for unrestricted divorce, for the retention of maiden names in marriage, and for the adoption of simple, uniform clothing.[14] A few radicals even called for the communalization of social institutions and espoused free sexual relations. Men and women in the anarchist movement did not marry on principle; instead, they lived in monogamous unions in which both partners preserved the freedom to have sexual relations with others. In print and in public lectures, Emma Goldman broadcast their ideas.

The feminist movement, then as in the 1960s, was international in scope. Swedish feminist Ellen Key advocated that mothers raise their children alone and that the state pay them to do so. English feminist Cicely Hamilton fulminated against marriage, which she viewed as an economic arrangement for women—a trade they entered for lack of any other. Olive Schreiner of South Africa, in

*Volunteers selling copies of the Birth Control Review. Margaret Sanger's pioneering publication first appeared in 1917.*

her influential *Women and Labor* (1911), turned Darwinian beliefs about women's evolutionary inferiority upside down by arguing that only self-reliant women could bear healthy children and that humanity was destroying itself by giving middle-class women nothing to do. Schreiner coined the much-used term "sex parasitism" to describe the position of married women.

Plays and novels that explored the relationship of women to men and to marriage reinforced this ferment of ideas, and in the novels of writers such as Charlotte Perkins Gilman, Susan Glaspell, and Neith Boyce, the message was openly feminist. Among playwrights, Danish writer Henrik Ibsen, in his famed *A Doll's House* (1879), portrayed a woman who slowly becomes aware of her oppression in a traditional marriage. George Bernard Shaw's plays about conflicts between strong-minded men and women—*Man and Superman, Saint Joan, Pygmalion*—also were produced and discussed. Lesser playwrights followed Ibsen and Shaw. Journalist Ben Hecht asserted that "novelists and playwrights were knocking the wind out of the public by presenting radical heroines who had been to bed with some man before their marriage."[15]

One play with such a theme—a minor vehicle named *Hindle Wakes*—was a hit on Broadway. In this play, a young woman spends a weekend in the country with the son of her father's employer. When discovered, the man, in time-honored fashion, offers to marry her "to save her honor." She refuses, and all are amazed. But she stands her ground. "Why did you go on the weekend?" she asks her paramour. "I'm a man," he replies. "It was just my fancy of the moment." "Well," she counters, in a statement that must have shocked audiences one step removed from Victorianism, "I'm a woman. It was just *my* fancy of the moment."[16]

## A New Breed of Scholars

Feminist scholars added their contribution to the crusade for women's emancipation. Much like feminist scholars in the 1970s, they scanned the past and the present for evidence of female oppression and activism. Emily Putnam produced a prototype of such works in *The Lady* (1910), an exploration of the upper-class female role over the ages. (Putnam, dean of Barnard College, retained her position when she married but was forced to resign it once she had a child.) In her book, Putnam traced women's history from the orientalism of ancient Greece, which confined women to the home while men exercised in the gymnasium and debated public issues in the forum, to the devaluation of women in the eighteenth-century French salons. There women brought the day's intellectuals together and then formed a backdrop to the male conversation. Putnam ended her book with the eighteenth-century English "bluestocking," the originator of modern feminism, and her oppressed contemporary, the lady of the Southern slave plantation. The former, according to Putnam, presaged the future; the latter was an ominous reminder of how a caste system could victimize women. However, Putnam only alluded to the oppression of black women under slavery, and she was seemingly unaware of that perpetrated by white mistresses.

Feminist scholars in science argued that men as well as women underwent periodic emotional disturbances based on bodily cycles. On the basis of new evidence that women were better able

*Author Charlotte Perkins Gilman, who advocated that professionals take over housework.*

to resist pain than men and that they lived longer, some feminists theorized that women were, in fact, superior to men. New anthropological data from early societies provided women scholars with the basis of a new interpretation of the origins of women's oppression. They speculated that the earliest societies had been matriarchal and that man's inherent and irrational drive for power, rather than any evolutionary inferiority of women, had led to the creation of patriarchal societies. Charlotte Perkins Gilman was critical of feminine passivity, but she judged the male-dominated world a regrettable evolutionary stage that had produced a host of ills, not the least of which was warfare. In war, wrote Gilman, we find maleness in absurd extremes. "Here is to be studied the whole gamut of basic masculinity, from the initial instinct of combat, through every form of glorious ostentation, with the loudest possible accompaniment of noise."[17]

### Feminist Action Groups: A Faint Voice

Despite their literary and scholarly endeavors, militant feminists did not translate ideology into action. There was no National Organization for Women; there were few local action groups focusing

*Elizabeth Gurley Flynn addresses striking textile workers in Lawrence, Massachusetts, in 1912.*

on gender equality similar to those of today. The WCTU had identified spousal abuse as a major problem for women, but only one local organization, in Chicago, was formed to deal directly with the issue. The Protective Agency for Women and Children, founded in 1885 and with a board composed of delegates from 15 women's associations in Chicago, provided diverse forms of legal aid and personal assistance to female and child victims of assault. The agency sometimes sent abused women to a shelter operated by the Woman's Club of Chicago, and it sought out alleged rape victims to assist with counseling and legal redress.

Several discussion and action groups emerged in New York City, but they did not spread to other areas of the nation. One of these was formed by Henrietta Rodman, a schoolteacher associated with Greenwich Village leftists. Her group, the Feminist Alliance, secured repeal of the New York City prohibition against the employment of married women as schoolteachers. The

Alliance also formed committees of doctors and lawyers, who wrote law and medical schools demanding an end to restrictions on the admission of women. These feminists discussed, but never pursued, constructing one of Charlotte Perkins Gilman's professionally staffed apartment buildings. For the most part, their actions were piecemeal. But their membership was small; many were career women with limited leisure time; and many were drawn into working for woman suffrage.

A second New York group, called Heterodoxy, was less inclined toward activism than the Feminist Alliance. Its members included Charlotte Perkins Gilman, Rheta Childe Dorr, Elizabeth Gurley Flynn, and other prominent women writers and reformers. They met to discuss their common problems and to provide mutual support. After attending a meeting of Heterodoxy, one observer wrote that its members seemed to be "in church, that they were worshipping at some holy shrine, their voices and their eyes were full of religious excitement."[18]

Yet many of these women were divided in their political and professional loyalties. Elizabeth Gurley Flynn was a socialist; Rheta Childe Dorr was a professional journalist active in woman suffrage. Margaret Sanger and Emma Goldman were difficult personalities who easily clashed with others. Goldman, too, was suspicious of the women's movement, partly because her anarchist principles led her to focus on society, not on women, and partly because she did not like arguments about women's superiority. In the end, leadership to unify women around a common cause came not from the radicals, but from the suffragists.

In general, however, militant feminism was a threat to the majority of Americans. They could accept Progressive women reformers because, as one analyst put it, most of them were "good wives and mothers" who had not taken up such "eccentricities of base quality" as free love.[19] But mainstream Americans were suspicious of behaviors and ideologies that deviated from the middle-class norm. Charlotte Perkins Gilman was vilified by the press for divorcing her husband and later sending their daughter to live with him; Margaret Sanger, who left her family to go to Europe, did not fare any better. Playwright Margaret Anderson invited Emma Goldman to dinner at her Chicago apartment, and the next day the manager of the building informed her of complaints from other tenants. "Emma Goldman has been here. We can't allow such a thing," he admonished. "By the public," commented Anderson, Goldman "was considered a monster, an exponent of free love and bombs."[20]

The support of the militant feminists added strength to the coalition of women that achieved woman suffrage. The radicals gave moral support to women and men who were trying to establish new roles in their lives. But the opposition to fundamental reform for women was strong. Margaret Sanger, for example, spent 20 years in achieving the legalization of birth control. Besides, as so often has been the case in the history of American feminism, other issues seemed more pressing than the achievement of equality for women.

## SHAKY GROUNDS FOR ARGUMENT

Seen in retrospect, there were weaknesses in the ideology and action of both the social feminists and the radical feminists. At the time, these deficiencies were not readily apparent, but they contributed to the decline of feminism in the 1920s. Most of these weaknesses stemmed from the conservative implications of their attitudes toward gender. In their own day, these women seemed to be innovators and radicals; to a different generation after the First World War, this meaning of their message was not so obvious.

### Women's Frailty and Special Legislation

The popularity of special legislation for working women among many organized women of this age provides insight into an underlying gender conservatism. For example, the Women's Trade Union League worked to organize women into unions, but it also lobbied for the passage by state legislatures of maximum-hour and minimum-wage laws that would apply only to women workers. Even socialist Elizabeth Gurley Flynn thought that working women needed special legislation and that an equal rights amendment, which would void this legislation, would be against their best interests. Behind this campaign lay certain pragmatic arguments. First, working women were difficult to organize into unions. Second, special legislation for women might force employers to improve conditions for male workers, too. Third, although the courts had overruled special legislation for men on the grounds that it violated the common-law doctrine of "freedom of contract" between worker and employer, they might be willing to validate such legislation for women.

But behind the special legislation campaign also lay conservative reasoning. Its supporters argued that the difficulties of factory labor were greater for women than for men because women were physically weaker and because they were potential mothers. In 1908, officials of the Consumers' League prepared the brief on the basis of which the Supreme Court rendered its first decision upholding a minimum-wage law for women (*Muller v. Oregon*). The brief declared that "besides anatomical and physiological differences, physicians are agreed that women are in general weaker than men in muscular strength and in nervous energy."[21] Overlooking the differing conclusions of feminist scholars, Consumers' League officials cited contemporary studies indicating that women who worked strained their bodies and bore unhealthy children. The Court agreed with the League. Yet this argument implied that men did not need such legislation, at a time of abysmal conditions of work for both men and women. It also gave added weight to the arguments of antifeminists that a woman's anatomy was her destiny.

### Housekeepers in Government—and Out

The social feminist rationale for the participation of women in reform and in government had similar conservative implications. Social feminists argued that women naturally took an interest in education, clean streets, and public parks because these matters were related to family life. This was a central theme in the writings of Jane Addams. "As society grows more complicated," she wrote, "it is necessary that women shall extend her sense of responsibility to many things outside of her home if she would continue to preserve the home in its entirety."[22] She contended that "city housekeeping has failed partly because women, the traditional housekeepers, have not been consulted. . . ."[23]

The problem with this argument was that, as in the argument for special legislation, it was based on a traditional image of women. Moreover, there was a counteractive side to this view of women as competent housekeepers. The belief was growing that mechanization and new scientific knowledge about, for example, child rearing and the effective utilization of time had made homemaking itself so complex that women needed extensive training for it. The unorganized domestic-science movement of the nineteenth century was becoming the organized home-economics movement of the twentieth century. In the early 1900s, social feminists regarded it with favor. It laid claim to being scientific in an age that celebrated science, while its advocates in universities were important women who were often friends of social feminists.

Nor were its practitioners in those early years without a feminist rationale. Ellen Richards was the first woman graduate of the Massachusetts Institute of Technology. In 1908 she was the founding president of the American Home Economics Association. According to her biographer, she believed that "because women had clung to antiquated ways of doing housework . . . and had failed to take hold of their own problems in a masterful way, they were handicapped when they tried to do systematic work outside the home."[24] Yet seen in retrospect, the home economists' message was not that women would become so highly trained in domestic management that they could leave the home for involvement outside of it, but rather that the job of running a home was so all-encompassing that women should not leave it to take up other concerns.

### Suffrage as a Cure-All

Similar ideological weaknesses were to be found in the arguments for woman suffrage. The contention that women needed the vote to protect the home helped to make suffrage respectable, just as it helped to disarm the opposition to women's participation in reform and to the special legislation campaign. It nonetheless implied that women's real place was in the home. "Women are the mothers of the race," wrote Inez Milholland, "and as such are admittedly more concerned than anyone else with all that goes to protect life."[25] For this reason, she argued, women should have the vote. Milholland was a Vassar graduate and a lawyer, known for her physical beauty. She gained widespread attention in 1913 when she rode a horse at the head of a New York City suffrage parade, inviting comparisons to Helen of Troy and Joan of Arc.

Women's use of the vote to effect social change was also couched in conservative rhetoric. A central theme in the suffrage argument

*Inez Milholland, lawyer and journalist, leading a suffrage parade.*

was that once women could vote, social reformation would ensue. What was on one level a practical argument, designed both to attract social feminists to suffrage and to express the realistic understanding that suffrage was only a step toward the emancipation of women, at times took on inflated, utopian dimensions. Thus, suffragists argued that women as voters would end corruption in government and prevent wars.

The danger in the assumption that women were natural reformers lay not only in its proximity to the conservative position but also in that if it proved incorrect in a specific situation, the feminists would appear to have engaged in irrational, "feminine" thinking. And in the 1920s, this is what happened, as women seemed to vote for the same party and candidates as their husbands and not for any woman-defined reform agenda.

### Sex versus Soul

During the prewar years, feminist positions on sexuality, marriage, and motherhood were also contradictory. "We are learning to be frank about sex," Inez Milholland wrote forthrightly in 1913.

*What more can a woman want?*

"And through all this frankness runs a definite tendency toward an assault on the dual standard of morality and an assertion of sex rights on the part of the women."[26] But what exactly did this assertion mean? To Margaret Sanger, for one, it meant women's recognition of their ability to enjoy sex. Mabel Dodge Luhan was a wealthy literary patron and friend of radicals in New York City. According to her, Sanger was "the first person I ever knew who was openly an ardent propagandist for the joys of the flesh."[27]

Other feminists were not so certain that sensuality was key to women's happiness. Living in an age before Freudian theories interpreted sex as a human necessity, many feminists preferred celibacy. Unmarried women often found emotional fulfillment in friendships with women. Reminiscences of professional women who never married express little regret. For romantic love and family devotion, these women substituted devotion to a cause and the close friendship of other women. They participated in the "women's separate culture" of the age.

Many feminists were suspicious of sensuality on other grounds. A major theme in the thought of nineteenth-century reformers—from free-love advocates to leaders of the WCTU—had been that excessive male sensuality lay at the heart of women's oppression, that men's inability to control their sexual urges had produced widespread prostitution and venereal disease. Such attitudes continued into the twentieth century. Charlotte Perkins Gilman wrote about the dangers of "excessive sex indulgence," and social feminists campaigned to make men sexually continent rather than to make women sexually free.[28] These women wanted what they called a "single standard" of morality. They wanted to eliminate neither marriage nor women's sensuality within marriage. Rather, they wished to make marriage a spiritual union.

"No one," wrote Inez Milholland, "least of all the advanced feminist thinkers, questions the imperative beauty and value of romantic love. Indeed, the hope is that marriage, far from being undermined or destroyed, can be made real and lasting."[29] Rheta Childe Dorr envisioned a time when marriage would become a matter of "soul selection."[30] Yet while preaching what seemed to them a revolutionary message, the feminists were also furthering the standard romantic ideal of passionate attachment to personal relationships—an ideal that interpreted women's lives as incomplete without a man's love.

Many feminists of all persuasions agreed that the chief fulfillment of a woman's life was motherhood. According to Ellen Key, "Women's best qualities . . . are inseparably bound up with the motherhood in her nature."[31] Emma Goldman wrote that "motherhood is the highest fulfillment of woman's nature."[32] And Charlotte Perkins Gilman echoed her: "In the line of physical evolution, motherhood is the highest process."[33]

From one point of view, such sentiments were radical. They implied a superiority of women that extended into the biological realm and suggested that women might live with children and other women separate from men. Inez Milholland asserted that the women's movement implied the most genuinely "radical revolution . . . of all history; for the relation of the sexes is the very material out of which the fabric of life is spun and woven."[34] Ellen Key contended that a women's revolution would "finally surpass in fanaticism any war of religion or race."[35] Yet ideas about the superiority of motherhood—together with feminist advocacy of special legislation, women's moral superiority, and a "single standard" of morality—were damaging to the feminist position, because they advanced the gender stereotypes that had always plagued women's emancipation.

## TWO GENERATIONS

Before the First World War feminists were not of one mind on the issues of organization, sexuality, and woman's nature. By 1910, two groups—one older and one younger—had emerged. The older generation, leaders of the suffrage movement and the settlement houses, subscribed to conservative ideas about sexuality and were primarily interested in ending discrimination against women in the public sphere. The younger generation—many dedicated careerists—were sexually more liberal and, according to one observer, they used conservative arguments because they were effective, not because the younger women believed them.[36]

More than anything else, however, the younger feminists were concerned with women's internal, psychological liberation. They argued that gaining the vote or entering the professions did not guarantee that women would feel differently about themselves. A psychological revolution, they argued, not only a social one, was needed. At Heterodoxy, for example, formal political papers were presented, but most of the discussions centered around the difficulties encountered in individual women's lives.

The ideas of these younger women were both radical and conservative. They seized on the new term "feminism," coined in France in the nineteenth century, to describe their ideas and to differentiate themselves from the older "woman's rights" advocates. They particularly praised the writings of Ellen Key, who proposed that men and women had different natures and that motherhood should be the center of women's lives. Yet how to combine marriage and motherhood with a career concerned them, and this question would become central to the exploration of personal life that would dominate feminist thought in the 1920s. On the one hand, an emphasis on the individual held out the possibility of a reorientation of the female psyche; on the other, it created the potential for diffusing women's focus on formal organization and the public sphere. And a falling away from organizational activity was a characteristic of the history of American women in the 1920s.

## SUFFRAGE ACHIEVED

Such ideological weaknesses were hardly apparent as the twentieth century approached its third decade. The suffrage crusade was emerging from its doldrums, bringing women together. Three factors were responsible. First, new leaders, some of whom had lived in England, where suffragists employed militant tactics, contributed new ideas and energy. Second, social feminists came to agree that votes more than moral arguments swayed politicians. Third, Progressives came to regard woman suffrage as part of their program, and the suffrage movement gained strength from an identification with the popular reform movement. Between 1910 and 1914, six additional states gave the vote to women. These states were Illinois, Washington, California, Arizona, Kansas, and Oregon.

### A United Front

By 1914, most activist women united around suffrage. The Woman's National Committee of the Socialist party, for example,

*Suffragists ride in a parade in New York City in 1912 (above) and march to the Capitol in Washington, D.C., in 1913 (below)*

*Carrie Chapman Catt during
her second term as president
of the National American
Woman Suffrage Association,*

began to devote most of its time to woman suffrage. In 1914, the
General Federation of Women's Clubs, a last holdout, endorsed
the measure. The suffrage coalition was extensive; it included
women from many groups. Jane Addams, active in the NAWSA,
painted a vivid picture of the variety of its supporters and the reasons for their support when she wrote that the association was
joined by

> a church society of hundreds of Lutheran women; . . . by organiza-
> tions of working women who had keenly felt the need of the municipal
> franchise in order to secure . . . the consideration which the vote alone
> obtains for workingmen; by federations of mothers' meetings, who
> were interested in clean milk and the extension of kindergartens; by
> property-owning women, who had been powerless against taxation;
> by organizations of professional women, of university students, and
> of collegiate alumnae; and by women's clubs interested in municipal
> reforms.[37]

### Tactics and Techniques

The new suffragist leaders first appeared in Massachusetts and
New York City and included such women as Rheta Childe Dorr
and Harriot Stanton Blatch. These women revived flagging

*Picketing the White House—a innovative strategy.*

organizations, introduced new lobbying techniques, standard-ized membership lists, and established state headquarters. They actively sought out contacts with working-class groups. They introduced the suffrage parade—a striking innovation that gained national attention. In addition to the New York and Massachusetts women, Carrie Chapman Catt and Alice Paul were crucial to the new suffrage strategy. Catt had been president of the NAWSA between 1900 and 1904, but she had resigned from the post to move to England due to ill health, leadership tensions in the organization, and an invitation to become president of the new International Woman Suffrage Association.

By 1915, Catt returned to the United States, and she was again elected president of the NAWSA. Alice Paul had also been living in England, as a student and a participant in the British suffrage movement. A woman of strong will and ambition, Paul found it difficult to play a subordinate role in the NAWSA. She was also more militant in her views than Catt and more sympathetic to the tactics of direct confrontation through civil disobedience, which

*Alice Paul makes a toast to suffrage in August 1920.*

British suffragists had employed. In 1913, Paul left the NAWSA to found her own group, the Congressional Union.

Both Catt and Paul possessed considerable ability. Under Catt, the NAWSA adopted the new tactics of parades, rallies, and tight administrative coordination. Paul used them, too; but in contrast to the NAWSA, which concentrated on passage of the suffrage amendment in state legislatures, Paul focused her efforts on Congress, where the suffrage amendment had lain dormant in both houses since 1893. Within one year of the formation of the Congressional Union, her group was able to pressure the Senate into voting on the amendment, although the measure was defeated in this initial attempt.

Six more years of agitation followed. Despite their differences, the NAWSA and the Congressional Union worked together during those years, even though the Congressional Union broadened its efforts to the state level and regrouped itself into a political party, the Woman's Party, in the election of 1916. As tension mounted and Congress repeatedly failed to pass the suffrage amendment, Alice Paul and the Woman's Party took extreme measures. In 1917, they organized round-the-clock picketing of the White House. Woodrow Wilson's administration played into their hands by having them arrested and jailed. The national press coverage they received embarrassed the administration by exposing the harshness of their treatment, including force-feeding when they refused to eat. Even this action did not bring an immediate congressional victory. Not until 1919, after numerous additional state victories seemed to provide the ultimate pressure, was passage of the amendment successful. Finally, on August 18, 1920, with its passage by the state of Tennessee, the Nineteenth Amendment, giving women the vote, became law.

### The Aftermath of Victory

To what extent the militant tactics contributed to the suffrage victory is difficult to determine. In her study of the suffrage movement, Eleanor Flexner splits the difference, giving equal plaudits to the NAWSA and to the Woman's Party. Jane Addams, however, discounted the efforts of the suffrage leaders. Addams thought women were given the vote because they had performed admirably during the First World War, keeping the economy going at home while men were at war. Woman suffrage, according to Addams, was "a direct result of the war psychology."[38] In 1917, the war mood produced a reaction against dissent. Aliens and political radicals were incarcerated without any major public outcry. Paul's militant tactics may have produced a reaction against feminism among an American public which by the 1920s was ambivalent about Progressivism.

The split between the NAWSA and the Woman's Party was to have future repercussions. Although the two groups agreed on goals, they differed on tactics. In 1919, Catt openly disavowed Paul's militancy. Once suffrage was achieved, the disagreement over tactics broadened to include a disagreement over goals.

*Miss Pauline Weschmeyer registers to vote in New York.*

Yet in 1920, activist women were euphoric. Not only had women been enfranchised but also during World War I, as the economy expanded and men left jobs for battle, women were promoted to previously male skilled-labor and administrative positions. Women were proving that they were capable of performing jobs believed to be impossible for them. They were working as streetcar conductors, as engineers on trains, as construction workers.

Furthermore, in 1917, the federal government formed the Women's Committee of the Council for National Defense to mobilize women behind the war effort. Both Anna Howard Shaw and Carrie Chapman Catt served on it with distinction. In 1919, the prohibition amendment became law. It had long been a goal of the WCTU and of rural Protestant women, many of whom ultimately supported woman suffrage. It, too, gave the impression that women had the power to effect reform. Viewing the scene in 1920, socialist Elizabeth Gurley Flynn was optimistic. Never before, she wrote, had women been so well-organized, so unified.[39] The future looked bright.

Flynn's optimism proved to be premature. In the 1920s, the feminist movement broke apart, and the interest of American women turned away from feminism and social reform. Looking back from the late 1920s, when conservatism seemed dominant, one analyst of prewar feminism could write as if the movement was unimportant, passing it off as the work of "women quite remote in purpose from the millions of census breadwinners." The growth in industrialism, she contended, had caused the advances for women. Before the First World War, feminism had been only a "little wave" on the broader flow of events.[40] Her point of view was not at all unique.

## NOTES

[1] Abigail Scott Duniway, *Path Breaking: An Autobiographical History of the Equal Suffrage Amendment in the Pacific Coast States* (1914; New York: Source Book Press, 1970), p. 60.

[2] Joseph Gilpin Pyle, "Should Women Vote?" in *Anti-Suffrage Pamphlets*, miscellaneous collection, Princeton University Library, p. 19.

[3] Harriot Stanton Blatch and Alma Lutz, *Challenging Years: The Memoirs of Harriot Stanton Blatch* (New York: G. P. Putnam's Sons, 1940), p. 109.

[4] Edith Finch, *Carey Thomas of Bryn Mawr* (New York: Harper & Row, 1947), pp. 249–50.

[5] Rheta Childe Dorr, *A Woman of Fifty* (New York: Funk & Wagnalls, 1924), p. 148.

[6] Mary Earhart, *Frances Willard: From Prayers to Politics* (Chicago: University of Chicago Press, 1944), p. 194.

[7] Ida A. Harper, "Women in Municipal Governments," in May Wright Sewall, ed., *The World's Congress of Representative Women: A Historical Resumé for Popular Circulation of the World's Congress of Representative Women, Convened in Chicago on May 15, and Adjourned on May 22, 1893* (Chicago: Rand McNally, 1894), II, 453.

[8] "Men's Views of Women's Clubs," *Annals of the American Academy of Political and Social Science*, XXVIII (July–Dec., 1906): 289.

[9] Blake McKelvey, *American Prisons: A Study in American Social History Prior to 1915* (Chicago: University of Chicago Press, 1936), p. 214.

[10] Alice Hamilton, *Exploring the Dangerous Trades: The Autobiography of Alice Hamilton* (Boston: Little Brown, 1943), p. 269.

[11] Robert L. Duffus, *Lillian Wald, Neighbor and Crusader* (New York: Macmillan, 1939), p. 71.

[12] Elizabeth Butler, *Women and the Trades: Pittsburgh, 1907–1908* (New York: Charities Publication Committee, 1909), p. 332.

[13] Marvin Lazerson, *Origins of the Urban School: Public Education in*

*Massachusetts, 1870–1915* (Cambridge: MA: Harvard University Press, 1971), pp. 36–73.

[14] W. L. George, "Feminist Intentions," *Atlantic Monthly*, CXII (Dec., 1913): 731.

[15] Ben Hecht, *A Child of the Century* (New York: Simon & Schuster, 1954), p. 48.

[16] Inez Milholland, "The Liberation of a Sex," *McClure's*, XL (Feb., 1913): 185–88.

[17] Charlotte Perkins Gilman, *The Man-Made World: or, Our Androcentric Culture* (New York: Charlton, 1911), p. 211.

[18] Hutchins Hapgood, *A Victorian in the Modern World* (New York: Harcourt Brace Jovanovich, 1939), p. 377.

[19] Marie Theresa Blanc, *The Condition of Women in the United States: A Traveller's Notes*, trans. Abby Langdon Alger (1895; Freeport, NY: Books for Libraries Press, 1972), p. 88.

[20] Margaret Anderson, *My Thirty Years' War: An Autobiography* (New York: Covici, Friede, 1930), pp. 55, 74.

[21] Josephine Goldmark, "The World's Experience Upon Which Legislation Limiting the Hours of Labor for Women is Based," in Josephine Goldmark, *Fatigue and Efficiency: A Study in Industry* (New York: Russell Sage Foundation, 1917), p. 1.

[22] Christopher Lasch, ed., *The Social Thought of Jane Addams* (Indianapolis: Bobbs-Merrill, 1965), p. 144.

[23] *Jane Addams: A Centennial Reader* (New York: Macmillan, 1960), p. 115.

[24] Caroline Hunt, *The Life of Ellen Richards* (Washington, DC: American Home Economics Association, 1958), p. 144.

[25] Winifred Scott Cooley, "The Younger Suffragists," *Harper's*, LVIII (Sept. 27, 1913): 6–7.

[26] Milholland, "Liberation of a Sex," 185.

[27] Mabel Dodge Luhan, *Intimate Memories* (New York: Harcourt Brace Jovanovich, 1936), III: *Movers and Shakers*, p. 69.

[28] Charlotte Perkins Gilman, *Women and Economics: The Economic Factor Between Men and Women as a Factor in Social Evolution* (1898; New York: Harper & Row, 1970), p. 30.

[29] Inez Milholland, "The Changing Home," *McClure's*, XL (March 1913): 214.

[30] Dorr, *Woman of Fifty*, pp. 450–51.

[31] Ellen Key, *Love and Marriage* (New York: G. P. Putnam's Sons, 1911), p. 124.

[32] Emma Goldman, "Marriage and Love," in Miriam Schneir, ed., *Feminism: The Essential Historical Writings* (New York: Vintage Books, 1971), p. 322.

[33] Gilman, *Man-Made World*, p. 245.

[34] Milholland, "Changing Home," 208.

[35] Key, *Love and Marriage*, p. 214.

[36] Cooley, "Younger Suffragists," 7.

[37] Jane Addams, *Twenty Years at Hull House* (1910; Urbana: University of Illinois Press, 1990), p. 196.

[38] Jane Addams, *The Second Twenty Years at Hull House* (New York: Macmillan, 1930), p. 103.

[39] Elizabeth Gurley Flynn, *I Speak My Own Piece* (New York: Masses and Mainstream, 1955), p. 267.

[40] Mary Ross, "The New Status of Women in America," in Samuel D. Schmalhausen and V. F. Calverton, eds., *Woman's Coming of Age, A Symposium* (New York: H. Liveright, 1931), pp. 545–48.


## BIBLIOGRAPHY

Although historians have long acknowledged the importance of the woman suffrage movement, a comprehensive study is still needed. Alan P. Grimes, *The Puritan Ethic and Woman Suffrage* (New York: Oxford University Press, 1967), argues that the desire for order in Western states brought the early vote for women there, although he pays insufficient attention to organized suffragist activity. Aileen S. Kraditor, *The Ideas of the Woman Suffrage Movement, 1890–1920* (New York: Columbia University Press, 1965), explores the flaws in the suffrage argument, although she slights its positive aspects. Sharon Hartman Strom, "Leadership and Tactics in the American Suffrage Movement: A New Perspective from Massachusetts," *Journal of American History*, 62 (Sept., 1975): 296–315, argues for an earlier date than 1910 for the reinvigoration of the suffrage movement.

The most recent study of the last years of the movement is David Morgan, *Suffragists and Democrats: The Politics of Woman Suffrage in America* (East Lansing, MI: Michigan State University Press, 1972). Eleanor Flexner, *Century of Struggle: The Woman's Rights Movement in the United States* (Cambridge, MA: Harvard University Press, 1959), is still a useful overview, and comparative perspectives are provided in Ross Evans Paulson, *Women's Suffrage and Prohibition: A Comparative Study of Equality and Social Control* (Glenview, IL: Scott, Foresman, 1973), and in Donald Meyer, *Sex and Power: The Rise of Women in America, Russia, Sweden, and Italy* (Middletown: CT: Wesleyan University Press, 1987). Personal experiences in the suffrage movement are recounted in Sherna Gluck (ed.), *From Parlor to Prison: Five American Suffragists Talk About Their Lives: An Oral History* (New York: Random House, 1976).

These sources should be supplemented by the many analyses of participants, including Harriot Stanton Blatch and Alma Lutz, *Challenging Years: The Memoirs of Harriot Stanton Blatch* (New York: G. P. Putnam's Sons, 1940); Carrie Chapman Catt and Nettie Rogers Shuler, *Woman Suffrage and*

*Politics: The Inner Story of the Suffrage Movement* (New York: Scribner's, 1926); Maud Wood Park, *Front Door Lobby*, (ed.) Edna Lamprey Stentiel (Boston: Beacon Press, 1960); and Elizabeth Cady Stanton et al., *History of Woman Suffrage*, 6 vols. (New York: Fowler & Wells, 1881–1922). These volumes have been excerpted in Mary Jo Buhle and Paul Buhle (eds.), *The Concise History of Woman Suffrage: Selections from the Classic Work of Stanton, Anthony, Gage, and Harper* (Urbana: University of Illinois Press, 1978).

Studies of the many women's organizations include Karen J. Blair, *The Clubwoman as Feminist: True Womanhood Redefined, 1868–1914* (New York: Holmes & Meier, 1980), on women's clubs, and Ruth Bordin, *Woman and Temperance: The Quest for Power and Liberty, 1873–1900* (Philadelphia: Temple University Press, 1981), on the WCTU. The YWCA and black women's clubs still await their historians. On the DAR, see Margaret Gibbs, *The Daughters of the American Revolution* (New York: Holt, Rinehart & Winston, 1969). The only existing history of the Consumers' League is Maud Nathan, *The Story of an Epoch-Making Movement* (Garden City, NY: Doubleday, Page, 1926). Material on a number of women's organizations is to be found in Glenna Matthews, *Rise of Public Woman: Woman's Power and Woman's Place in the United States, 1630–1970* (New York: Oxford University Press, 1992); William L. O'Neill, *Everyone was Brave: The Rise and Fall of Feminism in America* (New York: Quadrangle, 1969); and Ann Firor Scott, *Natural Allies: Women's Associations in American History* (Urbana: University of Illinois Press, 1991).

Much scholarship has recently appeared on women in the Progressive movement. See Paula Baker, "The Domestication of Politics: Women and American Society, 1780–1920," in Ellen Carol DuBois and Vicki L. Ruiz, *Unequal Sisters: A Multicultural Reader in U.S. Women's History* (New York: Routledge, 1990); Ellen F. Fitzpatrick, *Endless Crusade: Women Social Scientists and Progressive Reform* (New York: Oxford University Press, 1990); Noralee Frankel and Nancy S. Dye (eds.), *Gender, Class, Race, and Reform in the Progressive Era* (Lexington, KY: University Press of Kentucky, 1991); Robyn Muncy, *Creating a Female Dominion in American Reform* (New York: Oxford University Press, 1991); and Theda Skocpol, *Protecting Soldiers and Mothers: The Political Origins of Social Policy in the United States* (Cambridge, MA: Harvard University Press, 1992). An interesting comparative perspective is provided by Sonya Michel and Seth Koven, "Womanly Duties: Maternalist Politics and the Origin of Welfare States in France, Germany, Great Britain and the United States, 1880–1920," *American Historical Review,* 95 (Oct., 1990): 1176–1208. Material on the debate over protective legislation is found in many of these sources, but one might also consult Susan Lehrer, *Origins of Protective Legislation for Women, 1905–1925* (Albany: State University of New York, 1987).

Older, but still useful works include Allen F. Davis, *Spearheads for Reform: The Social Settlements and the Progressive Movement, 1890–1914* (New York: Oxford University Press, 1967); Davis, *American Heroine: The Life and Legend of Jane Addams* (New York: Oxford University Press, 1973); Kathleen D. McCarthy, *Noblesse Oblige: Charity and Cultural Philanthropy in Chicago*

(Chicago: University of Chicago Press, 1982); and David P. Thelen, *The New Citizenship: Origins of Progressivism in Wisconsin* (Columbus, MO: University of Missouri Press, 1972). For an interesting account of the relationship between college culture and settlement-house involvement, see John P. Rousmanière, "Cultural Hybrid in the Slums: The College Woman and the Settlement House, 1889–1894," *American Quarterly*, 22 (Spring 1970): 45–66. On the general subject of violence against women and attempts at reform, see Elizabeth Pleck, *Domestic Tyranny: The Making of Social Policy Against Family Violence from Colonial Times to the Present* (New York: Oxford University Press, 1987).

Two insightful works explore the relationships between reformers and clients; both critique reformers' paternalism and applaud clients' activism. See Linda Gordon, *Heroes of Their Own Lives: The Politics and History of Family Violence: Boston, 1880–1960* (New York: Viking Penguin, 1988), on family service agencies in Boston, and Peggy Pascoe, *Relations of Rescue: The Search for Female Moral Authority in the American West, 1874–1939* (New York: Oxford University Press, 1990), on four Western reform agencies: the Presbyterian Chinese Mission Home in San Francisco, founded in 1874 to "save" Chinese prostitutes; the Colorado Cottage Home in Denver, Colorado, founded in 1886 for unmarried mothers; the Industrial Christian Home in Salt Lake City, Utah, founded in 1886 for polygamous wives; and the mission to the Omaha Indians of Nebraska by the Connecticut branch of the Women's National Indian Association, beginning in the mid-1880s. See also Gordon's *Pitied But Not Entitled: Single Mothers and the History of Welfare* (New York: Free Press, 1994).

Biographies and autobiographies are available for most major women Progressives, who themselves wrote extensively on their work. See especially Jane Addams, *Twenty Years at Hull House* (New York: Macmillan, 1910), and Lillian Wald, *The House on Henry Street* (New York: Henry Holt, 1915). Also consult Mary R. Beard, *Women's Work in Municipalities* (New York: Appleton-Century-Crofts, 1915); Sophonisba Breckinridge, *Women in the Twentieth Century: A Study of Their Political, Social, and Economic Activities* (New York: McGraw Hill, 1933); and Rheta Childe Dorr, *What Eight Million Women Want* (1910; reprint ed., Boston: Kraus, 1971).

Several works underline the broad nature of the feminist movement in the early twentieth century. See Estelle B. Freedman, *Their Sisters' Keepers: Women's Prison Reform in America, 1830–1930* (Ann Arbor: University of Michigan Press, 1981), and Delores Hayden, *The Grand Domestic Revolution: A History of Feminist Designs for American Homes, Neighborhoods, and Cities* (Cambridge, MA: Massachusetts Institute of Technology, 1981). On racism in white women's organizations, see Nancie Carraway, *Segregated Sisterhood: Racism and the Politics of American Feminism* (Knoxville: University of Tennessee Press, 1991).

On militant feminism in the early twentieth century, see June Sochen, *The New Woman: Feminism in Greenwich Village, 1910–1920* (New York: Quadrangle, 1972), for information on some of the New York activists. On Margaret Sanger, the definitive biography is Ellen Chesler, *Woman of Valor:*

*Margaret Sanger and the Birth Control Movement in America* (New York: Simon & Schuster, 1992). On Sanger, also consult the works on birth control by Linda Gordon and James Reed cited in the bibliography to Chapter 1. On Charlotte Perkins Gilman, see Mary A. Hill, *Charlotte Perkins Gilman: The Making of a Radical Feminist, 1860–1896* (Philadelphia: Temple University Press, 1980), and Ann Lane, *To Herland and Beyond: The Life and Work of Charlotte Perkins Gilman* (New York: Pantheon Books, 1990), as well as Gilman's own autobiography, *The Living of Charlotte Perkins Gilman: An Autobiography* (New York: Appleton-Century-Crofts, 1935). For an insight into her thought, as well as a fascinating voyage into a feminist utopia, see Gilman's *Herland* (New York: Pantheon Books, 1979).

On Emma Goldman, see Alice Wexler, *Emma Goldman: An Intimate Life* (New York: Pantheon Books, 1984); Wexler, *Emma Goldman in Exile: From the Russian Revolution to the Spanish Civil War* (Boston: Beacon Press, 1989); and Candace Serena Falk, *Love, Anarchy, and Emma Goldman* (New Brunswick, NJ: Rutgers University Press, 1990).

On the First World War and working women, see Maureen Greenwald, *Women, War, and Work: The Impact of World War One on Women Workers in the United States* (Westport, CT: Greenwood Press, 1980).

# 4

## THE 1920s: FREEDOM OR DISILLUSIONMENT?

DURING THE 1920S, MOST MAJOR women's organizations continued in operation, and several new ones appeared. The National Federation of Business and Professional Women's Clubs (BPW) was established in 1919. The Women's Bureau in the Department of Labor, the Women's Joint Congressional Committee (WJCC), and the League of Women Voters dated from 1920. Although the Women's Trade Union League and the National Consumers' League declined in membership, a number of women's organizations gained huge memberships. By 1930, the YWCA had 600,000 members, and the National Congress of Parent and Teacher Associations had a membership of a million and a half. Historian Nancy Cott asserts that "the greatest extent of associational activity in the whole history of American women took place in the era between the two wars."[1] The situation seemed to promise major progress for women.

But this was not to be the case in the 1920s, as the women's movement divided into groups with separate concerns. Soon after the passage of the suffrage amendment, Anna Howard Shaw confided in Emily Newell Blair, a young suffragist and later vice-president of the National Committee of the Democratic Party: "I am sorry for you young women who have to carry on the work . . . for suffrage was a symbol, and now you have lost your symbol."[2] Shaw could not foresee that the political conservatism of the 1920s would imperil reform initiatives. But she did realize the potential for division within the women's movement. Four groups emerged: social feminists, pacifists, professional women, and feminists. Additionally, some activists focused on expanding women's role in politics.

The Progressive coalition of settlement-house and social workers was organized around issues pertaining to women and children. Coordinated through the Children's Bureau in the Department of Labor, it did remain active. Its major achievement was the 1921 Sheppard-Towner Act, which provided federal grants to states for maternity and pediatric clinics. The first federal program for social welfare, it was a predecessor to the Social Security Act of 1935. But growing 1920s conservatism led to its demise in 1927.

## WOMEN'S ORGANIZATIONS IN TRANSITION

With suffrage won, the NAWSA disbanded, and a new organization, the League of Women Voters, was formed. During the 1920s, the League concentrated on social reform, elimination of state laws discriminatory to women, and the education of women to effective citizenship.

As an agency of reform, the League was not ineffective. Its efforts at local, state, and national levels on behalf of municipal reform, conservation, women's legal rights, tighter consumer laws, the Child Labor Amendment, and public support of indigent mothers were impressive. The League often served as a training ground for women in politics. For example, after Lavinia Eagle served seven years as a field secretary for the NAWSA, she became director of the Maryland League in 1920. She was later elected to the Maryland Legislature. In 1936, she became an official in the federal Social Security Administration.

In approach, however, the League has usually been moderate. As former suffragists who expected voting women to spearhead a national reformation, League leaders were shaken when the turnout of women voters in the elections of the early 1920s was light and their voting patterns similar to those of men. In reaction, League leaders decided to concentrate on educating women for responsible citizenship. This concept was grounded in caution. Study often took the place of action. The League's approach, wrote one analyst, was to focus on "some definite, limited problem. . . . Conclusions and new ideas are tentatively held, are tested, and are revised."[3]

Yet, with organization, women could effectively challenge the male-dominated political system. In Ohio, Florence Allen won a seat on the state supreme court in 1922 and reelection in 1928 by organizing women activists. Her managers contacted former suffragists, who handled publicity, arranged meetings, and distributed campaign literature. (In 1934, Franklin D. Roosevelt appointed Allen to the Sixth Circuit Court of Appeals—the federal court level just below the Supreme Court.) And, in 1928, Ruth Hanna

*"Ma" Ferguson (seated) was elected governor of Texas in 1924 and 1932—one of the first women to hold the office.*

McCormick of Illinois won her deceased husband's House of Representatives seat by utilizing the network of state Republican women's clubs she had organized for her husband's successful House race in 1924.

But to form coalitions of women was difficult. Many former suffragists were exhausted. One Connecticut activist explained: "After we got the vote, the crusade was over. It was peacetime and we all went back to a hundred different causes and tasks that we'd been putting off all those years."[4] The national League of Women Voters' leadership complained of a lack of able women willing to take on leadership positions in local chapters; the League attracted to its membership only a fraction of the former membership of the suffrage organizations.

In the 1920s, the suffrage coalition fell apart. Alice Paul's Woman's Party refused to endorse the League of Women Voters' program of social feminism and education, while women's groups in general focused on issues other than mobilizing women around the political parties. The Woman's Party centered its efforts on attaining an Equal Rights Amendment (ERA). This amendment, they believed, would be the surest way to abolish the many laws still on the books that discriminated against women. The ERA was first introduced in Congress in 1923. Its text was short, simply stating that "men and women shall have equal rights throughout the United States and every place subject to its jurisdiction." But most women's organizations, including the League of Women Voters, opposed the ERA on the grounds that factory women required special legislation.

The membership of the Woman's Party was small, but it included wealthy and eminent women. It was not a radical group. Crystal Eastman was a socialist, a pacifist, and an associate of Henrietta Rodman in the prewar Feminist Alliance and of Alice Paul in the prewar Woman's Party. She charged that when in the 1920s she presented Paul with a list of militant demands, including the legalization of birth control, Paul refused to consider them.[5] The concern of the Woman's Party was the ERA. To this end the Woman's Party operated on several fronts, including support for women attempting to run for Congress.

The new Women's Bureau in the Department of Labor might have served as an agency to unify women's organizations, following the example of the Children's Bureau. But the Women's Bureau became primarily a fact-finding and publication service, concerned with women's employment. Its first and long-term president, Mary Anderson, came from the Women's Trade Union League and established its agenda firmly in support of special legislation for women. Always underfunded, the Bureau lacked influence with business and labor leaders. According to historian Judith Sealander, the networks its officials did establish with women reformers condemned the Bureau to the outer circles of male political power in Washington.

A number of organizations active in the Progressive coalition before the war turned away from activism. Local women's clubs, which had led the social-welfare coalition before the war, often made entertainment their priority, with their members focusing on playing the game of bridge, a national craze in the 1920s, or discussing fashions, gardening, and cooking rather than social problems. One ex-president of a suburban club in the Midwest bemoaned that her clubhouse, once filled with political speeches, "now . . . rings with such [bridge] terms as 'no trump' and 'grand slam.'"[6] The national office of the General Federation of Women's Clubs, reflecting the era's pride in technology and its emphasis on management efficiency, established program goals highlighting home economics and the use of electrical appliances in the home.

The primary concern of many former suffragists became pacifism. Carrie Chapman Catt established the National Conference on the Cause and Cure of War, and Jane Addams lent support to the Women's International League for Peace and Freedom (WILPF). As a result of the war, Rheta Childe Dorr found herself no longer interested in the women's movement but rather concerned with "humanity."[7] Organized women were outraged by the outbreak of World War I, which many traced to male aggressiveness. In pacifist rhetoric, women as mothers had a "peculiar moral passion against both the cruelty and the want of war."[8]

In the 1920s, the efforts of women pacifists were not without success. The WILPF, for example, was an important pressure group behind the decade's disarmament and peace conferences. Women pacifists were influential in pressuring the United States and overseas governments into signing the 1927 Kellogg-Briand Pact, which outlawed war as national policy. Only in retrospect, with the outbreak of World War II, do their actions appear futile. Yet their campaign for peace further scattered the feminist effort at home.

Professional women increasingly focused on equal pay and equal employment opportunity in their own professions. After the war, new professional women's associations appeared in a number of fields, including dentistry, architecture, and journalism. In 1919, under the sponsorship of the YWCA, the National Federation of Business and Professional Women's Clubs was formed. Composed primarily of teachers and clerical workers, its goal was gender equity in these professions. But despite this organizing, agitating for change was difficult. Women's struggle in male-dominated professions simply to maintain the status quo often absorbed all their energy, while the power of male supervisors in professions such as nursing and librarianship, where women held numerical superiority, made progress toward equity difficult even in these "feminized" fields.

The situation for social workers and settlement-house workers was also complex. Some dropped out of the social-activist coalition.

To postwar college graduates, settlement work—now in its fourth decade—no longer held the appeal of newness. In many cities, Community Chests, founded in the early 1920s to coordinate charitable giving, became the major financial backers of settlements. Because conservative businessmen usually controlled the Community Chests, settlement workers became cautious about innovation. Moreover, the movement of African Americans from the South into the formerly Jewish, Italian, and Slavic neighborhoods that the settlements served created new challenges, given the nation's overriding racism. The field of social work itself was going through a process of professionalization, of concern with issues of standards, training, and pay that focused attention away from clients and their needs. Still, the idealism inspired by the founders of the profession did not entirely dissipate. Many of these women pioneers were still teaching in schools of social work and mentoring young careerists in the 1920s.

In 1920, a number of women's organizations, under the leadership of Julia Lathrop of the Children's Bureau, formed the Women's Joint Congressional Committee to work as a common lobby. The League of Women Voters, the National Federation of Business and Professional Women's Clubs, and the General Federation of Women's Clubs were members of the WJCC, as were the National Congress of Parents and Teachers, the WCTU, the AAUW, and the National Council of Jewish Women. In many states, similar legislative councils emerged. The national committee worked for improved education, an amendment to the Constitution regulating child labor, and U.S. membership in the World Court. They especially were concerned about maternal and infant health care, given statistics showing that the United States had one of the highest infant mortality rates in the industrialized world.

## The Sheppard-Towner Act: Successes and Failures

The major success of the WJCC was the 1921 Sheppard-Towner Act. This legislation provided matching federal grants to states to set up maternity and pediatric clinics. It was administered by the Children's Bureau. At least 75 percent of the directors of the state programs were women, and the programs employed over 800 public nurses. In each state, these nurses traveled from

*A Sheppard-Towner visiting nurse working among Negro families, circa 1928.*

county to county, working with local doctors and women's groups to organize health conferences to examine and evaluate mothers and their preschool children. The Sheppard-Towner nurse might initiate needed follow-up visits, or she might attempt to catalyze local groups into setting up their own clinics.

The Sheppard-Towner administration was sensitive to its clients. In the Southwest, Mexican-American nurses were sent into Mexican-American counties and Native-American nurses to Native Americans. In the South, African-American nurses served black communities. Sheppard-Towner nurses taught many women hygiene and infant care: Children's Bureau files contain testimonials from these clients. On the other hand, the public health nurses were suspicious of the midwives and folk healers of local communities, and they often encouraged domesticity in their clients. They typically counseled women to remain at home and raise their own children, no matter their situation.

In 1927, Congress refused to reallocate Sheppard-Towner funding. Part of the difficulty stemmed from the lack of a women's voting bloc, which might have forced Congress to pay more attention to social-welfare and feminist issues. More than that, male physicians, organized through the powerful American Medical Association, worried about possible loss of income from the competition of the visiting nurses, and they lobbied to end the program. Most important, however, the increasing conservatism of the decade militated against government spending programs.

During the 1920s, federal legislators were sympathetic neither to reform nor to feminism. Attempts to secure passage of even such moderate measures as an amendment restricting child labor and one outlawing lynching failed to succeed. Historian Stanley Lemons contends that women's organizations were primarily responsible for whatever Progressive impulse carried over to the conservative 1920s. The wartime antiradical hysteria that culminated in the "Red Scare" of 1919, with deportations and jailings, colored the decade. "The business of America is business," intoned Calvin Coolidge, enunciating one of the era's major themes. And business seemed in control. In Connecticut, for example, the women's movement experienced no factionalization and remained unified under the leadership of the League of Women Voters. In fact, the effort for social reform there, as in New York, where by the mid-1920s Eleanor Roosevelt was beginning her work in social feminist reform, was concentrated at the state level. But in Connecticut, the far-reaching reform agenda, including birth control, was regularly defeated by a legislature controlled by Republican businessmen.

## ANTIFEMINIST UNDERCURRENTS AND FEMINIST CONSERVATISM

Reflecting business sentiment, the mood of the country was not especially reform-minded. Americans in the 1920s were dazzled by seem-

*Helen Wills, tennis star of the 1920s.*

ing prosperity and mass-produced consumer goods: automobiles, radios, and, for women in particular, washing machines, vacuum cleaners, and electric kitchens. What need was there for social service when industry was apparently fulfilling its promise of providing material prosperity to all? What concerned Americans—at least of the middle class—were their cars, the radio serials and the latest movies, the exploits of sports stars and cultural heroes, and the pursuit of beauty and youth. The women's clubs that turned from social service to bridge were indicative. Vida Scudder, a Wellesley College professor active in Boston settlements and in the Women's Trade Union League, concluded that "those ten exhausted years [the 1920s] were the worst I have ever known."[9]

By the mid-1920s, it had become a matter of belief—proclaimed by press and radio—that women had achieved liberation. Suffrage had been won. The number of women's organizations had not diminished. Women had been employed in large numbers during World War I in positions of responsibility; they had become men's comrades in offices and factories, or so it seemed. Legions of Vassar and Smith graduates descended on New York City every year to become secretaries, copy editors, and management trainees in department stores. Women were smoking in public, wearing short skirts, and demanding and gaining entry into speakeasies, men's clubs, and golf courses. Female sports stars, such as Helen Wills in tennis and Gertrude Ederle in swimming, were challenging any remaining notions that women could not excel in athletics. Journalists Jane Grant and Ruth Hale formed a Lucy Stone League in New York City to encourage married women to continue to use their maiden names, as had Lucy Stone, the nineteenth-century suffrage leader. Even Suzanne LaFollette, author of one of the few militant feminist treatises of the decade, wrote in 1926 that the woman's struggle "is very largely won."[10]

The premise that women had achieved liberation gave rise to a new and subtle antifeminism. By the late 1920s, articles appeared in popular journals contending that in gaining their "rights," women had given up their "privileges." What these privileges involved were self-indulgence and freedom from working. The new antifeminists did not openly question women's right to work. They simply proclaimed that women were incapable of combining marriage and a career. They pictured women's world

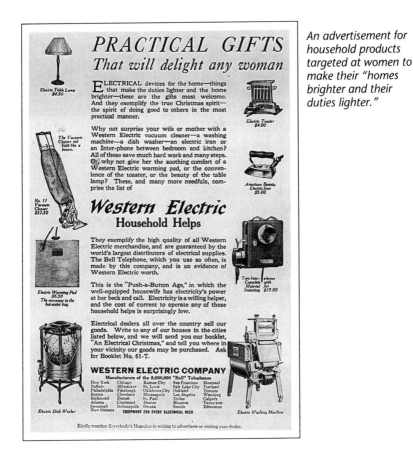

*An advertisement for household products targeted at women to make their "homes brighter and their duties lighter."*

in the home as exotic, contending that working women did not have the "delightful" experience of taking "an hour to dress," of "spending the day in strictly feminine pursuits," of "actually making the kind of cake that [now] comes from the bakery."[11]

These new antifeminists not only borrowed the rhetoric of the prewar feminists but also claimed that they were the real feminists of the 1920s. "It [the return to the home] is going to be almost as long and hard a struggle . . . as the struggle for women's rights."[12] In 1927, writer Dorothy Dunbar Bromley defined a "new-style feminist" who bore no relationship to "the old school of fighting feminists who wore flat heels and had very little feminine charm, or the current species who antagonize men with their constant clamor about maiden names, equal rights, women's place in the world." The "new-style" feminist was well-dressed, openly liked men, avoided women in groups, and instinctively knew that "a full life calls for marriage and children as well as a career."[13]

Molders of public opinion spread the message. Advertising, which expanded dramatically in volume in the 1920s, found its major market in women, who spent much of the family income. To sell domestic items like kitchen appliances and cleaning products, advertisers pictured women as model consumers devoted to improving family life through purchasing new products. The clothing and cosmetics industries advertised their way to a phenomenal growth in the 1920s, and in their ads fashion and sex appeal were women's most important concerns.

New writings on women's sexuality validated this message. Marriage manuals advocating sexual pleasure for women and spelling out techniques now were readily available. The theories of Sigmund Freud underlined their message, for he had argued early in the century that unconscious drives, especially sex, were central motivators of human behavior. A number of doctors and Greenwich Village intellectuals knew Freud's work before the war, but not until the 1920s did Freudian theories became popular. Yet Freud's ideas were as constraining for women as liberating. His crucial factor in female personality development, for example, was the female child's envy of the male sex organ. This envy, according to Freud, made women always dissatisfied, with motherhood their only real avenue to happiness.

However, the influence of Freudian theories in the 1920s should not be overemphasized. In the later years of the decade, the behaviorist ideas of John B. Watson were in vogue. Watson played down the notion of suppressed desires influencing human actions and contended that, through will power, behavior could be controlled. His message to women was nonetheless ambiguous. In his *Psychological Care of Infant and Child* (1928), the standard reference on child rearing for a decade or more, Watson argued that most women were failures as mothers. Consequently, they should either not have children or recognize that proper child rearing required extensive training and complete dedication.

In the 1920s, notions of the pleasures of sex permeated the culture. Women's magazines were full of it. Films made it a stock device. Sex-story magazines like *True Confessions* exploited it and garnered huge sales. Mabel Dodge Luhan's Greenwich Village Salon was a gathering place for intellectuals and radicals in the 1910s. Her psychoanalysis in 1915 set an example for her friends. Luhan laid clear the underlying message of the new ideas about sex. "The sex act," she wrote, is "the cornerstone of any life, and its chief reality," especially for women. "It is indeed the happy woman who has no history," because she has lived for erotic gratification, for her husband or lover, and for her children.[14]

To these ideas, the feminist rebuttal was weak. The arguments of those feminists who had wanted a "single standard" of sex behavior and who had attacked male sexuality seemed antiquated. Charlotte Perkins Gilman, for one, found it almost impossible in the 1920s to secure speaking engagements or to sell her books. No longer did friendships among women suffice; the marriage rates of women college graduates escalated in the 1920s. The argument about women's special morality, important to nineteenth-century reform, and the reality of women's separate culture, important to women's bonding during that century, were fractured, if not destroyed.

Yet the advent of freer views about sexuality encouraged sexual experimentation and allowed some acknowledgment of lesbianism. In the 1920s, lesbian subcultures emerged in cities such as San Francisco and New York. In Greenwich Village, cultural leaders like Mabel Dodge Luhan openly espoused bisexuality, and Heterodoxy's membership included a number of lesbian couples. In her 1929 study of women's sexual behavior, Katherine Bement Davis found that nearly 50 percent of her respondents admitted to having had intense emotional relationships with women, and 25 percent admitted that a sexual component was involved.[15]

Feminists, like others, took an interest in the new theories. By the mid-1920s, Charlotte Perkins Gilman reported that Heterodoxy was holding sessions on the new sex psychology—a topic that, she noted, did not interest her.[16] Yet more than anything else, feminists focused on how to combine careers and marriage. This issue was appropriate to an individualistic era in which women's work-force participation was highly visible. But it was basically a middle-class issue—one that did not address matters of class or racial discrimination.

Still, conservatism in the 1920s ran deep. The excesses of wartime antiradicalism resulted in Emma Goldman's deportation to Europe. Before the war Margaret Sanger had organized rallies, distributed mass propaganda, and courted jail sentences in her campaign for the legalization of birth control. During the 1920s Sanger confined her efforts to lobbying campaigns before legislatures and groups such as the American Medical Association. Greenwich Village feminists, who before the war had formed the Feminist Alliance, were dispirited as a result of the war experience and left New York City. Greenwich Village women of the next generation were primarily interested in the pursuit of pleasure, not the reorganization of society.

Finally, antifeminism was aided by accusations of communism lodged against many feminist leaders by organizations like the American Legion and the DAR (which had evolved from a sometime advocate of social feminism into a right-wing supporter of military preparedness). Jane Addams was charged with being a communist because she was involved in pacifist causes; Florence Kelley was similarly accused because she had a socialist past and was identified with the attempt to secure passage of a child labor amendment to restrict children's working, which the extreme right saw as a socialist measure designed to undermine the family. Such charges contributed to a popular suspicion of feminism.

One powerful ultra-conservative organization during the 1920s was the Ku Klux Klan. Its female membership, numbering about 500,000, constituted a significant minority of total Klan membership. The 1920s Klan was anti-Semitic, anti-Catholic, and anti-black. Women's role in it was to mobilize "poison squads" to spread rumor and slander about the groups it despised through churches, families, and community networks and to organize consumer boycotts against them. Yet like the prewar female antisuffragists, the women of the Klan were not always conservative on women's issues: they supported a range of equal rights for women in politics and employment. According to their most recent historian, these Klan women "recalled their years in United States history's most vicious campaigns of prejudice and hatred primarily as a time of solidarity and friendship among like-minded women."[17]

*Playwright Lillian Hellman.*

## "FLAMING YOUTH"—NEW LIBERTIES, OLD ATTITUDES

Feminism also failed to take root in the 1920s because it had limited appeal for young women. No movement can prosper long without attracting younger members. In 1910, the suffrage campaign had been reactivated by a group of younger women, including Alice Paul and Rheta Childe Dorr. However, this was not true of the feminist cause in the 1920s—indeed, not until the 1960s.

Rarely before or since the 1920s has a generation been so conscious of its identity and of its perceived difference from an older generation. Their attitude was cavalier toward the achievements of their elders, including the hard-won gains in woman's rights. Lillian Hellman, playwright and member of this generation, has described their attitude:

> By the time I grew up the fight for the emancipation of women, their rights under the law, in the office, in bed, was stale stuff. My generation didn't think much about the place or the problems of women, were not conscious that the designs we saw around us had so recently been formed or that we were still part of that formation.[18]

*Flappers compete in a Charleston dance contest.*

Young people had other interests. Foremost was their rebellion against the mores of Victorian culture, especially its sex taboos. They set a tone in the 1920s. They were the leaders in fashion, in dance, in the introduction of a freer morality. Young women were flappers, living for fun and freedom, for short skirts, cigarettes, automobiles, dancing, and speakeasies. Young middle-class women adopted the freer behavior already observable among the working class before World War I.

Artist John Held, Jr., captured the "flapper" for the *New Yorker* magazine in a series of drawings that were widely reprinted. Like the Gibson girl for the 1890s, Held's flapper became the symbol of the 1920s generation of youth. With her short, straight skirt, her lean torso and her cropped hair, and with a cigarette in her mouth, she was the epitome of rebellious, sexualized youth.

To what extent this appearance indicated a true sexual revolution is debatable. Some rudimentary surveys of sex attitudes were

1896                    1926

Thirty Years of "Progress"!

*John Held, Jr.'s answer to the Gibson girl appears in a 1926 issue of Life magazine.*

attempted during the 1920s; they point to a limited, rather than an extensive, change in behavior. Katherine Bement Davis found that only 7 percent of the married women she interviewed admitted to having had heterosexual sexual relations before marriage and 10.5 percent of the unmarried women admitted to having had a sexual experience with a man. Moreover, 80 percent of both groups saw no justification for premarital sex.[19] Judge Ben Lindsey of the Juvenile Court in Denver, Colorado, gained a national reputation for his work among teenagers. Based on the young people he saw, he reported little evidence of a vast change in sexual values, although he thought that after the war young men were more likely to have sexual relations with their school classmates rather than go to prostitutes, as they had before the war. Yet, in his opinion, no more than 10 percent of Denver's young women were sexually permissive.[20] After all, the "flapper" image hardly appears sexual; more than anything else she resembles a boy.

Far from all young women adopted the new standards of behavior. If they had, the "sexual revolution" would have emancipated their generation, and their daughters and granddaughters would not have reported conflicts with their mothers over sexual behavior. Novelist Mary McCarthy, raised in the 1920s in a strict Catholic

*Anne Morrow Lindbergh.*

family, was forbidden to date until she was 18. She disobeyed this rule only once when she had a secret, although unconsummated, affair with a married man who gallantly preserved her "virtue."[21] Author Anne Morrow Lindbergh, wife of the famed aviator Charles Lindbergh, spent her time at Smith College working hard at her studies, hoping to win the poetry prize, seeing numerous men, and worrying about whether she would ever marry.[22]

The path that Anne Morrow Lindbergh followed was, more often than not, the characteristic one. Sexual emancipation in the end most often led to marriage. Divorce statistics continued to rise, as they had throughout the previous decade. But the number of marriages remained equally high, and the median age of first marriage remained constant. Some historians contend that the real sexual revolution during the 1920s occurred among married women, who began to demand sexual fulfillment in marriage and to use birth control in larger numbers than ever before. One participant in the youth culture of the 1920s later remembered debating free love and companionate marriage, bobbing hair and carrying hip flasks. But there the rebellion stopped. Ten years later, these "rebellious" women were respectable citizens, "worried about the interest on the mortgage; making poor Aunt Ida feel she really isn't a burden; and fervently hoping Junior will escape the epidemic of measles ravaging the fourth grade."[23]

And, this generation had not overcome what is perhaps women's greatest impediment to achieving equality: the feminine sex-role conditioning of their upbringing. Then, as before and after, little girls played with dolls; their brothers, with cars. Boys were encouraged toward bodily freedom and emotional repression; girls, toward ladylike behavior and emotional expression. Girls who stepped out of line were considered "tomboys." According to the biographer of Amelia Earhart, the famed aviator, her "masculine" spirit of adventure was the result of an upbringing that differed from the norm for girls: she was encouraged to engage in such "tomboy" behavior as exploring the out-of-doors. Psychologist Floyd Allport, writing in 1929, called for an end to the indoctrination of rigid sex roles in the rearing of children. Woman, he wrote, "not through nature but by early training . . . becomes a reflection of a feminine image which men carry around in their heads."[24]

Those women who tried to combine marriages and careers still found it difficult. Nonetheless, the percentage of married women in the work force continued to rise—from 5.6 percent in 1900 to 10.7 percent in 1910 to 11.7 percent by 1930. Moreover, the percentage of professional women who were married was also rising—from 12 percent in 1910 to 27 percent in 1930. Many of these women worked due to economic necessity or the influence of the decade's consumerism. "The two-car family," noted economist Lorine Pruette, "demands the two-wage family."[25] Among working-class women a number of factors decreased homework options. The immigration restriction legislation of the 1920s diminished the numbers of men looking for boarding situations, while the passage of "anti-sweating" ordinances in many localities ended industrial homework. Moreover, with stricter enforcement of local and state child labor laws during the 1920s, mothers' work outside the home often replaced their children's labor.

Still, the increasing participation of married women in the work force constituted one of the major long-term trends in the employment of women. It also directly challenged the traditional beliefs that linked women with the home and defined masculinity partly in terms of a man's ability to provide unaided for his family—the so-called "breadwinner ethic."

But it was not always easy for married women to work. Late in the decade, popular journals featured a number of "autobiographies" and "confessions" by self-styled "liberated" women and "ex-feminists." The revelations were similar. All began marriage with their husbands' agreement that family responsibilities were to be shared. But both husband and wife soon reverted to conventional roles. One woman admitted that the problem was partly her own lack of strength, but she also blamed her husband. "He has given lip service to my aspirations," she wrote, "but when it has come to the difficulty of putting them into practice, he has not helped me."[26] Another woman, who married a socialist she met while working in Socialist Party headquarters, had the same problem of lack of support from her husband. Bitterly she wrote that "feminism as a personal religion was as interesting to him as . . . socialism," but not when it interfered with his own comfort. The many women who wanted not only a career but also, in the words of one of these "ex-feminists," "the rich domestic life of husband, home, and babies that my mother's generation enjoyed" faced substantial problems.[27]

## WOMEN AT WORK: PROGRESS AND SETBACKS

### Professional Women

The popular evidence of women's emancipation in the 1920s—the number of women at work, the freer sexuality, the new clothing styles—masked the discrimination against women that still existed. At the height of women's employment during the First World War, for example, only 5 percent of all women workers had not been in the labor force before the war. What seemed to demonstrate new employment actually reflected the fact that women who were already members of the work force were promoted to higher-paying, higher-skilled jobs during the war. In some cases, this meant a permanent transfer into clerical work, on the increase in the 1920s as throughout the twentieth century. In other cases, women who had replaced men were demoted or fired when the war ended. In Cleveland, Ohio, the women who became streetcar operators were cultural heroines for a time but were laid off when returning male operators went on strike against the women's continued employment. And, according to

Women's Bureau analysts, the opening of some new employment areas to women and the advancement of a few women to skilled positions were offset by the wage discrimination that existed in every category of women's employment.[28]

Similarly, the common assumption that the proportion of women who worked increased during the 1920s is inaccurate. It is true that an additional two million women had jobs, but this was a reflection of general population growth. In fact, whereas 23 percent of American women were employed in 1920, 24 percent were employed in 1930—an increase of only 1 percent. Furthermore, with the exception of women's movement into clerical work, they did not improve their position in the labor force in the 1920s. Although the number of women increased in most professions, women still held jobs that were less prestigious and lower-paying than those of men. For example, although women yearly received about one-third of the graduate degrees awarded, only 4 percent of the full professors in American colleges and universities were women. Most colleges were reluctant to promote women beyond the lower ranks; Mary Ellen Chase, novelist and distinguished scholar of English literature, left the University of Minnesota in 1926 for Smith College because Minnesota would not promote her beyond the rank of assistant professor.

In medicine, the proportion of women to men declined. Dr. Alice Hamilton thought that women could more easily become doctors earlier in the century, when feminism was still powerful and "a woman doctor could count on the loyalty of a group of devoted feminists who would choose a woman [doctor] because she was a woman."[29] Most medical and law schools admitted women, but most applied quotas to female admission. (Until 1945, the standard quota was about 5 percent.) Most women lawyers and doctors continued to cluster in the less lucrative specialties or to serve women and children. The few women dentists were primarily children's orthodontists. But they dominated that lucrative specialty only briefly; by the 1950s, men had taken over the field.

Even the expanding fields of business administration and advertising offered limited opportunities for women aside from clerical work. Female Horatio Algers could always be found to bolster the nation's success mythology and the belief that feminism had achieved its goals. Often, these businesswomen made their money by marketing products designed for women. Industries like apparel

*Helena Rubinstein, to whom personal beauty was a source of both power and profit.*

and cosmetics have always been open to career-minded women. Helena Rubinstein, who parlayed her mother's home beauty cream into a cosmetics empire, was only one of a number of such women. Another was her competitor Elizabeth Arden.

For women to make their way in the masculine world of business was not easy. M. Louise Luckinbill, a secretary at the Schultz-McGregor Advertising Agency in New York City, declined a promotion to vice president. Businessmen, she wrote, "would throw up their hands in horror at the idea of a woman being . . . vice-president of an [advertising] agency . . . ."[30] Edith Mae Cummings, who built her job as an insurance saleswoman into her own firm, contended that, with perseverance, any woman could succeed in business. Yet, she admitted, businessmen were hostile to women entrepreneurs because they feared that these women would lose their "feminine daintiness."[31] Helena Rubinstein recalled that "it was not easy being a hard-working woman in a man's world." To survive in the business world, she became a tyrant, indulging in legendary rages. She married a count, lived in lavish style, and was known as "madame." For "added courage," she wore elaborate, expensive jewelry. To Rubinstein, the quest for beauty, central to both her business and her personal life, was not oppressive but rather was a "force. . . to make you feel greater than you are."[32]

*Isadora Duncan, pioneer of the modern dance movement of the 1920s.*

In keeping with women's continuing participation in the professions in the 1920s, many women writers and artists appeared and received critical acclaim. In the field of dance, Ruth St. Denis, Isadora Duncan, and Martha Graham were key figures in the emergence of "modern dance," which utilizes natural body movements and soft shoes in place of the fixed poses and toe dancing of classical ballet. The greatest patron of the arts in the 1920s was Gertrude Vanderbilt Whitney, herself a sculptor and, as a Vanderbilt, the possessor of great wealth. When the Metropolitan Museum in New York City refused her offer to build a new wing to house modern art, she funded the building of the Whitney Museum.

In literature, Emily Dickinson and Edith Wharton in the late nineteenth century developed complex personal styles, initiating a trend away from the sentimentalism of Harriet Beecher Stowe and the scores of other best-selling women authors of that century. In the 1920s, poet Edna St. Vincent Millay, with her candle burning "at both ends," became the symbol of the nihilism and emancipated life-style of writers in Greenwich Village. Willa Cather continued her distinguished career as a writer of frontier fiction and a

*Regina Andrews played an important role in encouraging black writers during the Harlem Renaissance.*

critic of technology. Dorothy Parker dominated the New York City intellectuals and wits who gathered at the famed "round table" at the Algonquin Hotel. Gertrude Stein's Parisian salon was a center for American artists abroad.

In Harlem, Regina Andrews made the 135th Street Branch of the New York Public Library a gathering place for African-American intellectuals, and Jessie Fauset as literary editor of the *Crisis,* the magazine of the NAACP, encouraged young black writers. Both thus made important contributions to the Harlem Renaissance—the outpouring of writings by black authors living in Harlem that established an African-American claim to literary eminence. Black writers Nella Larsen and Jessie Fauset wrote realistic novels about the tensions of gender and race, often about the dilemma of people of mixed blood and light skin who attempt to "pass" as white. They thereby overcame the white publishing world's prejudice that African-American novels would sell only if violent or exotic.

Zora Neale Hurston was the seventh of eight children of a Southern tenant farm family that moved to the Alabama town of Eatonville, the first all-black town in the United States. There

Hurston's father became a Baptist preacher and a town leader. Hurston came to New York City in 1925 and studied anthropology with Franz Boas, Margaret Mead's famed mentor. Between 1927 and 1932 Hurston journeyed through the South as an ethnographer, studying African-American folkways. Her 1937 novel, *Their Eyes Were Watching God*, was an outgrowth of this research and is today considered one of the finest of American literary productions.

Yet for most women artists and authors, difficulties still existed. In the 1920s painter Georgia O'Keeffe began her distinguished career, which spanned seven decades. But gaining recognition was not easy. Her friendship with, and eventual marriage to, Alfred Steiglitz, the famed photographer, was initially important in securing New York shows for her and in attracting critics' attention. Even then, her work was judged more in terms of gender than artistic ability. Her canvases, filled with huge exotic flowers, sometimes resembling female genitalia, confounded critics; the paintings violated the canon that women were expected to do small and fragile works of art.

Despite a tradition that identified amateur music with women, major symphony orchestras included few women musicians, and the field of conducting was closed to them. When conductor Antonia Brico returned to the United States in the 1930s after an acclaimed European debut, few orchestras engaged her; ultimately, she founded her own orchestra of women players. What woman, it was said, possessed either the authority or the musicianship to mold 80 or more instrumentalists into an effective ensemble?

## LATINA IMMIGRATION; WOMEN, WORK, AND ACCULTURATION

On the surface, the decade of the 1920s seemed to be a time of economic prosperity. But many workers did not participate in the prosperity. Sectors of the economy were depressed; at least 50 percent of farm and industrial workers earned survival wages. This group especially included African-American and Mexican workers. On the surface both groups profitted from the cut-off of overseas immigration during World War I and from restrictive immigration laws passed in the early 1920s. These laws, by establishing

*Mexican itinerant workers.*

national quotas favoring Northern Europeans, vastly decreased immigration from Eastern Europe and the Mediterranean region, creating labor shortages and thus potential jobs for African Americans and Mexicans. In the case of African Americans, their movement northward escalated, energized by the Northern need for labor and by the devastation of Southern cotton crops by the boll weevil. Despite the availability of jobs in Northern cities, exploitation and a system of de facto segregation awaited them.

In the case of Mexicans, powerful farmers and industrialists in the Southwest and the West had secured an exemption from the immigration restriction laws, so that they could continue to use Mexican migrants as cheap labor. After World War I, an increased demand for processed food due to urbanization stimulated farm production and the canning industry in the West and Southwest. Among Mexican migrants, entire families worked—picking the crops at piecework rates and living in substandard housing provided by their employers. In Texas, they often worked as tenant farmers for absentee landlords, in a system of peonage similar to Southern sharecropping. Owners in Texas preferred Mexicans to white tenants because the wives and children of Mexicans would work in the fields, while white tenant farmers' wives would not. According to historian

Rosalinda González, the independence which employment outside the home could foster in women did not occur in this case because of poverty, isolation, and serflike social conditions. In fact, owners pressured tenant wives to have many children, since cotton required intensive labor for picking. The attitude of landlords was that a tenant must have "at least eight children and a wife who worked in a field 'like a man.'"[33]

Growers throughout the Southwest preferred to hire families rather than single workers, even when tenant farming was not involved. To work the sugar beet fields of the South Platte Valley of Colorado, the Great Western Sugar Company had at first relied on German families. World War I, with Germany the enemy, ended their availability. The company then turned to single Japanese-American and Mexican-American men, so-called "solos," and finally to Mexican and Mexican-American families. They were a more stable labor force in which children constituted an especially inexpensive labor pool. Without citizenship, these Latino people could easily be exploited as workers. They could also be used as a divisive wedge against Anglo workers and their potential for unionization. At a time when the federal government considered an annual income of $800 to be the subsistence minimum for a family, many Mexican families made less than $100 a year.

Large numbers of Mexicans migrated to the United States in the 1920s. So sizable was their movement into Los Angeles that its barrio became the largest Mexican community in the world outside of Mexico City. In response, both industrialists and reformers, many of them women, launched "Americanization" campaigns. In contrast to the settlement-house response to European immigrants before World War I, little value was given to Mexican culture in these campaigns. In Los Angeles, the campaign targeted mothers in the home through home teachers sent out by schools. The Mexican women were taught "American" standards of diet and health, and they were encouraged to take on work as unskilled laborers for clothing manufacturers and in laundries and as domestic workers in Anglo homes. This advice reflected capitalism's need for cheap labor, although it violated domestic ideals glorified in mainstream culture.

Because Puerto Ricans were U.S. citizens, East Coast manufacturers and Hawaiian planters actively recruited them as workers in a time of immigration restriction. Their largest *colonias* (neighborhoods) were in New York City, where many Puerto Rican women took in piece work in their homes and provided child care for pay, while others worked in domestic service and factory work. They were shocked by the color division between blacks and whites in the United States, for the Puerto Rican identification of a number of additional types, including browns and Indians, resulted in lessened racism.

## WORKING-CLASS WORKING WOMEN

During the 1920s, most unskilled laborers—not just immigrants—experienced difficult economic conditions. Sizable wage increases went primarily to skilled laborers. The income of many unskilled workers, which included the majority of women workers, rose hardly at all. And the relative position of these women worsened. According to one study, the differential between the hourly wages paid to unskilled male and female workers rose from 6.3 cents in 1923 to 10.2 cents in 1929.[34]

Within unskilled employment, non-Anglo women encountered the greater discrimination. Over 70 percent of all Asian women workers and over 90 percent of all Latina and African-American workers were employed as domestics or in agriculture, while less than 40 percent of white women workers were so employed. In the 1920s, factory work began to open up to nonwhite women, but pay differentials still existed. In Texas, for example, white factory women were paid about $7.50 a week, while Mexican Americans earned about $5.50 and blacks earned $3.75.

Working-class mothers who worked away from home faced particular difficulties. For the most part, they left young children with relatives or neighbors, and their older children often fended for themselves after school. In 1930 there were approximately 800 nursery schools in the nation.[35] Charitable organizations ran most of these schools specifically for lower-income working women, but most mothers were suspicious of them. This suspicion stemmed partly from the tendency of welfare agencies to place the children of indigent families in asylums and foster homes. And many social workers opposed establishing nursery centers on the grounds that county and state relief programs to mothers with children should be expanded so that mothers could stay at home. Such programs, however, were usually badly underfunded.

*Telephone operators were primarily women in the 1920s.*

These conditions of low pay and little relief for working mothers partly resulted from the disarray of the union movement in the 1920s. Membership had plummeted, and there was not much strike activity. Women workers, as well as men, were reluctant to challenge employers, who promised (but generally did not deliver) a new welfare capitalism under which employers would assume responsibility for the welfare of their workers. But workers were constantly threatened by unemployment during the decade and chastened by the defeats that unions suffered in a series of major strikes after the end of the war. By 1919, for example, telephone operators in New England, who were primarily women, finally managed to form a union, but an unsuccessful strike in 1921 proved its undoing. Membership in the union evaporated, and the telephone company fired and blacklisted union members.

Even the ILGWU fell on hard times. The rise in demand for ready-to-wear clothing for women was a boon to the garment industry, but individual companies—and their workers—became dependent on the caprice of fashion. When a dress style failed, worker layoffs could follow. Such worker insecurity made organization difficult. Also difficult for the ILGWU was the appearance of a strong communist faction among its membership in the 1920s. Instead of concentrating on organization and strike activity, the union spent the decade engaged in infighting. The struggle nearly destroyed the union. Its membership dropped from 250,000 to 40,000.

The Consumers' League and the Women's Trade Union League, the Progressive organizations that focused on working women, continued operations in the 1920s, but problems beset them. The WTUL, dependent on the regular unions for its funds, had a modest yearly budget of $20,000, and most of this money went to lobbyists working for special legislation for working women. The Consumers' League also focused on special legislation, but the 1923 Supreme Court decision in *Adkins v. Children's Hospital,* which outlawed federal minimum-wage laws for women on the grounds of violating freedom of contract between worker and employer, made advances in special legislation difficult.

Moreover, to persuade well-to-do women to support programs for working women was difficult, for they easily believed businessmen's propaganda about providing benefits for their workers. In 1920, Maude Nathan, a wealthy founder of the New York Consumers' League, wrote that there had been a "metamorphosis" in working conditions for women in urban department stores. Merchants, she contended, were "vying with each other in giving [their employees] humane attention." The Consumers' League, she implied, was no longer necessary. Yet the improvements she cited were hardly definitive. Sales clerks may have won the right to sit down on occasion and to take a week's vacation a year, but pay was still low and they still worked a 12-hour day.[36] Nathan's attitude was representative of the popular view that women were achieving equality on a variety of fronts and that little more needed to be done for them.

## THE NEW HEROINES

Every age has its heroines, and those in the 1920s reveal much about attitudes towards women. In the 1910s, Jane Addams had been the national heroine—the secular saint whose compassion endeared her to a generation of humanitarian Americans. The heroines of the 1920s were different. Assuredly, women of uncommon achievement were not unknown: In 1928, 27-year-old Margaret Mead published her first book, *Coming of Age in Samoa,* to instant acclaim. She thus began a life of anthropological travel

*Anthropologist Margaret Mead at the time of her investigation of Pacific tribes.*

and commentary on public events that would not flag for 40 years. Yet among female models in the 1920s, pilot Amelia Earhart, movie actress Mary Pickford, and the "vamp," a standard film character, stand out. Although on the one hand they seem emancipated, together they signaled the decline of feminism as the prewar generation had known it.

In her way, Amelia Earhart was a feminist manqué. Her early career was split between social feminism and flying. A graduate of Barnard College, she became a settlement worker in Boston. Meanwhile, she learned to fly. She searched out women instructors, because she found male pilots insulting and overprotective. In 1927, Amy Phipps Guest, a wealthy New York flying enthusiast, persuaded Earhart to accept her financial backing for a solo flight across the Atlantic, in imitation of Lindbergh's flight the year before. With the flight a success, Earhart was welcomed by impressive crowds and national fame. Yet on the flight Earhart served only as navigator; a male pilot was at the controls.

*Amelia Earhart, whose solo flight on a Lockheed Vega monoplane from Newfoundland to Ireland in 1932 made her one of the most celebrated women of her time.*

Earhart's life was an eloquent testimony to women's abilities. But in the long run, her achievements had a limited feminist impact. Part of the difficulty was that she was shy and self-effacing. She was popularly known as "Lady Lindy" because she bore a striking physical resemblance to Lindbergh, and some said she had been chosen for the flight because of this. Despite her membership in the Woman's Party, her feminism was modest. She wrote, "probably my greatest satisfaction was to indicate by example, now and then, that women can sometimes do things themselves if given the chance." But it was flying above all that thrilled her and that she publicized. Her books describe her flights in detail and celebrate the dangers and glories of aviation.

Earhart's last flight, on which she disappeared, took place in 1937. After her presumed death, there were other women flyers, but none captured the public imagination in quite the same way.

*Theda Bara, the star of Cleopatra, was promoted as the "wickedest force in the world."*

As aviation became professionalized, male pilots came to dominate flying. Finally, in 1931, an innovation was added to commercial air flights that determined the future position of women in aviation. Airline stewardesses, then called "hostesses" and required to have a nursing degree, made their appearance. Now, as doctors had nurses as subordinates and businessmen had secretaries, pilots also had female subalterns. Once again, women were relegated to their traditional service role.

The settlement worker was the heroine of prewar America; the public of the 1920s thrilled to Earhart's individual daring. Mary Pickford and the "vamp" expressed other sides of the American character—sides implicitly antifeminist. Pickford was the virginal child-woman, "America's Sweetheart," its "Little Mary;" the vamp was the sexual temptress, the Eve who led men astray.

Between World War I and the 1930s, Pickford triumphed. Golden-haired and impish, she played adolescents on the verge of maturity, in roles similar to those that Shirley Temple would play at an even younger age in the next decade. Often, she was portrayed as athletic and rebellious; sometimes, as a working woman. In this

*Margaret Gorman, Miss Washington, D.C., becomes the nation's first "Miss America" in 1921.*

regard, she mirrored those trends of the age which validated women in sports and in the work force. As a person she was tough and shrewd; she was the first in her profession to demand and receive the high salaries that have become standard in the movie industry. She was less successful in convincing the public to accept her as other than the personification of youth—a role she came to hate. When in the late 1920s she cut off the long blonde curls that were her trademark, she almost lost her audience. As much as movie audiences thrilled to the femme fatale and the sex dramas of the 1920s, they wanted Pickford to show them an idyllic America, where women never grew up.

The opposite character, the "vamp," appealed to the nation's new fascination with sexuality. Her origins can be traced to the days of prewar burlesque and vaudeville, to music-hall stars like Lillian Russell and the Florodora girls, who bared shoulder and ankle. As was often the case, the war speeded up a trend already under way. As a type, the "vamp" underwent several transformations during the course of the decade. For a time she was the seductress, pure and simple. With the rise of the youth cult and the appearance of censorship codes that restricted sexuality on the screen, she became the "flapper." Finally, she emerged as the *femme fatale*, a major screen character in the 1930s, particularly as personified by Greta Garbo and Marlene Dietrich.

The vamp first appeared in 1915 in a movie entitled *A Fool There Was*. It starred Theda Bara, who became famous overnight for sultry sexuality. Press agents transmogrified her typical American background into a saga of Oriental exoticism: She was the daughter of an Algerian soldier and an Egyptian dancer; she was kidnapped and raised by a band of cutthroats; she had occult powers. (Bara was the first screen personality to wear eye makeup; Helena Rubinstein designed it for her to create a new cosmetic market.) After the war, the mantle of "sex queen" passed to Gloria Swanson. She was more sophisticated than Bara, but she fulfilled the same role of seductress. The flapper was different. She was the flirt—a sex tease who promised sex play but not mature passion. Although the flapper smoked and danced, she was honest at heart and deserved the hero's love. Still, the end in life for her was a man.

Yet another screen image for women existed. In popular prewar screen serials, the main character was sometimes a woman who could solve any predicament on her own. The most famous of these serials was the *Perils of Pauline*, starring Pearl White. Pauline could ride and shoot a gun as well as any man. And in *The Goddess*, made in 1915, the heroine was raised on a desert island to believe that she was a goddess destined to solve the world's ills.

Such feminist themes were muted in the decade of the 1920s. The emblem of change was the "beauty queen." In 1920, hotel owners in Atlantic City, New Jersey, concocted a promotional scheme to lengthen their summer season into the fall. In late September they hosted a contest to crown America's reigning beauty, its "Miss America." These promoters raised the beauty contest to a national level and enshrined it as a venerated American institution. And they provided the ultimate symbol of the American woman, one constructed around competing for an evanescent beauty ideal, just as men competed in business, in the professions, on football fields, or in war.

## NOTES

[1] Nancy Cott, *The Grounding of Modern Feminism* (New Haven: Yale University Press, 1987), p. 97.

[2] Emily Newell Blair, "Wanted—A New Feminism," *Independent Woman* (Dec. 1930): 499.

[3] Sara Barbara Brumbaugh, *Democratic Experience and Education in the National League of Women Voters* (New York: Teachers College Press, 1946), p. 45.

[4] Marion K. Sanders, *The Lady and the Vote* (Boston: Houghton Mifflin, 1956), pp. 141–42.

[5] June Sochen, *The New Woman: Feminism in Greenwich Village, 1910–1920* (New York: Quadrangle, 1972), pp. 115–16.

[6] Anna Steese Richardson, "Is the Women's Club Dying?" *Harper's*, CLIX (Oct. 1929): 607.

[7] Rheta Childe Dorr, *A Woman of Fifty* (New York: Funk & Wagnalls, 1924), pp. 280ff.

[8] Marie Louise Degen, *The History of the Women's Peace Party* (Baltimore: Johns Hopkins University Press, 1939), p. 20.

[9] Vida Scudder, *On Journey* (New York: E. P. Dutton, 1937), p. 300.

[10] Suzanne LaFollette, *Concerning Women* (New York: Albert and Charles Boni, 1926), p. 10.

[11] Elizabeth Onatavia, "Give Us Our Privileges," *Scribner's*, LXXXVII (June 1930): 593–94.

[12] *Ibid.*, p. 597.

[13] Dorothy Dunbar Bromley, "Feminist—New Style," *Harper's*, CLV (Oct. 1927): 552–60.

[14] Mabel Dodge Luhan, *Intimate Memories* (New York: Harcourt Brace Jovanovich, 1936), Vol. III: *Movers and Shakers*, p. 263.

[15] Katharine Bement Davis, *Factors in the Sex Life of Twenty-Two-Hundred Women* (New York: Harper & Bros., 1929), p. 248.

[16] Charlotte Perkins Gilman, *The Living of Charlotte Perkins Gilman: An Autobiography* (New York: Appleton-Century-Crofts, 1935), pp. 332–33.

[17] Kathleen M. Blee, *Women of the Klan: Racism in the 1920s* (Berkeley: University of California Press, 1990), p. 1.

[18] Lillian Hellman, *An Unfinished Woman: A Memoir* (Boston: Little, Brown, 1969), p. 35.

[19] Davis, *Factors in the Sex Life*, pp. 231–32; 350–51.

[20] Ben B. Lindsay and Evans Wainwright, *The Revolt of Modern Youth* (New York: Boni and Liveright, 1925), pp. 66–7.

[21] Mary McCarthy, *Memories of a Catholic Girlhood* (New York: Harcourt Brace Jovanovich, 1957).

[22] Anne Morrow Lindbergh, *Bring Me a Unicorn: Diaries and Letters of Anne Morrow Lindbergh, 1922–1928* (New York: Harcourt Brace

Jovanovich, 1972), passim.

[23] Maxine Davis, *The Lost Generation: A Portrait of American Youth Today* (New York: Macmillan, 1936), pp. 25–6.

[24] Floyd Allport, "Seeing Women as They Are," *Harper's*, CLVIII (March 1929): 406.

[25] Lorine Pruette, "The Married Woman and the Part-Time Job," *Annals of the American Academy of Political and Social Science* (1929): 302.

[26] "Confessions of an Ex-Feminist," *New Republic*, XXII (April 14, 1926): 218ff.

[27] Worth Tuttle, "Autobiography of an Ex-Feminist," *The Atlantic Monthly*, CLII (Dec. 1933): 645.

[28] Alice Rogers Hager, "Occupations and Earnings of Women in Industry," *Annals of the American Academy of Political and Social Science* (1929): 65–73.

[29] Alice Hamilton, *Exploring the Dangerous Trades: The Autobiography of Alice Hamilton* (Boston: Little, Brown, 1943), p. 268.

[30] *Women of Today* (1926): 235.

[31] Edith Mae Cummings, *Pots, Pans, and Millions: A Study of Women's Right to Be in Business; Her Proclivities and Capacity for Success* (Washington, DC: National School of Business Science for Women, 1929).

[32] Helena Rubinstein, *My Life for Beauty* (London: Bodley Head, 1964), p. 22.

[33] Rosalinda M. González, "Chicanas and Mexican Immigrant Families 1920–1940: Women's Subordination and Family Exploitation," in Lois Scharf and Joan M. Jensen, (eds.) *Decades of Discontent: The Women's Movement, 1920–1940* (Westport, Conn.: Greenwood Press, 1983), p. 63.

[34] Irving Bernstein, *The Lean Years: A History of the American Worker, 1920–1933* (Boston: Houghton Mifflin, 1960), p.69.

[35] The White House Conference on Child Health and Protection, *Nursery Education* (New York: Century, 1931).

[36] Maude Nathan, *The Story of an Epoch-Making Movement* (Garden City, NY: Doubleday, Page, 1926), pp. 105–109.

## BIBLIOGRAPHY

Historians disagree over the unity of organized women in the 1920s. J. Stanley Lemons, *The Woman Citizen: Social Feminism in the 1920s* (Urbana: University of Illinois Press, 1973), and Nancy F. Cott, *The Grounding of Modern Feminism* (New Haven, CT: Yale University Press, 1987), stress the positive aspects, while an opposite position is taken by Dorothy M. Brown, *Setting a Course: American Women in the 1920s* (Boston: Twayne, 1987), and Judith Sealander, *As Minority Becomes Majority: Federal Reaction to the Phenomenon of Women in the Workforce, 1920–1963* (Westport, CT: Greenwood Press, 1983). (Sealander's work is primarily a history of the federal Women's Bureau.) Also consult Susan Becker, *The Origins of the*

*Equal Rights Amendment: American Feminism Between the Wars* (Westport, CT: Greenwood Press, 1981), and interesting works by Carole Nichols and Sandra Schackel. Carole Nichols, "Votes and More for Women: Suffrage and After in Connecticut," *Women & History* (Spring 1983); and Sandra Schackel, *Social Housekeepers: Women Shaping Public Policy in New Mexico, 1920–1940* (Albuquerque: University of New Mexico Press, 1991).

Several recent biographies address this issue: Kristie Miller, *Ruth Hanna McCormick: A Life in Politics, 1880–1944* (Albuquerque: University of New Mexico Press, 1991); Elizabeth Israels Perry, *Belle Moskowitz: Feminine Politics and the Exercise of Power in the Age of Alfred E. Smith* (New York: Oxford University Press, 1987); and Susan Ware, *Partner and I: Molly Dewson, Feminism, and New Deal Politics* (New Haven, CT: Yale University Press, 1987).

On the social-work profession, the settlement houses, and social reform in general, see Jane Addams, *The Second Twenty Years at Hull House* (New York: Macmillan, 1930); Clarke A. Chambers, *Seedtime of Reform: American Social Service and Social Action, 1918–1933* (Minneapolis: University of Minnesota Press, 1963); and the 1929 issue of the *Annals of the American Academy of Political and Social Science*, "Women in the Modern World." On cultural attitudes, Frederick Lewis Allen, *Only Yesterday: An Informal History of the 1920s* (New York: Harper & Row, 1931), and Helen Merrell Lynd and Robert S. Lynd, *Middletown: A Study in Contemporary American Culture* (New York: Harcourt Brace Jovanovich, 1929), are still indispensable. Walter Lippman, *A Preface to Morals* (New York: Macmillan, 1929), is insightful. On conservatism and women in the 1920s, see Kathleen M. Blee, *Women of the Klan: Racism in the 1920s* (Berkeley: University of California Press, 1990).

On advertising in the 1920s, see Roland Marchand, *Advertising the American Dream: Making Way for Modernity, 1920–1940* (Berkeley: University of California Press, 1985). As yet, there are no comprehensive studies of the impact of Freudian ideas, of the participation of women in the peace movement, or of the exact dimensions of the youth "rebellion" in the 1920s. One could consult Grace Adams, "The Rise and Fall of Psychology," *Atlantic* CLIII (1934): 82–92; Lucille C. Birnbaum, "Behaviorism in the 1920s," *American Quarterly*, 7 (Spring 1955): 15–30; and Gertrude Bussey and Margaret Tims, *Women's International League for Peace and Freedom, 1915–1965* (London: Allen & Unwin, 1965). The culture of college students in this period has been explored by Paula Fass, *The Damned and the Beautiful: American Youth in the 1920s* (New York: Oxford University Press, 1977). Specific cultural attitudes are effectively traced by Beth Bailey, *From Front Porch to Back Seat: Courtship in Twentieth-Century America* (Baltimore: Johns Hopkins University Press, 1988); Ellen K. Rothman, *Hands and Hearts: A History of Courtship in America* (New York: Basic Books, 1984); and Virginia Scharff, *Taking the Wheel: Women and the Coming of the Motor Age* (New York: Free Press, 1991).

Several works have begun to address the antifeminism of the era, especially directed toward lesbians, unmarried women, and aging women. Lois W. Banner, *In Full Flower: Aging Women, Power, and Sexuality: A History*

(New York: Alfred A. Knopf, 1992), pp. 273–310; Christina Simmons, "Modern Sexuality and the Myth of Victorian Repression," in Kathy Peiss and Christina Simmons (eds.), *Passion and Power: Sexuality in History* (Philadelphia: Temple University Press, 1989), pp. 157–77; and Carroll Smith-Rosenberg, "The New Woman as Androgyne," in Carroll Smith-Rosenberg, *Disorderly Conduct: Visions of Gender in Victorian America* (New York: Alfred A. Knopf, 1985).

To what extent a change in sexual attitudes occurred during the 1920s has occasioned much debate. The classic view for change is presented in Allen, *Only Yesterday*. The popular impression of change is partly based on the well-publicized exploits of several well-known women, especially Zelda Fitzgerald, the tragic wife of F. Scott Fitzgerald. On her, see Nancy Milford, *Zelda: A Biography* (New York: Harper & Row, 1970). Most historians now question the extent of the change and look on the pre-World War One era as crucial and the working class as introducing the new behavior patterns. For contemporary points of view on morality, see Phyllis Blanchard and Carolyn Manasses, *New Girls for Old* (New York: Macauley, 1937); V. F. Calverton, *The Bankruptcy of Marriage* (New York: Macauley, 1928), and Ben B. Lindsey and Evans Wainwright, *The Revolt of Modern Youth* (New York: Boni & Liveright, 1925). Also consult V. F. Calverton and S. C. Schmalhausen, *Sex in Civilization* (New York: Macauley, 1929); Floyd Dell, *Love in the Machine Age: A Psychological Study of the Transition from Patriarchal Society* (New York: Farrar & Rinehart, 1930); and Freda Kirchway (ed.), *Our Changing Morality: A Symposium* (New York: Albert & Charles Boni, 1924).

On women and work see Irving Bernstein, *The Lean Years: A History of the American Worker, 1920–1933* (Boston: Houghton Mifflin, 1960); Philip S. Foner, *Women and the American Labor Movement: From World War One to the Present* (New York: Free Press, 1980); Winifred D. Wandersee, *Women's Work and Family Values, 1920–1940* (Cambridge, MA: Harvard University Press, 1981), and studies by the Women's Bureau of the Department of Labor. Dorothy Sue Cobble's interesting *Dishing It Out: Waitresses and Their Unions in the Twentieth Century* (Urbana: University of Illinois Press, 1991), focuses on the decades after World War One, since the majority of commercial food and lodging establishments employed only men until the 1920s. On the participation of the working class in the consumerism of the 1920s, see Susan Levine, "Workers' Wives: Gender, Class, and Consumerism in the 1920s United States," *Gender & History*, 3 (Spring 1991): 45–64.

Several works of literary criticism provide an introduction to the subject of women writers. These include Nina Baym, *Feminism and American Literary History: Essays* (New Brunswick, NJ: Rutgers University Press, 1992), and Elaine Showalter, *Sister's Choice: Tradition and Change in American Women's Writing* (New York: Oxford University Press, 1991). For an interesting argument about the centrality of "blackness" to the American literary imagination, see Toni Morrison, *Playing in the Dark: Whiteness and the Literary Imagination* (Cambridge, MA: Harvard University Press, 1992). On individual writers, see Sharon O'Brien, *Willa Cather: The Emerging Voice* (New York: Oxford University Press, 1987), and Robert Hemenway, *Zora Neale Hurston:*

*A Literary Biography* (Urbana: University of Illinois Press, 1977). Also interesting is Hurston's autobiography, *Dust Tracks on a Road: An Autobiography* (Urbana: University of Illinois Press, 1970). On women writers and the Harlem Renaissance, see Gloria T. Hull, *Color, Sex, and Poetry: Three Women Writers of the Harlem Renaissance* (Bloomington: University of Indiana Press, 1987), specifically on the poets Alice Dunbar-Nelson, Angelina Grimké Weld, and Georgia Douglas Johnson.

On women and music, see Christine Ammen, *Unsung: A History of Women in American Music* (Westport, CT: Greenwood Press, 1980). A moving study of the career of Antonia Brico, *Antonia: A Portrait of a Woman* (1977), has been made by Judy Collins and Jill Bodmillow and is available from Phoenix Film, 470 Park Avenue South, New York, NY 10016.

On women and art, see Eleanor Munro, *Originals: American Women Artists* (New York: Simon & Schuster, 1979); Claire Richter Sherman and Adele M. Holcomb (eds.), *Women as Interpreters of the Visual Arts, 1820–1979* (Westport, CT: Greenwood Press, 1981); and Ellen Perry Berkeley (ed.), *Architecture: A Place for Women* (Washington, DC: Smithsonian Institution Press, 1989). On Georgia O'Keeffe, see Laurie Lisle, *Portrait of an Artist: A Biography of Georgia O'Keeffe* (New York: Harper & Row, 1980). In *The "New Woman" Revised: Painting and Gender Politics on Fourteenth Street* (Berkeley: University of California Press, 1993), Ellen Wiley Todd links an important group of painters known as the Fourteenth Street School with significant gender trends of the 1920s and 1930s.

For interesting studies of women and the development of modern dance, see Elizabeth Kendall, *Where She Danced: American Dancing, 1880–1930* (New York: Alfred A. Knopf, 1979), and Suzanne Shelton, *Divine Dancer: A Biography of Ruth St. Denis* (Garden City, NY: Doubleday, 1981).

On Amelia Earhart, see George Palmer Putnam, *Soaring Wings: A Biography of Amelia Earhart* (New York: Harcourt Brace Jovanovich, 1939). On women in sports, see Allen Guttmann, *Women's Sports: A History* (New York: Columbia University Press, 1991); and Stephanie L. Twin (ed.), *Out of the Bleachers: Writings on Women and Sport* (Old Westbury, NY: Feminist Press, 1979). On women in films, see Jeanine Basinger, *A Woman's View: How Hollywood Spoke to Women, 1930–1960* (New York: Alfred A. Knopf, 1993); Molly Haskell, *From Reverence to Rape: The Treatment of Women in the Movies* (New York: Holt, Rinehart & Winston, 1973); Lary May, *Screening out the Past: The Birth of Mass Culture and the Motion Picture Industry* (New York: Oxford University Press, 1980); and Marjorie Rosen, *Popcorn Venus: Women, Movies, & the American Dream* (New York: Coward, McCann & Geoghegan, 1973). The autobiography of actress Louise Brooks, *Lulu in Hollywood* (New York: Alfred A. Knopf, 1982), addresses broad cultural themes, as does Betty H. Fussell in her biography of Mabel Normand, *Mabel: Hollywood's First I-Don't-Care-Girl* (New York: Ticknor & Fields, 1982). On Margaret Mead, see Jane Howard, *Margaret Mead: A Life* (New York: Simon and Schuster, 1984), and especially Mary Catherine Bateson, *With A Daughter's Eye: A Memoir of Margaret Mead and Gregory Bateson* (New York: William Morrow, 1985).

A compilation of interesting articles on the 1920s and 1930s is contained in Lois Scharf and Joan M. Jensen (eds.), *Decades of Discontent: The Women's Movement, 1920–1940* (Westport, CT: Greenwood Press, 1983). Elaine Showalter, *These Modern Women: Autobiographical Essays from the Twenties* (Old Westbury, NY: Feminist Press, 1978), has reprinted a set of moving autobiographies by contemporary women indicating the depths of the difficulties women experienced in this decade. For an argument that women's "separate culture" was seriously undermined in the 1920s, see Estelle Freedman, "Separatism as Strategy: Female Institution Building and American Feminism, 1870–1930," *Feminist Studies*, 5 (Fall 1979): 512–529.

# 5

## WOMEN IN DEPRESSION AND WAR

WOMEN'S NEW FREEDOM IN THE 1920s to compete in organized sports, to wear comfortable clothes, and to expect sexual fulfillment constituted significant progress. But underlying these gains was the predominance of the traditional belief that home, husband, and the pursuit of beauty should be women's paramount concerns. During the 1930s and 1940s, these attitudes continued, but some countervailing forces appeared. The federal government demonstrated an increased concern about poor and working women. Labor unions made greater efforts to organize women workers. Women's organizations began to unite around the Equal Rights Amendment. And World War II, like World War I, opened up extensive employment opportunities to women. Once again, it seemed that war might bring women a liberation that peace had not provided.

## FEMINISM AND WOMEN'S ORGANIZATIONS

On the whole, feminist causes were not the central concern of organized women during the 1930s. The Depression cut across class and gender and focused attention on general social problems. By the winter of 1932–33, 38 states had closed all banks, local governments could no longer meet relief payments, breadlines stretched outside of Red Cross and Salvation Army food distribution centers, and thousands of homeless families lived in makeshift shacks. Unemployment had reached 25 percent of the work force, and many employed workers had suffered pay cuts.

In this situation social feminism came to the fore. The League of Women Voters worked for the extension of the civil service merit system at national and state levels and campaigned for the 1936 Social Security Act and the 1937 Food, Drug, and Cosmetic Act. "We of the League are very much for the rights of women," wrote one leader, "but . . . we are not feminists primarily; we are citizens."[1] The General Federation of Women's Clubs continued its campaign to familiarize housewives with labor-saving devices and efficient housework techniques. Many women activists continued to work for pacifist groups like the Women's International League for Peace and Freedom, and they did achieve some success. In 1931, Jane Addams won a Nobel Peace Prize. The 1934–35 congressional investigation of the munitions industry, conducted by Senator Gerald Nye, was largely the result of the lobbying of women's pacifist groups.

Women's organizations did not abandon feminist efforts. In 1936 their leaders considered uniting around a charter of women's rights promoted by Margaret Anderson of the Women's Bureau. But this initiative floundered because of divided sentiment over special legislation and the ERA. Women's organizations came together to lobby against state bills prohibiting the employment of married women who were not heads of households and against federal legislation that disallowed employing both husband and wife in federal civil service positions. "The apprehensions caused by this assault," writes historian Lois Scharf, "created a unity among women's organizations and institutions unmatched since the passage of the Nineteenth Amendment."[2] But the criticism of this legislation advanced by many women's groups was conservative. The League of Women Voters' primary objection to the federal nepotism legislation was not that it discriminated against women but rather that it violated the merit principle. Other groups argued for women's right to work on the basis of need or family interest, not on the feminist principle of equal employment opportunity.

## Southern Women and the Antilynching Movement

In contrast to Progressive women, reformers in the 1930s worked through existing organizations and emphasized influencing government legislation. An exception was the Association of Southern Women for the Prevention of Lynching, founded in 1930.

Since Reconstruction, the lynching of African-American men by white male mobs in Southern communities had been a grievous social ill and a means of controlling blacks. This vigilantism implicitly involved women as well as men, because the crime usually incorrectly charged to the black victim was the rape of a white woman. Lynching revealed the sexual attitudes at the heart of race and gender control. Because according to the racist

*Jessie Daniel Ames, founder of the Association of Southern Women for the Prevention of Lynching. This movement enlisted housewives to report the formation of mobs sent on lynchings.*

stereotype, blacks were oversexed. White women ought to fear African-American men, while white men had to guard the virtue of white women. But at this time, sexual approaches to African-American women by white men were not considered violations of social mores.

Since the late nineteenth century, black and white Southern women had taken tentative steps toward cooperation through their churches. From 1920 on, through the auspices of the Methodist Women's Missionary Council and black YWCAs, annual women's interracial conferences were held. In 1922, in connection with the National Association of Colored Women, the NAACP had formed a women's group called the Antilynching Crusaders to mobilize support for its antilynching bill before Congress. The most important group working on the lynching issue, however, was the Council for Interracial Cooperation. It had been formed in response to race riots which had occurred in many cities in the aftermath of World War I. Texan Jessie Daniel Ames, a widowed mother of three who supported her family by operating a local telephone exchange, was the linchpin for change. In her organizational activities, Ames worked through the Women's Committee of the Council for Interracial Cooperation, forming the Association of Southern Women for the Prevention of Lynching.

Ames and her association mounted a massive educational campaign directed toward women's organizations. These women sent out speakers, wrote articles, passed out pamphlets, and lobbied legislatures for antilynching legislation. Working through the churches, the women's antilynching association collected 40,000 signatures on an antilynching petition, gathering women's signatures in most counties throughout the South.

By 1933, the incidence of lynching, which had increased with the onset of the Depression, began to decline. Even though Congress refused to pass an antilynching bill, in 1942 the Association of Southern Women for the Prevention of Lynching was disbanded. Yet before its demise, its achievements were impressive. Not only had it played a role in ending a brutal form of violence, but also it had persuaded white Southern women to stand up against the sexual intimidation that kept them in their place. Jessie Daniel Ames called this intimidation "the crown of chivalry which has been pressed like a crown of thorns on her head."[3] Yet the Southern women's antilynching organization included only white members; the integrationist impulse of the Council for Interracial Cooperation did not extend to this organization.

## ELEANOR ROOSEVELT: EXEMPLAR OF HER ERA

The social-welfare concern of the 1930s, prominent during the New Deal administrations of Franklin Delano Roosevelt, did not exclude women. The primary spokesperson for women both inside and outside the government was Eleanor Roosevelt, Franklin's wife. Through her radio broadcasts, newspaper columns, books, and speeches, she molded public opinion.

Eleanor Roosevelt was a feminist with traditional values. Above all, she felt that women should focus on providing qualities of compassion which she saw as female and as lacking in male insti-

*Eleanor Roosevelt at the age of 23, holding one of her children.*

tutions. Women had "understanding hearts," she wrote; men had "ability and brains." Because in a crisis men easily concluded "that they must fight," women's natural pacifism was needed to moderate male aggressiveness.[4] Such reasoning resembled that of Jane Addams and other Progressive social feminists. The appeal to gender traditionalism offered a justification for widening women's sphere, but it ran the risk of conceding ground to those who wanted women to remain in the home.

Eleanor Roosevelt's attitudes reflected her Victorian upbringing by a strict grandmother and her early experience of marriage to her cousin Franklin Roosevelt, in which she was dominated by his mother. For the first 15 years of her marriage, Eleanor Roosevelt was a dutiful wife, regularly bearing children, acceding to the wishes of her mother-in-law, and performing the social duties of a political wife while her husband served as Assistant Secretary of

*Eleanor Roosevelt opens the Grandmothers' War Bond League campaign.*

the Navy between 1913 and 1920 and ran for vice president on the unsuccessful Democratic ticket of 1920.

Two events transformed her life. The first was her discovery in 1917 of her husband's love for another woman; the second was his crippling attack of polio in 1921. The first experience disillusioned her with marriage; the second gave her the strength to defy her mother-in-law, to persuade her husband to continue in public life, and to take on a public role in her own right. She became active in the League of Women Voters, the Consumers' League, the Democratic Party, and especially the Women's Trade Union League. Through her, many women leaders came to know Franklin Roosevelt and to counsel him on labor and social-welfare decisions, especially when he served as governor of New York State between 1928 and 1932.

The transformation of her life was not easy for Eleanor Roosevelt. By nature, she was retiring. The media deprecated her looks. But she found experts to coach her, and she learned through experience. In the end, she developed into a skilled politician. She became, for example, FDR's unofficial adviser on domestic matters and his frequent representative on public business during his presidential administrations. For emotional support, she turned to other women, to whom she wrote passionate letters and with whom she spent much time. Estranged emotionally from her husband, she demonstrated behavior typical of women of the nineteenth-century culture in which she had been raised. Like Jane Addams and others, she turned to women for affection as well as for political and reform support.

By the end of the 1930s, polls showed that Eleanor Roosevelt was very popular among the public. After her husband died in 1945, there was talk of her running for the presidency. But like other social feminists, her interest turned to internationalism, especially, in her case, to the United Nations, founded in the aftermath of World War II. In 1946, she served as the United States representative to the United Nations General Assembly and from 1947 to 1952, as U.S. representative to the United Nations Human Rights Commission and its Economic and Social Council.

Aside from her formative role in the Federal Theatre Project (the government's first subsidy to the arts) and in conceiving the building of planned communities in rural areas, Eleanor Roosevelt was not involved in the central planning of New Deal programs. Rather, she became a special lobbyist for those groups—African Americans, the poor, and women—whose interests were easily overlooked in power-oriented Washington. She personally served as a clearing agent for proposals submitted by women to agencies like the Works Progress Administration (WPA), and she lobbied for numerical guidelines for women's employment in New Deal programs. Democratic Party chairman James Farley estimated that she was responsible for the appointment of over 4,000 women to post-office jobs, many of which were then patronage positions. She admitted only female reporters to her press conferences, in order to generate more newspaper jobs for women. She regularly appeared at NAACP gatherings, and in a celebrated 1939 incident, she publicly resigned from the DAR when that organization refused to allow famed African-American singer Marian Anderson to appear in its

*Frances Perkins, FDR's Secretary of Labor and the first woman cabinet member.*

Washington, DC, Constitution Hall. Meanwhile, she arranged a public concert for Anderson at the Lincoln Memorial.

Under Eleanor's influence, Franklin Roosevelt appointed a number of women to important government offices. These appointments included the first women ministers to foreign countries (the rank directly below ambassador) and the first woman judge on a Circuit Court of Appeals. Ruth Bryan Owen, daughter of William Jennings Bryan, served as minister to Denmark; Florence Jaffray Harriman, widow of the railroad magnate, served as minister to Norway; Florence Allen moved from the Ohio Supreme Court to the Sixth Circuit Court of Appeals. Women from the Consumers' League and the Women's Trade Union League were employed in every New Deal agency. In these agencies, women constituted about one-third of the administrators; in the regular bureaucracy, they constituted about one-sixth. These figures reflected not only Eleanor Roosevelt's influence but also women's domination of the profession of social work, from which New Deal welfare bureaucrats were often recruited.

*Mary McCleod Bethune, second from the right, with Marian Anderson and three shipyard workers. Bethune was a prominent African-American leader of her time.*

## THE WOMEN'S NETWORK AND NEW DEAL PROGRAMS

In addition to Eleanor Roosevelt, prominent New Deal women came together to advance the participation of women in New Deal programs. So close were the connections among about 30 of them that historian Susan Ware contends they formed an informal "network" of women activists. The network included Eleanor Roosevelt; Mary Dewson, head of the Women's Division of the Democratic Party; Frances Perkins, Secretary of Labor and FDR's most important female appointee; and Ellen Woodward, head of Women's and Professional Projects of the Works Progress Administration, the New

*Author Zora Neale Hurston was editor for the Works Progress Administration's Federal Art Project in Florida.*

Deal's major employment program. Other activist women were involved in the Democratic Party, New Deal agencies, and the Women's and Children's Bureaus of the Labor Department. They mobilized women within the Democratic Party, furthered relief programs for women, and were influential in attaining Social Security legislation.

On the periphery of the women's network was Mary McCleod Bethune—an important African-American leader. The daughter of slaves, Bethune became a prominent educator, president of the National Association of Colored Women, and founder, in 1935, of the National Council of Negro Women. This organization pursued a program of protesting discrimination in contrast to the National Association's self-help program. The National Council of Negro Women was a coordinating group for some 20 national and 95 local organizations, representing almost 850,000 African-

American women. As director of Negro Affairs under the National Youth Administration, Bethune founded the Federal Council on Negro Affairs. This organization was dubbed the "black cabinet" because it safeguarded African-American concerns under the New Deal just as the women's network looked out for women's concerns.

The social and economic reforms of the New Deal directly affected women. In 1933, Eleanor Roosevelt and other administration women worked with the Women's Trade Union League, the League of Women Voters, and the Consumers' League to call a White House Conference on the Emergency Needs of Women, which publicized women's economic problems and set priorities for relief. The earliest 1933 relief agencies—the Federal Emergency Relief Administration (FERA) and the Civil Works Administration (CWA)—included women in their programs. By 1935, WPA rolls included about 350,000 women, or about 15 percent of the agency's total employment. Under FERA and later under the National Youth Administration (NYA), resident job-training camps were set up for unemployed women which paralleled the Civilian Conservation Corps (CCC) for young men. In addition to old-age pensions, the 1935 Social Security Act provided federal funding for state and local aid-to-dependent children programs and for state programs for maternal and pediatric care reminiscent of the 1920s Sheppard-Towner clinics.

Moreover, the WPA employment projects for out-of-work artists and writers employed women. Although women were overlooked by the Federal Music Project (renowned for transcribing folk music), they formed an important part of the Federal Art Project and the Federal Theatre Project. The former was dedicated to enriching the nation's artistic heritage through murals in public buildings, such as post offices and train stations. The latter attempted, through its productions, to bring theater to all classes, not just to the elites. The Federal Art Project employed Louise Nevelson; the Federal Writers' Project, Tillie Olsen. Black writer Zora Neale Hurston was editor for the Federal Art Project in Florida.

In an age drawn to documentary accounts of social conditions that might explain the era's economic breakdown, the Farm Security Administration employed photographer Dorothea Lange to record the grim conditions of life for rural Americans. Her brilliant photographs were a famed and moving exhibit of human dignity in the midst of economic despair. And, the Federal Writers' Project's encouragement of artistic social relevance sparked the proletarian novel, the typical writer's production of the 1930s, which focused on the working class. Mary Heaton Vorse's *Strike!* is a fictionalized account of a textile strike in Gastonia, North Carolina, in which Vorse worked as an organizer for the Amalgamated Clothing Workers of America. In her many articles and short stories, Meridel LeSueur described life in radical farmers' strikes and on picket lines, as well as the experiences of women working in strike kitchens and trying to live on welfare.

### The NRA: Benefits and Drawbacks

Any description of the New Deal's attention to women must include the National Industrial Recovery Act of 1933. This act provided that representatives of labor and management in each industry would meet with government negotiators to draft production codes under the auspices of a National Recovery Administration (NRA). Under the National Industrial Recovery Act, maximum-hour and minimum-wage standards were established for both men and women workers. In 1938, after the Supreme Court declared the NRA unconstitutional, Congress passed the Fair Labor Standards Act, which reaffirmed maximum-hour and minimum-wage legislation for interstate industries. State legislatures followed suit for intrastate commerce.

Such legislation represented a dramatic reversal in the way the government viewed workers. For all workers, the old common-law doctrine of the inviolability of contract between worker and employer was overruled. For women, the New Deal legislation brought into question the campaign for special legislation for women, which had divided organized women for over a decade. By 1933, even the Women's Trade Union League had reversed its stand to join other reform groups in advocating general labor legislation for minimum wages and maximum hours. The way was now open for an eventual rapprochement of women's groups around the Equal Rights Amendment.

Antifeminism had not, however, been exorcised, nor had the unequal treatment of women been ended. Sex segregation in work opportunities characterized most New Deal work programs. In keeping with a general New Deal discrimination against minorities, the WPA and other work-relief agencies barred women from construction jobs—the major employment they offered—and shunted them into sewing and other traditional types of women's work. In comparison with the male CCC camps, the women's resident camps were small in number and their purpose was never entirely clear; the reforestation and service projects designed for young men were deemed inappropriate for women. Nor was the welfare aid under the Social Security Act necessarily of benefit to the women who qualified for it. Once it was available, many local WPA officials fired women with children from the higher-paying WPA jobs, despite the women's protests.

Moreover, many of the codes drawn up by the NRA permitted industries to pay less to women workers than to men employed in similar jobs. In general, the minimum wages established by NRA codes did increase women's salaries. Yet fully one-fourth of these codes contained some measure of salary discrimination, particularly the codes written for industries that employed large numbers of women. Such discrimination, of course, had long been the unofficial practice. And the Fair Labor Standards Act of 1938 exempted from its provisions many job categories, such as domestic service, in which women were clustered. The argument was that such marginal work might disappear if wages were raised; on the other hand, the lack of regulation invited exploitation. Furthermore, despite the protest of women's organizations, the federal government ruled that only one member of a family could work in the federal civil service, anticipating thereby more jobs for heads of families. The result was the resignation of thousands of women with civil service jobs, who usually earned less than their husbands. Bills prohibiting the employment of married women were introduced in the legislatures of 26 states, and only the determined opposition of women's organizations defeated them. The state of Louisiana passed such a law, but the courts declared it unconstitutional.

Whether or not Eleanor Roosevelt or other women in the administration could have prevented these discriminatory New Deal measures is doubtful, for they reflected the gender traditionalism of New Deal thinking. Grace Abbott, historian of New Deal welfare programs and head of the Children's Bureau, contended that most male administrators disregarded the opinions of women administrators.[5] Rose Schneiderman, a WTUL official and FDR's female appointee to the Labor Advisory Board of the NRA, never accepted the monthly dinner invitation issued to members of the labor board by the employer's advisory board. She thought that the presence of a woman among these men would "cramp their style" and prevent them from being "chummy" with one another.[6]

Frances Perkins hit these prejudices head-on. Businessmen and politicians who did not like the pro-labor legislation of the New Deal accused Perkins of being a typically incapable woman, "bewildered, rattlebrained, befuddled," and "scared" of John L. Lewis, the militant labor leader. Moreover, Congress often required Perkins to testify before its committees. "Dragging Frances Perkins up to the Hill before congressional hearings, with accompanying ballyhoo in the press," according to Eleanor Roosevelt, "became a kind of game."[7]

On the other hand, Perkins, like Eleanor Roosevelt and other New Deal women, held traditional views. She had followed a typical social feminist career path—from settlement work through paid employment with a voluntary agency (the New York Consumers' League) to government bureaucracy, especially as New York State Industrial Commissioner under Governor Al Smith. Yet she did not want to be held up as an example to women. Perkins "never recommends a public career" for women, reported the BPW journal, because she believes that "the happiest place for most women is in the home."[8] By and large, New Deal women leaders were silent on the issue of New Deal discrimination against women. They were social feminists willing to compromise on issues of gender equality.

More than that, they did not seem cognizant of their crucial position as the transmitters of the Progressive social-feminist tradition to later generations. Born in the 1880s and 1890s, many of them had worked in Progressive reform as young women. When they entered New Deal agencies, most were in their 50s and a decade or so away from retirement. They had lived through the 1920s; they had witnessed the self-involvement of that generation. Yet they did little to ensure the survival of their network—or of social feminism more generally—by recruiting younger women to it. For the most part married and with families, they neither challenged prevailing gender traditionalism nor ensured that their efforts on behalf of women within the federal government would continue. When they retired, the "female dominion" that historian Robyn Muncy identified as a creation of Progressive women reformers largely ceased to exist.

Still, these women were crucial to the New Deal's social-welfare legislation, and their contributions merit recognition. Before Frances Perkins accepted her assignment as Secretary of Labor, she demanded and received FDR's support for a social security program, for which she worked assiduously throughout her tenure in office. Women had been central to the direction and success of Progressive social-welfare reform; they played a similar role during the New Deal.

## CHANGES FOR THE WORKING WOMAN

During the 1930s, working women encountered severe difficulties. It is true that unemployment figures were higher for men than for women until the late 1930s. Yet this situation partly reflected the fact that the consumer-goods industries and the clerical field, both employers of large numbers of women, were initially less affected by the economic downturn than industries that employed primarily men. Ironically, the sex-segregated work force helped women retain their jobs. However, the unemployment figures, which included only individuals who were actively seeking work, may not provide an accurate statistic. When finding employment seemed impossible, women may have retreated from the work force into the home more readily than men.

Throughout the Depression, official unemployment statistics rarely rose above 30 percent, although they sometimes were much higher in hard-hit areas. Older women and minority women, those with the least resources, dominated the percentage of unemployed women. Many companies refused to hire women over 35 years of age. This "ageism" made the campaign for social security legislation especially compelling. And even younger single women encountered difficulties. Although they were often given preference over married women in hiring, families were given preference in relief payments.

According to one observer in 1934, there were 75,000 single, homeless women in New York City alone. The pattern of their lives was similar. They spent mornings making the rounds of employment agencies. Afternoons they rested in train stations. At night, they rode the subways. They ate in "penny kitchens," cheap eateries spawned by the Depression.[9] Some of them—like the poor and unemployed more generally—began to organize. An Association of Unemployed Single Women was formed. Although small in membership, it put pressure on local and state agencies. However, one study of the many teenage girls who had left home to join the legions of tramps who roamed the nation concluded that prostitution was often their only livelihood.[10]

Even women who were employed encountered hardships. In most occupations, wages and hours were cut and advancement limited. This trend especially affected professional women. Men entered the feminized professions of teaching, librarianship, and social work in larger numbers than ever before. During the 1930s, the number of male librarians grew from about 9 percent of the profession to 15 percent; the number of male teachers, from 19 percent to about 24 percent; the number of male social workers, from 20 percent to over 35 percent. And, men continued to dominate the high-level administrative positions in all these fields.

With regard to male-dominated professions, the percentage of women remained stable. But a deeper reality existed in which women were often demoted from high-level positions and replaced by men. In business, positions held by two women were often combined into one, and the new post was given to a man. In university teaching, the numbers of women faculty declined. This decline was especially evident at women's colleges, in past eras teaching havens for academic women.

By and large, professional women accepted the discriminatory situation and lowered their expectations. Women scientists, for example, gave up vying for academic work and found employment in government agencies or as research assistants. Personnel managers became secretaries; secretaries became file clerks. Clerical occupations increased 24 percent during the decade, but advancing technology lessened the need for education and skills in the new positions. Private secretaries who took shorthand, for example, were often replaced by stenographers who used dictating machines. Although women seemed to accept such demotions without protest, many internalized discontent. Experiencing the humiliation of downward mobility, many of them, according to recent analysts, lost self-confidence and acceded to a male domination of the professions that would not be challenged until the 1960s.

Laws against married women working especially affected women schoolteachers. By 1940, only 13 percent of communities nationwide would hire wives as teachers and only 30 percent would retain women who married. Such discrimination against a group highly visible in local communities seems to indicate the strength of traditional attitudes about women's proper role. Indeed, a 1930 Gallup poll found that nearly 80 percent of Americans felt that wives should not work if their husbands were employed. Among women, the figure was 75 percent. And, the argument was not uncommon in the 1930s that women had caused the Depression by going to work and taking jobs away from men. Or, by leaving home, the argument went, women had weakened the moral fiber of the nation and rendered inevitable a crisis of the spirit.[11]

## LATIN- AND AFRICAN-AMERICAN WOMEN

For African-American and Latin-American women, the situation was especially severe. Employment on federal work-relief projects was often closed to them, especially to Latin-American women without citizenship. Traditional discriminatory practices in employment still existed. A Women's Bureau study in 1938 found that only 10 percent of African-American working women were employed in manufacturing—only a 7 percent gain over the statistic for 1890. Downwardly mobile white women pushed women of color even out of domestic work. In 1930, 42 percent of black women were employed; by 1940, the figure was 37.8 percent. In 1935, 42 percent of the nonwhite population of New York City was on relief. And even most disadvantaged whites were better off than African Americans: in 1939, the median annual earnings for nonwhites were 38 percent of those for whites. In many large cities, black women's only hope of employment was to gather on street corners, where white women would drive by offering a day's work, often at no more than two dollars a day. In New York City there were 200 such locations, called "slave markets."

Clerical labor and office work were still largely closed to African-American women. Social worker Ellen Terry noted that in 1930 in Harlem all the salesclerks in the stores on 125th Street, the African-American shopping center, were white.[12] Ultimately black men and women picketed these stores, mostly owned by whites, shouting "don't shop where you can't work." And in Brooklyn, YWCA leader Anna Arnold Hedgemann led protests against the major department stores until she opened up clerking positions to African-American women.

Latin-American women also encountered severe exploitation. In 1935 in Chicago, 32 percent of Mexican Americans were unemployed in comparison to 47 percent of the black population and 11 percent of all foreign-born residents. Among Latin-American female heads of households in Chicago who reported that they had worked at some past time, only 25 percent were actively seeking work and almost none had found employment. In San Antonio, Texas, the labor of men and women became even cheaper than machines. The Southern Pecan Shelling Company scrapped the machines it had introduced to employ Mexican families as laborers there, and the NRA code for pecan shelling was never put into effect. In Puerto Rico, capitalists extracted large sugar and garment profits while the average income of workers was among the world's lowest and Depression unemployment was high.

Moreover, the economic downturn brought an official movement to repatriate Mexicans living in the United States back to Mexico. About 500,000 individuals of Mexican descent left, and there were mass raids by immigration authorities in which children who had been born in the United States and thus were citizens were also swept up and taken to the border. In 1940, the Mexican-American population in the United States was about half what it had been in 1930.

Yet some scholars have found increasing evidence of assimilation among Mexican Americans and of militancy within this group in the 1930s, as higher proportions of young Mexican-American women than ever before enrolled in public school, while older women went to adult school. In Chicago, according to Louise Kerr, employed women first joined Mexican-American mutual aid societies before going on to join multiethnic unemployed worker groups and then craft and industrial organiza-

*The wives of United Auto Workers strikers back up their husbands' demands during the 1936–1937 steel and automobile strikes.*

tions.[13] This situation in Chicago was replicated in other instances, particularly in some striking examples of union organization among Mexican-American women workers.

## UNIONS IN AN AGE OF DEPRESSION

As the economic situation worsened, one avenue of relief for workers appeared. Massive unemployment and government sympathy produced a new, more militant labor movement. The International Ladies' Garment Workers' Union (ILGWU), which by 1930 had nearly ceased to exist, underwent a transformation. The passage of the 1933 National Industrial Recovery Act, which recognized labor's right to organize, prompted the union's leadership to call a series of successful strikes. Throughout the clothing industry, hours were reduced and wages were increased by as much as 50 percent. During 1934, union membership increased from 45,000 to over 200,000.

*More than 1,000 women storm an office building in St. Louis in answer to a newspaper advertisement for 150 jobs as soap demonstrators.*

Of great importance for women workers was the formation in 1935 by a faction within the AFL leadership of what would become by 1938 the Congress of Industrial Organizations (CIO). The militant CIO abandoned the skilled-craft orientation of the AFL to focus on all workers in a given industry. Under its leadership, mass-production industries such as auto and steel, which employed small numbers of women workers, were finally organized. Inroads were even made in the textile industry, largely located in the traditionalist South, in which 40 percent of the workers were women. Through effective and often bloody strikes, as well as through the mediation of the National Labor Relations Board, employers were forced to recognize worker demands. In 1939 and 1940, black and white women workers in the textile mills of Durham, North Carolina, came together in strike activity to force the largest textile mill in the South to sign its first contract with its workers.

Women were involved in many of these strikes. When police fired into a picket line during the famed 1937 "Memorial Day Massacre" at the Chicago Republic Steel plant, women were at the head of the line. In the Flint, Michigan, strike which finally unionized the automobile industry, women formed an Emergency Brigade and armed themselves with clubs and blackjacks. They broke windows to keep strikers from being gassed inside the plants, and they took injured pickets to the first-aid station. In one situation, a diversion by the women was crucial to the successful takeover of a new plant by the strikers.

In department stores, hosiery mills, restaurants, and hotels, women adopted the tactic of sit-down strikes. Refusing to leave the work location proved to be the most effective strike weapon yet devised. The sit-down action would be a major influence on civil rights protesters in their "sit-in" demonstrations during the 1960s.

Because factory women were clustered in the mass-production industries, the new labor movement became valuable to them. The CIO cannot be credited with any extensive pro-woman sentiment. But in many industries the CIO had to include women workers in its organizing efforts to gain majority control. Not surprisingly, few women breached the leadership ranks of the new labor organization. Nor was the new union organization among women workers extensive. Even in 1973, only one-third as many women as men belonged to unions; domestic servants and most women clerical workers have never been unionized. The CIO was no more willing to support the WTUL than the AFL had been. In 1947 the WTUL was dissolved. The reason given by its leaders was that the sympathetic attitude of the unions toward women made its existence unnecessary. But WTUL official Rose Schneiderman contended that the real reason for its demise was the unwillingness of the male-dominated unions to provide funding.[14]

A striking exception to this record of lack of union interest in working women was to be found among Mexican-American unions in the Southwest. Important here was the CIO's United Cannery, Agricultural, Packing, and Allied Workers of America (UCAPAWA). This union dated from 1937, and it was centered in the food-processing industry. Because 75 percent of workers in this industry were women, UCAPAWA was a women's union: "women organizing women" was the key to its success. Forty-four percent of its local union offices were filled by women.

Louisa Moreno, a native of Guatemala who had migrated to the United States in 1928, was a leader in this union. Working as a seamstress in the appalling conditions of New York sweatshops had radicalized her. Moreno helped organize San Antonio pecan shellers, Texas cotton pickers, Colorado beet workers, and California cannery workers. In 1938 she was instrumental in organizing in Los Angeles the National Congress of Spanish Speaking People, an important effort bringing Mexican Americans together as a political pressure group.

The impact of the Communist Party on unionization in the 1930s deserves mention. Dedicated to the class struggle, Communists were strong union activists, and the contrast between apparent economic success in Stalinist Russia and the breakdown of the world capitalist system increased Communist Party membership, particularly among intellectuals. The "common front" enunciated by the Soviet Communist Party in the 1930s made them more receptive to working with others of differing political persuasions, and thus the ideological divisions of the 1920s evident in the ILGWU did not emerge in the 1930s. At the same time, during the 1930s the Socialist Party was only a shadow of its former self.

Communists encouraged the discussion of women's issues. Elizabeth Gurley Flynn joined the party in 1936 and subsequently wrote a regular feminist column on politics for the *Daily Worker*. On the other hand, feminism was not a Communist priority; class issues were what mattered. Communists focused on union organization, on aiding the African-American cause, and on forming associations of the unemployed and of community groups to fight high prices and rents. One such organization, the New York Women's Council, began a housewives' boycott against high meat prices which mushroomed into a national consumer's movement.

By the 1940s, knowledge of Stalin's purges and his nonaggression pact with Hitler disillusioned American members, and Communist Party membership plummeted, vastly reducing the organization's influence. Yet of the parties of the left, the Communists seemed willing to confront the issues of poverty and discrimination when other groups avoided them.

*A West Virginia coal miner and his wife spend an evening listening to the radio.*

## THE SECURITIES OF MARRIAGE IN AN INSECURE AGE

A significant trend in women's employment during the Depression was the increased employment of married women. Despite hostility against their leaving the home to work, their employment increased from 11.7 percent in 1930 to over 15 percent in 1940, continuing a trend that had begun during the 1920s. By and large,

*This photograph of the mother and two children of a migrant family en route to California in search of work was taken by Dorothea Lange for the Farm Security Administration.*

economic motives, not feminist ones, dictated married women's working. Many families tried to maintain consumption standards established during the affluent 1920s. That gasoline sales and automobile registrations did not diminish during the 1930s indicates that the automobile—once viewed as a luxury—was now considered a necessity. At the same time, due to compulsory-education laws and state regulations prohibiting child labor, families were less able to put children to work. All of these factors placed pressure on wives to supplement the family income.

Contrary to conservative predictions that working wives would destroy the home, the family seemed to become stronger during the decade. Gallup polls demonstrated that the majority of married women still defined domesticity as their primary responsibility. And, in this time of economic insecurity, the family assumed a new importance. The home was one place where the individual could find emotional sustenance. The number of divorces declined during the early 1930s, as did attendance at public events, travel, and club memberships. In part, people were staying home and staying married because they could not afford to do otherwise. Also, the radio had become a popular form of home entertainment. In their study of Muncie, Indiana, Helen and Robert Lynd found an increasing incidence of teenage marriage. Emotional insecurity, they thought, produced this trend.[15]

Many sociologists who studied the response of families to the Depression were surprised to find that economic adversity did not, as they had expected, destroy families. On the contrary, it often welded them together into more closely knit units. Families unaffected by unemployment often gave money to indigent relatives and shared living space with them. One city editor in the Lynds' *Middletown* expressed a general sentiment when he wrote: "More families are now acquainted with their constituent members than at any time since the log-cabin days of America." And, he continued, in an antifeminist vein: "Society is not made poorer because mother is now neglecting the encyclopedia from which sprang full blown the club papers with which she formerly bored her fellow clubwomen, and is devoting more of her time to cookbooks."[16]

Economic adversity, however, often undermined traditional family roles. According to one analyst, a long-term loss of income could create an "epic demoralization" within the family.[17] Sometimes wives could find jobs when husbands could not, and this situation could increase women's power in families. One psychiatrist who observed long-unemployed miners in Pennsylvania found that the structure of the family there had shifted. The men hung out on street corners and dreaded returning home. Within this culture, both a jobless man and his family considered him worthless. Wives punished their unemployed husbands by withholding themselves sexually, and according to this observer, "by belittling the men . . . [and] undermining their parental authority."[18] One thinks, however, of the Joad family in John Steinbeck's *Grapes of Wrath*, torn apart by the process of migration from Oklahoma to California and by the difficult conditions of work for migrant families there, yet held together by the strength of the mother, in Steinbeck's scenario a loving matriarch.

The Lynds identified a similar pattern in Muncie, Indiana. The majority of the wives were much less disrupted by the Depression than their husbands. Women who remained at home had a familiar household routine. Women who worked often gained increased status within the family. Men who were out of work "lost much of their sense of time and dawdled helplessly and dully about the streets." In such situations, women became the centers of stability within the family and often the arbiters of family decisions. In general, the Lynds concluded, "All sorts of temperamental variations have appeared, with women sometimes showing perspective and steadfastness under stress and men sometimes dissolving into pettiness . . . and personal rancor."[19]

Given women's increased authority within the family and in response to lowered incomes and employment, the birth rate dropped during the 1930s. More couples were using contraceptive measures, and by 1940, every state in the union, with the exceptions of Massachusetts and Connecticut, had legalized birth control. At the beginning of the decade, there were 28 family-planning clinics in the nation. By 1941, there were 746, and almost one-third were receiving government assistance.

The increasing availability of contraceptives probably did not lead to an increase in sexual promiscuity. Among the young, a vanguard for liberated sexual attitudes in the 1920s, most studies showed that premarital intercourse was on the increase but that both men and women expected it to lead to marital fidelity. The "emancipated" young women in Mary McCarthy's novel *The Group* are knowledgeable about sex, but they are shocked by the one member of the group who lived with her lover before marriage. They expect that a sexual encounter will lead to a permanent liaison, if not marriage.

The 1930s witnessed the demise of America's so-called "flaming youth." The national concern was over jobs and housing, and the rebellion of youth was no longer interesting. What concerned people was that a generation of young Americans could not find jobs, that these future citizens might become permanently embittered. Young middle-class women did not demand liberation. Caroline Bird, author of several feminist studies in the 1960s, reminisced about her Vassar College class in the 1930s that "we did not think we had a right to a private life until we had first straightened out society."[20] A 1936 *Fortune* magazine survey of college campuses found that economics had replaced liquor, sex, and religion as the dominant issue.[21] Leftist movements emerged on many college campuses. Critic Pauline Kael, a student at the University of

California at Berkeley in the late 1930s, remembered that Berkeley was then a "cauldron" of radical discontent.[22]

But most young people were probably not so oriented. While acknowledging student discontent, Kael also recalled that the conservative fraternities and sororities were powerful and that they supported the university administration in quelling dissent. The *Fortune* study showed that three out of every five college women wanted to marry immediately after graduation. Writer Doris Fleischman agreed. The "charming and lovable fire-eating youngsters" of the 1920s were gone, she wrote. The young women of the 1930s, Fleischman thought, were tired of the "sport of their elder sisters." But in her view, they had not found much to take the place of the older interests:

> They go to college in great numbers, but they are ashamed of being regarded as highbrows. They enter the professions and place an enormous compensation emphasis on their social activities. They seem to be stabilizing their interest into a feminine preoccupation with the essentials of marriage and motherhood.[23]

Author Pearl Buck thought that in the face of the Depression, women in general—old as well as young—more than ever before were retreating into domesticity and femininity. "Women's interest in work and a profession, wrote Buck, "has not been lower in the last half century than it is now."[24] In contrast to the Chicago Columbian Exposition of 1893, the New York World's Fair of 1939 contained no separate women's building. Rather, in keeping with a decade of feminist retreat, the attempt to integrate women's contributions to culture in the displays resulted in exhibits of women's fashions and cooking and not much else. Based on such evidence, some historians propose that the retreat to marriage and motherhood of the 1950s was already evident in the 1930s and that an earlier return to prosperity would have ended the 1930s' low fertility rates and precipitated a "baby boom" two decades before it occurred in the 1950s.

Still, this was the decade in which Nancy Drew was invented and in which Blondie appeared in the comic strips. Carolyn Keene created Nancy Drew, the detective whose skillful sleuthing in many novels became favorite reading for girls. Blondie, the daffy housewife, dominated Dagwood, her worried, bumbling

*Jean Harlow in Dinner at Eight: the sales of peroxide skyrocketed.*

husband. How do we interpret Scarlett O'Hara, the famed fictional character, renowned in print and on the screen, in Margaret Mitchell's *Gone With the Wind*, published in 1936? Her tempestuous involvement with two men, one fair and gentle and the other dark and virile, mirrored the stereotypes of women's romantic fiction. But during the crisis of the Civil War and Reconstruction, the historical period in which the novel is set, Scarlett casts off traditional womanhood to pursue any means to survive. Identifying with her self-made immigrant father, she becomes a successful businesswoman and the main financial support of her family. Of indomitable spirit, she is calculating and ruthless. A nation of women assessing conflicting models of domesticity and assertiveness adored her. Yet at the same time,

*Mae West, the voluptuous independent siren of the 1930s, was an exception to the rule about immorality.*

they seemed to overlook Mitchell's false characterization of African-American women under slavery as either scatterbrained dimwits or mammies, loyal to the family which owned them.

## FASHIONS AND MOVIES: OLD AND NEW IMAGES

Among all women, working or not, a return to tradition was evident in their dress. Women no longer wore the short skirts and the flat-chested frocks of the 1920s. Although clothing remained loose, skirts became longer and waistlines and bosoms reappeared. Indeed, to look just right, well-groomed women again donned some form of figure-molding undergarment. In the 1927 spring-summer Sears, Roebuck catalog, a source of fashion for rural women and other mail-order customers, corset advertising had been directed to the overweight woman who wanted the "stylish 'uncorseted' effect

*A 1936 movie billboard in Atlanta, Georgia: women controlled by violence.*

without allowing [her] figure to spread."[25] By the fall of 1930, however, the catalog directed corset advertising to all women: "The new mode calls for a definitely higher indented waistline, long tapering hips, and the molded bust. To wear the new frocks, you must wear the smart, new corsetry."[26]

The most influential model for women in the 1930s was the movie star. Author Maxine Davis found that in every section of the country and within every social group, the most common subject

*Young women "clicking" with young men at a luncheonette in New York.*

of conversation was the cinema queen.[27] Particularly in a time of social despair, people were living their lives vicariously through films. Unlike other types of entertainment, movies still attracted sizable audiences. First Greta Garbo was the rage; then, Marlene Dietrich and Bette Davis. When Jean Harlow dyed her hair blonde, it started a fad that has lasted for decades.

The films of the 1930s continued trends begun in the 1920s. There was the vamp turned temptress, like Marlene Dietrich in *The Blue Angel,* and the sweet virginal blonde, like Janet Gaynor in a series of films beginning with her best-known, *Seventh Heaven* (1927). A new twist was the "good-bad girl," who was both temptress and angel and whose good qualities, through the help of a man, triumphed in the end. Yet during the 1930s, a strict censorship code was in force, and although violence was not prohibited, any hint that immorality was condoned could bring down the wrath of the powerful censorship board. Endings had to be happy and sex outside of marriage punished, particularly when it was on the part of a woman.

One female film star of the 1930s paid little attention. Weighty and buxom, Mae West mimicked contemporary standards of female beauty; she even padded her hips to make them larger. In voice and movement, she exuded sexuality, and no man could resist her. No man could manipulate her, either. A range of men from Cary Grant to W. C. Fields chased her; and to Grant's question, "Haven't you met a man who could make you happy?" her answer was classic West, "Sure, lots of times." She was strong and confident, always in command. She wrote much of her dialogue herself, and she took a hand in directing and editing some of her films. Her sardonic, salacious dialogue was so cleverly worded that, for a time, it even slipped by the censorship board.

Mae West movies were exceptions. The prevailing movie plots continued to deny real power to women. In gangster films, a favorite genre of the 1930s, gangster lovers regularly mistreated their leading ladies. In 1930, James Cagney established the pattern by hitting Mae Clark in the eye with a grapefruit in the movie *Public Enemy*. Critic Gilbert Seldes attributed the stir created by this scene to its effect in reinforcing the image of strong masculinity which, he contended, feminism and the Depression had undermined.[28] By 1938, one analyst of movie trends thought that the mistreatment of women stars had become standard. "Today, a star scarcely qualifies for the higher spheres," she wrote, "unless she has been slugged by her leading man, rolled on the floor, kicked downstairs, cracked over the head with a frying pan, dumped into a pond, or butted by a goat."[29]

A consistent theme from the 1930s through the 1950s involved a professional woman or a wealthy woman who was taught by a man that sex and marriage were all that really mattered in life. The movie was made again and again. Occasionally, as in the sophisticated 1936 comedy *Wedding Present*, with Cary Grant and Joan Bennett, marriage itself was satirized and the professional woman was sympathetically portrayed. More often, the opposite was the case. In *Take a Letter, Darling* (1942), Rosalind Russell gives up a glamorous career as the head of an advertising agency to travel around Mexico in a trailer with Fred MacMurray. In

*Lady in the Dark* (1944), magazine executive Ginger Rogers relinquishes all to marry her assistant, Ray Milland, after her psychoanalyst convinces her that only through marriage can she find fulfillment. Spencer Tracy and Katharine Hepburn wage the war of the sexes in eight films; in most of them, the battle is charmingly intense until Hepburn capitulates in the last frames. And in *It Happened One Night* (1934), one of the most successful films of the 1930s, wealthy Claudette Colbert finds Clark Gable, a virile journalist of indeterminate origins, irresistible.

Although not gender equal in viewpoint, these films did strike a new note. The women in them were strong-minded, quick-witted, even aggressive. Despite the fact that Bette Davis, Rosalind Russell, and Katharine Hepburn regularly gave in to men on screen, their intelligence and strength shows through. In fact, so much does the personality of these women dominate their films that their final surrender seems almost irrelevant. In *Middletown*, the Lynds document the effect of one of these film stars on the first generation of women who viewed her. Joan Crawford, they wrote, "has her amateur counterparts in the high-school girls who stroll with brittle confidence in and out of 'Barney's' soft-drink parlor, 'clicking' with the 'drugstore cowboys' at the tables; while the tongue-tied young male learns the art of the swift confident comeback in the face of female confidence."[30]

The high-school girls at Barney's in *Middletown* became the Army WACS and war workers of the Second World War, and then the wives and mothers of the postwar era. Joan Crawford and Bette Davis did not hold out the vista of a feminist future to them. But these actresses became part of the mythology of the culture. Their movies continued to be shown, and the emergence of the feminism of the 1960s is not unrelated to the strong image these women projected.

## AFRICAN-AMERICAN WOMEN AND POPULAR CULTURE

The complexities of the movie image of white women in the 1930s were abandoned in the case of black women. Consistent with older stereotypes and in keeping with the age's persistent racism, black

*Famed singer of the blues, Bessie Smith.*

women in mainstream films were invariably servants, content to be caretakers and domestics, simple in affection and intellect. Hattie McDaniel was the most famous movie mammy; she won an Academy Award for her portrayal of the character in the film version of *Gone With the Wind*.

Another type of African-American entertainer was popular in the 1920s and 1930s, although she did not appear on the screen. On records and in roadhouses, in nightclubs and on the vaudeville stage, black female vocalists bellowed and crooned jazz and the blues—the shouts, laments, and often ribald rhapsodies that grew out of the reality and tragedy of the African-American experience in America as well as of their own lives. Ma Rainey began the tradition of the black female blues singer in the 1900s. Bessie Smith continued it in the 1920s. Ethel Waters and Ella Fitzgerald carried it into the 1930s.

Many of these women had fought their way out of poverty, sometimes through a period of prostitution. Extravagantly dressed, often overweight by white standards, they mirrored a nouveau-riche prosperity and sang songs of pathos, sexuality, economic despair and female strength that contrasted sharply with the idealized love refrains of white popular music. Where whites sang songs like "You're My Everything" and "Lover Come Back to Me," African-American blues singers sang "Don't Fish in My Sea," "Sweet Rough Man," and "Freight Train Blues," with its lines: "When a woman gets the blues she goes to her room and hides/When a man gets the blues he catch the freight train and rides."[31]

Exactly what role these women played in an emerging African-American consciousness is hard to say. They challenged oppression not directly but by subversion; they pointed toward racial pride. The advent of World War II increased employment opportunities for blacks, and the mechanization of cotton picking, which ended Southern tenant farming, accelerated the movement of African Americans to cities and to the North. These factors underlay what would become a revolution in black expectations and a civil rights movement of epic dimensions. By the 1940s and 1950s, light-skinned women such as Lena Horne and Dorothy Dandridge were being allowed some latitude in film roles; by the 1960s, African Americans were proclaiming that "black is beautiful," even as the racist and sexist attitudes of Americans were beginning to erode.

## WOMEN AS PART OF THE WAR EFFORT

Both world wars stimulated major changes in the female work force. However, whereas few additional women entered the work force during World War I, more than six million women went to work for the first time during World War II. The United States'

*"Rosie the Riveter"—an arc welder at the Bethlehem–Fairfield Shipyards in Baltimore, Maryland, May 1943.*

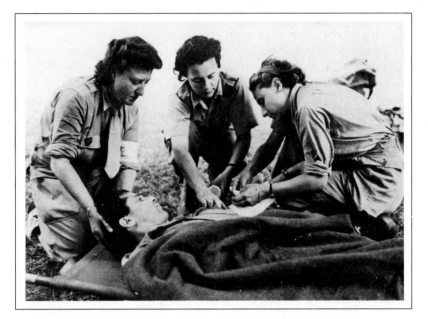

*Three American nurses recruited for the Free French Army Service treat a wounded French soldier near Eshouche, France, in 1944.*

participation in World War I lasted 19 months; World War II, and thus the need to employ women, lasted four years, from 1941 to 1945. The proportion of women in the labor force increased from 25 percent in 1940 to 36 percent in 1945. This increase was greater than that of the previous four decades combined.

Initially, women were not easily persuaded that they ought to transgress traditional standards and fill the jobs vacated by men. To accomplish this task, the molders of public opinion in newspapers, magazines, and radio created "Rosie the Riveter," the lauded symbol of the woman at work. The media praised working women, and the woman who did not at least raise a "victory garden" or work as a Red Cross volunteer was as criticized as the working woman in times past. Even the movies joined in. As part of their effort to bolster national morale, moviemakers churned out a steady stream of propaganda films. In these films, the wife or sweetheart who stayed behind and went to work in a regular job or for an agency like the USO, which provided entertainment and friendship for soldiers, became as familiar a figure as the valiant soldier-lover for whom she waited.

Government policy backed the propaganda for the employment of women. During the war years, four times as many women as men found employment in the federal bureaucracy. The War Manpower Commission, established to utilize labor resources more effectively, sponsored vocational training programs in high schools, storefronts, and on job sites, and encouraged women of all ages to enter these programs. State governors and legislatures suspended protective legislation for women so that they would not be barred from any jobs. The War Manpower Commission repeatedly urged a policy of equal pay for women, and the National War Labor Board, established to mediate labor disputes, for a time enforced this principle. The government supported day care for the children of working mothers: By 1945, 100,000 children were enrolled in federal child care facilities. The noncombatant Women's Army Corps (WAC), the Navy WAVES, the Women Marines, and the Coast Guard's SPARS were founded. Americans could observe women in military uniform—a traditional symbol of masculinity.

Although women were courted to join the work force, they were slotted primarily into clerical and factory jobs, particularly in war-related industries. Some opportunities opened in medicine and law, but few women moved into professional careers during the war years. Women were not hired for high-level positions in business or in government; these were left for men. A shortage of teachers and school administrators occurred, not so much because male instructors and supervisors went off to war, but because industry and business, lacking administrative talent, lured men away with higher salaries.

As for government directives that women's wages should be the same as men's, imprecise wording and lax enforcement on the part of the National Labor Relations Board allowed employer violations with impunity. And, although Women's Bureau studies showed that a majority of working women with children had inadequate child care, the 100,000 children enrolled in federal day-care centers constituted only 10 percent of the children who needed such care. In general, women leaders charged that the government showed little interest in their recommendations. The War Manpower Commission, for example, composed entirely of men, shunted women into a Woman's Advisory Committee, which was rarely consulted.

The concern for women lacked impetus because, for the most part, no one really expected women to continue working after the war ended. The unstated assumption was that women, like men, were enlisting in the national service during a time of crisis and that, like men, they would take up their "normal" roles again when the crisis ended. Thus, factory labor was often described in pro-work propaganda as akin to housework. Women, it was said, could adapt to factory machines "as easily as to electric cake-mixes and vacuum cleaners."[32] The implication was that the transition back to domesticity would be equally easy. Typical of the national attitude, all federal funds for day-care facilities were discontinued in 1946.

When the war ended, many women left jobs in factories and offices without complaint to return to the homes and marriages denied them during the war years. Yet a Women's Bureau study in 1944 concluded that 80 percent of working women wanted to continue in their jobs when the war ended. After all, many women had moved into high-paying men's work as railroad switchmen, precision toolmakers, and even lumberjacks. The manpower crisis had especially aided African-American women; the number of black women who worked as servants fell from 72 percent to 48 percent, while the proportion of black women working in factories grew to nearly 19 percent. According to historian William Chafe, the war represented for them almost a "second emancipation."[33]

Yet cutbacks among women workers, particularly in industry, began as soon as peace was declared. This was not unexpected; in the period of conversion from wartime to peacetime production, businesses and factories did not need as many workers. What was surprising was the large number of women who were laid off in comparison with men. For example, in aircraft-engine plants, women had made up 39 percent of the work force but comprised 51 percent of those laid off. In keeping with these trends, the percentage of women in the labor force in general dropped from 36 percent in 1945 to 28 percent in 1947.

After 1947, the number of working women again began to rise. By 1951, the proportion had reached 31 percent. Yet women in manufacturing generally did not regain the skilled jobs they had held during the war. Without equal rights legislation, there was little they could do, and state protective laws, suspended only temporarily during the war years, could easily be interpreted as meaning that women were not capable of performing whatever labor was defined as "men's work."

In some instances, the unions were willing to aid women members; the movement of women into war industries had caused their membership in the CIO to quadruple. During the war years, for example, Detroit unions had negotiated an equal pay agreement for women with General Motors. But once the war ended, the male-dominated unions were only too willing to acquiesce to agreements that reserved higher paying positions for men. In the late 1940s, some women filed lawsuits demanding back pay as a result of these practices. Most of these suits were denied, but 31 women in 1948 won a retroactive wage settlement of $55,000 from the Chrysler Corporation because the company had laid them off after World War II in violation of their seniority.

After 1951, the percentage of women in the labor force steadily continued to increase. By 1973 it reached 42 percent. The percentages of employed married women and older women continued to rise accordingly. Thus, many women retained their tie to a world outside the home. The experience of war had lasting effects on the lives of women—at least on the lives of those who were now relatively permanent members of the work force.

## NOTES

[1] William H. Chafe, *The American Woman: Her Changing Social, Economic, and Political Roles, 1920–1970* (New York: Oxford University Press, 1972), p. 115.

[2] Lois Scharf, *To Work and To Wed: Female Employment, Feminism, and the Great Depression* (Westport, CT: Greenwood Press, 1980), pp. 59–60.

[3] Quoted in Jacquelyn Dowd Hall, " 'A Truly Subversive Affair': Women Against Lynching in the Twentieth-Century South," in Carol Ruth Berkin and Mary Beth Norton (eds.), *Women of America: A History* (Boston: Houghton Mifflin, 1979), p. 366.

[4] Eleanor Roosevelt, *It's Up to the Women* (New York: Frederick A. Stokes, 1933), pp. 202–06.

[5] Grace Abbott, *From Relief to Social Security: The Development of the New Public Welfare Services and Their Administration* (Chicago: University of Chicago Press, 1941), pp. 361–62.

[6] Rose Schneiderman (with Lucy Goldthwaite), *All for One* (New York: Paul S. Erickson, 1967), p. 197.

[7] Eleanor Roosevelt and Lorena A. Hickok, *Ladies of Courage* (New York: G. P. Putnam's Sons, 1954), p. 192.

[8] *Independent Woman* (April 1933): 123.

[9] Grace Hutchins, *Women Who Work* (New York: International, 1934), p. 191.

[10] Thomas Mineham, *Boy and Girl Tramps of America* (New York: Farrar, Straus, & Giroux, 1934), pp. 75, 139–40.

[11] Margaret Culkin Banning, "They Raise Their Hats," *Harper's*, CLXXI (August 1935): 355; Alma Lutz, "Why Discharge Women First?" *Independent Woman* (Dec. 1931): 534.

[12] Ellen Terry, *The Third Door: The Autobiography of an American Negro Woman* (New York: David McKay, 1955), p. 88.

[13] Louise Año Nuevo Kerr, "Chicanas in the Great Depression," in Adelaida R. Del Castillo, (ed.), *Between Borders: Essays on Mexicana/Chicana History* (Encino, CA: Floricanto Press, 1990), pp. 257–268.

[14] Schneiderman, *All for One*, p. 246.

[15] Helen Merrell Lynd and Robert S. Lynd, *Middletown in Transition: A Study in Cultural Conflicts* (New York: Harcourt Brace Jovanovich, 1937), p. 152.

[16] Ibid., p. 146.

[17] Paul L. Benjamin, "The Family, Society, and the Depression," *Annals of the American Academy of Political and Social Science* CLX (March 1932): 142.

[18] Studs Terkel, *Hard Times: An Oral History of the Great Depression* (New York: Pantheon Books, 1970), pp. 196–97.

[19] Lynd and Lynd, *Middletown in Transition*, pp. 178–79.

[20] Caroline Bird, *The Invisible Scar* (New York: David McKay, 1966), p. 139.

[21] Dorothy Dunbar Bromley and Florence Britten, *Youth and Sex: A Study of Thirteen-Hundred College Students* (New York: Harper & Row, 1938), p. 20.

[22] Terkel, *Hard Times*, p. 346.

[23] Doris E. Fleischman, "Women: Types and Movements," in Fred J. Ringel (ed.), *America as Americans See It* (New York: Literary Guild of America, 1932), p. 117.

[24] Pearl Buck, *Of Men and Women* (New York: John Day, 1941), p. 91.

[25] *Sears, Roebuck Catalog*, CLIV (Spring/Summer 1927): 88.

[26] *Sears, Roebuck Catalog*, CLVII (Fall/Winter 1930): 79.

[27] Maxine Davis, *The Lost Generation: A Portrait of American Youth Today*

(New York: Macmillan, 1936), p. 87.

[28] Gilbert Seldes, "The Masculine Revolt," *Scribner's* XCV (April 1934): 279–282.

[29] Margaret Thorp, *America at the Movies* (New Haven, CT: Yale University Press, 1939), p. 76.

[30] Lynd and Lynd, *Middletown in Transition,* p. 262.

[31] Hazel V. Carby, " 'It Jus Be's Dat Way Sometime': The Sexual Politics of Women's Blues," in Ellen Carol DuBois and Vicki L. Ruiz, *Unequal Sisters: A Multicultural Reader in U.S. Women's History* (New York: Routledge, 1990), p. 245.

[32] Leila J. Rupp, *Mobilizing Women for War: German and American Propaganda, 1936–1945* (Princeton, NJ: Princeton University Press, 1978), p. 152.

[33] Chafe, *American Woman,* p. 142.

## BIBLIOGRAPHY

For the history of women in the 1930s, see Lois Scharf, *To Work and to Wed: Female Employment, Feminism, and the Great Depression* (Westport, CT: Greenwood Press, 1980), and Susan Ware, *Holding Their Own* (Boston: Twayne, 1982). Also interesting are Richard Lowitt and Maurine Beasley (eds.), *One-Third of a Nation: Lorena Hickok Reports on the Great Depression* (Urbana: University of Illinois Press, 1981), and Jeanne Westin, *Making Do: How Women Survived the '30s* (Chicago: Follett, 1976). Also consult with Mary Beard, *America Through Women's Eyes* (New York: Macmillan, 1933); Caroline Bird, *The Invisible Scar* (New York: David McKay, 1966); Helen Merrell Lynd and Robert S. Lynd, *Middletown in Transition: A Study in Cultural Conflicts* (New York: Harcourt Brace Jovanovich, 1937); and Studs Terkel, *Hard Times: An Oral History of the Great Depression* (New York: Pantheon Books, 1970).

Information on the League of Women Voters and women's political behavior can be found in Martin Gruberg, *Women in American Politics: An Assessment and Sourcebook* (Oshkosh, WI: Academia, 1968), and Eleanor Roosevelt and Lorena A. Hickok, *Ladies of Courage* (New York: G. P. Putnam's Sons, 1954). On women's role in New Deal administrations, see Susan Ware, *Beyond Suffrage: Women and the New Deal* (Cambridge, MA: Harvard University Press, 1981). The standard biography of Frances Perkins is George Martin, *Madame Secretary: Frances Perkins* (Boston: Houghton Mifflin, 1976). Mary Anderson's autobiography, *Women at Work: The Autobiography of Mary Anderson, as Told to Mary N. Winslow* (Minneapolis: University of Minnesota Press, 1951), sheds light on the situation for New Deal women administrators. For a compilation of letters of an important 1930s activist and early feminist historian of women, see Nancy F. Cott (ed.), *A Woman Making History: Mary Ritter Beard Through Her Letters* (New Haven, CT: Yale University Press, 1991).

Insightful studies of gender and New Deal programs include Grace Abbott, *From Relief to Social Security: The Development of the New Public Welfare Services and Their Administration* (Chicago: University of Chicago Press, 1941); Josephine Chapin Brown, *Public Relief, 1929–1939* (New York: Henry Holt, 1940); Clarke A. Chambers, *Seedtime of Reform: American Social Service and Social Action, 1918–1933* (Minneapolis: University of Minnesota Press, 1963). For an interesting discussion of constructions of masculinity and femaleness in New Deal artistic productions, see Barbara Melosh, *Engendering Culture: Manhood and Womanhood in New Deal Public Art and Theater* (Washington, DC: Smithsonian Institution Press, 1991).

Among the most insightful of the numerous biographies of Eleanor Roosevelt are Joseph Lash, *Eleanor and Franklin: The Story of Their Relationship* (New York: W. W. Norton, 1971), and *Eleanor: The Years Alone* (New York: W. W. Norton, 1972). On her relationships with women and involvement with women's groups, see Blanche Wiesen Cook, *Eleanor Roosevelt*, Vol. I: 1884–1933 (New York: Viking, 1992), the first volume of a projected two-volume biography. For a sample of her ideas, see *It's Up to the Women* (New York: Frederick A. Stokes, 1933). On her internationalism, see Jason Berger, *A New Deal for the World: Eleanor Roosevelt and American Foreign Policy, 1920–1962* (New York: Columbia University Press, 1982).

On women at work and on the labor movement in the 1930s, see Irving Bernstein, *Turbulent Years: A History of the American Worker, 1933–1941* (Boston: Houghton Mifflin, 1970); Philip S. Foner, *Women and the American Labor Movement: From World War One to the Present* (New York: Free Press, 1980); Grace Hutchins, *Women Who Work* (New York: International, 1934); Alice Kessler-Harris, *Out to Work: A History of Wage-Earning Women in the United States* (New York: Oxford University Press, 1982), and Women's Bureau studies of the subject. Several excellent movies are available. *Union Maids* (1977) focuses on an exploration of the work situation for women of various ethnicities in Chicago. *With Babies and Banners* (1977) is a moving exploration of women's participation in the 1937 automobile strike in Flint, Michigan. Both films are available from New Day Films, P.O. Box 315, Franklin Lakes, NJ 07417.

On ethnicity and race in the 1930s, see the works cited in the bibliography for Chapter II, and also Julia Kirk Blackwelder, *Women of the Depression: Caste and Culture in San Antonio, 1929–39* (College Station, TX: Texas A&M University Press, 1984); Louise Año Nuevo Kerr, "Chicanas in the Great Depression," in Adelaida Del Castillo, (ed.), *Between Borders: Essays on Mexicana/Chicana History* (Encino, CA: Floricanto Press, 1990), pp. 257–68; and Vicki L. Ruiz, *Cannery Women, Cannery Lives: Mexican Women, Unionization, and the California Food Processing Industry, 1939–1950* (Albuquerque: University of New Mexico Press, 1987).

The subject of women's involvement in radical movements in the 1930s awaits its historian. Two insightful autobiographies of women radicals are Ella Reeve Bloor, *We Are Many: An Autobiography* (New York: International Publishers, 1940), and Dorothy Day, *The Long Loneliness:*

*The Autobiography of Dorothy Day* (New York: Harper & Row, 1952). Day was a leader in Catholic radicalism. See also Sara Alpern, *Freda Kirchwey: A Woman of the Nation* (Cambridge, MA: Harvard University Press, 1987), and L. Dee Garrison, *Mary Heaton Vorse: The Life of an American Insurgent* (Philadelphia: Temple University Press, 1989). Bertha Thompson, *Sister of the Road: The Autobiography of Box Car Bertha, as Told to Dr. Ben L. Reitman* (New York: Macaulay, 1937), is the fascinating story of a woman who rode the rails.

On the family and the Depression, contemporary sociologists produced insightful studies. See *Annals of the American Academy of Political and Social Science* (March 1932); Robert Cooley Angell, *The Family Encounters the Depression* (New York: Scribner's, 1936); Mirra Komarovsky, *The Unemployed Man and His Family: The Effect of Unemployment upon the Status of the Man in Fifty-Nine Families* (New York: Institute of Social Research, 1940); Winona Morgan, *The Family Meets the Depression: A Study of a Group of Highly Selected Families* (Minnesota: University of Minnesota Press, 1939); and Samuel Stouffer and Paul Lazarsfeld, *Research Memorandum on the Family in the Depression* (New York: Social Science Research Council, 1937). More recent studies include Winifred D. Wandersee, *Women's Work and Family Values, 1920–1940* (Cambridge, MA: Harvard University Press, 1981).

On youth during the Depression, see Dorothy Dunbar Bromley and Florence Britten, *Youth and Sex: A Study of Thirteen-Hundred College Students* (New York: Harper & Row, 1938); Maxine Davis, *The Lost Generation: A Portrait of American Youth Today* (New York: Macmillan, 1936); and Thomas Minehan, *Boy and Girl Tramps of America* (New York: Farrar, Straus & Giroux, 1934). For a study of a major Southern group, see Margaret Jarman Hagood, *Mothers of the South: Portraiture of the White Tenant Farm Woman* (Chapel Hill: University of North Carolina Press, 1939). In *Like a Family: The Making of the Southern Cotton Mill World* (Chapel Hill: University of North Carolina Press, 1987), Jacqueline Dowd Hall and her associates have produced a moving oral history of worker communities in the Southern textile mills, which by the 1930s were the world's leading producer of yarn and cloth, only to fall into a minor position by the 1950s. See also Delores Janiewski, *Sisterhood Denied: Race, Gender, and Class in a New South Community* (Philadelphia: Temple University Press, 1986), on textile workers in Durham, North Carolina. On the women's crusade against lynching, see Jacquelyn Dowd Hall, *Revolt Against Chivalry: Jessie Daniel Ames and the Women's Crusade Against Lynching* (New York: Columbia University Press, 1979), and Lillian Smith, *Killers of the Dream* (Garden City, NY: Anchor Books, 1963).

On fashion and physical appearance, see Lois W. Banner, *American Beauty* (New York: Alfred A. Knopf, 1983). On film, the studies listed in the bibliography to Chapter IV pertain, as well as Andrew Bergman, *We're in the Money: Depression America and Its Films* (New York: Harper & Row, 1971). However, nothing substitutes for seeing the films themselves. On blues singers and black women in film, see Donald Bogle, *Brown Sugar: Eighty*

*Years of America's Black Female Superstars* (New York: Harmond, 1980), and Hazel V. Carby, "'It Jus Be's Dat Way Sometime': The Sexual Politics of Women's Blues," in Ellen Carol DuBois and Vicki L. Ruiz (eds.), *Unequal Sisters: A Multicultural Reader in U.S. Women's History* (New York: Routledge, 1990), pp. 238–249.

On black women, see Zora Neale Hurston, *Their Eyes Were Watching God*, a 1937 novel, and Maya Angelou, *I Know Why the Caged Bird Sings* (New York: Random House, 1969), a superb autobiography.

On women in the Second World War, see Karen Anderson, *Wartime Women: Sex Roles, Family Relations, and the Status of Women During World War Two* (Westport, CT: Greenwood Press, 1981); Beth Bailey and David Farber, *The First Strange Place: The Alchemy of Sex and Race in World War II Hawaii* (New York: Free Press, 1992); D'Ann Campbell, *Women at War with America* (Cambridge, MA: Harvard University Press, 1984); Susan M. Hartmann, *The Home Front and Beyond: American Women in the 1940s* (Boston: G. K. Hall, 1982); Ruth Milkman, *Gender at Work: The Dynamics of Job Segregation by Sex During World War Two* (Urbana: University of Illinois, 1987); and Leila Rupp, *Mobilizing Women for War: German and American Propaganda, 1936–1945*. A superb film, *Rosie the Riveter*, is available from Clarity Educational Productions, P.O. Box 315, Franklin Lakes, NJ 07417.

# 6

## FEMINISM COMES OF AGE: 1945–1970

Women's lives were influenced by two differing trends during the era that followed World War II. The first was a resurgent emphasis on domesticity and femininity. The second was women's continued participation in the work force—a participation which reflected changing economic, demographic, and medical factors.

During the postwar decade, women's interest in organized feminism was limited. Yet by the 1960s, a new and powerful women's movement emerged. Historians have named this movement the "second wave" because of its resemblance to the dynamic feminist crusade of the first decade of the twentieth century.

## A GENERAL CONSENSUS ON WOMAN'S ROLE

### Women Under Attack

During the war, the nation lauded women for their participation in the national effort, and they emerged from the war, in the words of a contemporary, "noble, impeccable, and shining."[1] But soon after this, many opinion makers turned against women, criticizing them not only for having gone to work during the war but also for having, as they saw it, destroyed the American family in the process. As in the past, antifeminism remained strong.

As early as 1942, in his best-selling *Generation of Vipers*, Philip Wylie accused American women of being tyrants in their homes and emasculating their husbands and sons. Taking an opposite tack in *Modern Woman: The Lost Sex* (1947), sociologist Marynia Farnham and historian Ferdinand Lundberg argued that the problems of modern society were caused by women's leaving the home. In their view, women had renounced their femininity to compete with men, causing their children to become delinquent or neurotic and their husbands to become alcoholic or sexually impotent. Wylie and Farnham and Lundberg based their cases on studies that seemed to show high rates of neurosis among Army draftees and

*In the postwar 1940s, women were expected to return to the home. Those who did not were branded by antifeminists as responsible for society's ills.*

career women and increasing alcoholism and impotence among American men. The antifeminists concluded that career women were neurotic because they had rejected their natural role and that the other evils were traceable to neurotic housewives.

Their arguments, however, grew out of their ideology. Farnham and Lundberg were Freudians. In the 1920s, Freudianism had begun to influence Americans. But Watson's behaviorism offered an alternative, and the Depression, which made psychoanalysis unaffordable except for the well-to-do, diluted the Freudian impact. Among psychiatrists and psychologists in the postwar years, however, Freudianism prevailed. The Freudians argued that women could attain emotional stability only through domesticity and motherhood. Women who worked denied their deepest needs and risked being unable to experience love or sexual satisfaction. This, in turn, threatened the family, and, according to apocalyptic thinkers, the whole of Western civilization.

Meanwhile, Freudian theory, especially as developed by Helene Deutsch in her influential *Psychology of Women* (1945), posited that women were naturally masochistic and thus secretly enjoyed physical abuse. Girls subjected to incest were often labeled as seductive and their molesters as sexually deprived. These beliefs, which both private therapists and public agencies applied in treating their clients, were an extension of Freud's theory that women were by nature psychologically impaired. Thus, as has not been uncommon in the history of women, the victims were blamed for the crimes committed against them.

In addition, menopausal women were commonly diagnosed as having re-entered a phase of strong sexual desire, like that of adolescence, in which both their sexuality and their emotions were out of control. Almost invariably, by this reasoning, they would engage in bizarre behavior, like attempting to seduce young men.

### Expert Opinion: Freud and Functionalism

The virulent antifeminism of the immediate postwar years was transitory. But its arguments, and its supporting Freudianism, continued throughout the 1950s. In 1956, sociologists Alva Myrdal and Viola Klein commented that conferences of such varied groups as school headmasters, juvenile magistrates, probation officers, and welfare workers invariably blamed mothers, especially working mothers, for the problems of the young.[2] Child-care experts recommended that mothers stay at home as long as their children were in school. Dr. Benjamin Spock, whose *Baby and Child Care* (1946) became the standard authority, recommended that the federal government pay women to stay at home and raise their children.[3] College educators recommended the adoption of new curricula for women stressing courses on marriage and the family.

Within the fields of sociology and anthropology, the approach known as functionalism was predominant. Functionalism, which reflected postwar conservatism, involved a value-free analysis of existing institutions that left little room for criticism. Not all sociologists, however, were functionalists or Freudians. In her influential *Women in the Modern World: Their Education and Their Dilemmas* (1953), sociologist Mirra Komarovsky critiqued the Freudians and the functionalists and argued that female personality traits and women's lack of accomplishment in comparison to men's were due

*Out of slacks and back into skirts: Christian Dior's 1947 "new look."*

to cultural conditioning, not to biological inferiority. She did not deny women the right to work, but she inferred that wives should assume major responsibility for the home and the family. "Everything we know and believe today about the development of the child points to the importance of mother-child relations."[4] In his popular *The Natural Superiority of Women* (1952), anthropologist Ashley Montague reviewed the evidence that women were superior to men because of factors like women's greater life span. But, contending that "mother love" was key to successful human development, he implied that mothers should stay at home. Even anthropologist Margaret Mead was ambivalent. In *Male and Female* (1955), she criticized the rigid sex-role categories of American culture, but she also glorified woman's role as mother and homemaker.

### The Evidence from Popular Culture

On a popular level, the new emphasis on domesticity was everywhere. In newspapers and magazines, on radio and billboards, the homemaker replaced "Rosie the Riveter" as the

*Marilyn Monroe at the pre-
miere of her film The Seven-
Year Itch.*

national female model. Advertisers were quick to exploit the
expanded market for domestic products offered by the return to a
peacetime economy and the appearance of a new affluence. As
before, their model woman was either a housewife displaying the
presumed benefits of the newest home products or a seductress
connecting the accompanying product with sexuality. In addition, Freudian attitudes infused many articles in mass-circulation
women's magazines, while the majority of the heroines in their
short stories were housewives. Nonfiction articles featured food
recipes and child-care advice.

Women's dress styles reflected the decade's conservatism.
During the war, women had worn mannish clothes: skirts were
narrow; suits were popular; padded shoulders were in vogue. But
in 1947, Parisian designer Christian Dior introduced the "new
look." It featured long, full skirts and emphasized a defined bosom
and a tiny waist. Women abandoned their masculine garb in a
rush to femininity. By the mid-1950s, these fashions reached their
height in the "baby doll" look, with a cinched-in waist, a full
bosom, and bouffant skirts held out by crinoline petticoats.
Girdles and padded bras were popular; for evening, women wore

"merry widow" waist cinchers. Shoe styles emphasized spike heels and pointed toes. Not since the Victorian era had women's fashions been so confining.

Reinforcing the belief that women functioned best as sweethearts and wives, female film stars of the 1950s were sweet and saccharine, like Debbie Reynolds and Doris Day. Or, they projected a complex blend of innocence and sexuality, like Marilyn Monroe. "Social problem" films, like *Come Back, Little Sheba* (1953) and *The Country Girl* (1955), explored issues like alcoholism. Typically, they featured female protagonists who helped male deviants find salvation through heterosexual love and marriage. On the other hand, in "women's films," like the popular *Magnificent Obsession* (1954), young and virile male heroes solved the female protagonists' problem: always the lack of a man.

In addition, by the mid-'50s, ownership of a television set was becoming ubiquitous. The message of TV, in countless situation comedies and dramas, was to glorify the nuclear family—a message backed by an advertising industry, which early became television's main financial supporter. Television shows were early divided into segments organized around advertising spots; critic Ella Taylor asserts that "television became a home appliance that could be used to sell other home appliances. . . ."[5]

There was a pronounced emphasis on domesticity in long-running, popular TV shows like *Father Knows Best* and *I Love Lucy*. But in every episode of the latter, comedienne Lucille Ball, playing Lucy, attempted to outwit her Cuban band leader husband, Ricky Ricardo. Although she was always defeated, still she never gave up the attempt. And, in an analysis of 13 movies, Brandon French asserts that movies in the 1950s recorded women's dissatisfaction. In her estimation they contain evidence of "women on the verge of revolt."

### The Back-to-the-Home Movement

After the war, traditionalism was in vogue, and the patriarchal past took on a romantic hue. The deprivation of the war years made family life attractive, and women responded to the returning soldiers' desire to re-create a secure environment within the family. Rates of marriage and remarriage after divorce remained high, and the age of first marriage dropped. In 1900, the average

*A relaxation technique for labor is demonstrated to a natural childbirth class in San Francisco in 1978 by childbirth educator and author Sheila Kitzinger.*

age of first marriage for women was 22 years; by 1940, it had lowered to 21.5 years. The World War II years and the postwar era occasioned the most rapid decrease over the course of the century: By 1962, women's average age of first marriage was 20.3 years.

In addition, the size of families increased. Families with four and five children were common; the 1940s and the 1950s witnessed a period of family formation unparalleled since the early nineteenth century. Within a few years, the trend toward smaller families, in evidence since the early nineteenth century, was reversed. The children of this mass reproduction came to be known as the "baby boom" generation. In keeping with these developments was the widespread influence of two movements that exalted the joys of motherhood. One, the La Leche League, was dedicated to helping mothers nurse their infants. The other movement promoted the Lamaze method of natural childbirth, which combined a humanitarian desire to free women from the pain of childbirth with a fervor to make it the most important experience of their lives.

*A suburban ritual: waiting at the station for the commuter train.*

Even college-educated women saw marriage as the most important goal in life. From her vantage point at Barnard College, Mirra Komarovsky noted that, far from taking a feminist position, college women were defending marriage and motherhood with Freudian arguments.[6] In her best-selling *The Feminine Mystique*, Betty Friedan estimated that by the mid-1950s, 60 percent of female undergraduates were dropping out of college to marry.[7] One educator traced this development to the influence of movies, television, and popular magazines, with their glorification of romantic love and marriage. To the young, marriage seemed both a haven and an escape from parental restraints.[8] Among teenagers, the new practice of "going steady," of dating exclusively one individual, came into being, a middle-class borrowing from a previous working-class custom. Before World War II, the typical middle-class teenager had prized the number and variety of dates, not the taking on of a quasi-marriage.

Other factors reinforced the desire to create a stable life around a romanticized version of the family, in many ways a middle-class luxury made possible by postwar affluence. The fear that the

*The revered model of mother-hood: the young white woman of the 1950s.*

decrease in population due to the war had weakened the nation prompted some authorities to call for a return to large families. Also, affluent Americans increasingly clustered in suburban areas, where jobs for women were limited and domestic help was in short supply. Husbands were away from home longer because they had to commute to work, leaving their wives responsible for the family—including the task of transportation. With schools, stores, and train stations rarely within walking distance from homes, suburban housewives could spend their days behind the wheel of a station wagon, suburbia's typical means of transportation. The American dream of affluence in a natural, bucolic setting away from urban crowding made it difficult for women to be anything other than housewives and mothers.

In addition, the superficially tranquil postwar decade had its own tensions. International affairs, entering the period known as the "Cold War," a stand-off between the communist Soviet Union and the capitalist United States, brought a series of crises and wars, including the Korean conflict. The perceived threat of communism was fed by the Soviet Union's domination of Eastern European countries, achieved as a result of the peace settlements of World War II, and by China's espousal of communism in 1949. Within the

United States, a virulent anticommunist movement led by the vituperative Wisconsin senator Joseph McCarthy flourished. Hovering above all was the knowledge of the destructive capability of the atomic bomb and the fears of nuclear annihilation. Recurring cycles of inflation and depression cast an air of unease over the new affluence. As early as 1945, one analyst contended that the postwar attack against women was a classic case of scapegoating—of blaming vague fears on a definable villain.[9] Soon thereafter, woman as virtuous wife replaced woman as villain in popular gender mythology. But to a populace that had undergone an exhausting war and was living in a troubled peace, home and family offered security. Historian Elaine May has concluded that during this era the home was a refuge from a "world gone amok."[10]

The celebration of the home was also related to fears that the movement of women into the work force during World War II might have irreparably threatened male dominance. In an interesting analysis of an overlooked subject, Rickie Solinger sees this fear as foremost in the policy toward unwed mothers and their "illegitimate" children. In keeping with the neo-Victorianism of the 1950s, sexuality outside of marriage was reprobated, and unwed mothers were vilified as having violated patriarchal norms by "getting themselves pregnant" and thus threatening the patriarchal nuclear family with the specter of women raising their children alone. The men involved were never mentioned.

Indicative of differing attitudes toward race, however, policies about illegitimacy varied between white women and black women. White unwed mothers who wanted to keep their babies were diagnosed as mentally ill and were pressured into giving up their offspring for adoption. Conversely, African-American unmarried women who became pregnant were diagnosed as suffering from uncontrollable sexual urges. Outside official respectability, many of these women kept their babies, and some of them entered the welfare rolls. In a racist response which Solinger thinks was not unrelated to fears of the growing civil rights movement, 18 states enacted or attempted to enact laws mandating imprisonment or sterilization of women on welfare who had more than one illegitimate child. Yet figures for the decade between 1950 and 1960 show that the percentage of nonwhite, unmarried mothers on welfare actually declined from 25 percent to 19 percent.

***Sex and Child Rearing***    The new emphasis on Freudianism also was central to the return to the home. Americans have always respected experts, particularly when "science" is their justification and when sexuality is the issue. Sex and marriage manuals have never wanted for sales in the twentieth century. After World War II as after World War I, Americans were eager to learn the techniques of physical gratification—so long as, in this era, they were confined to marriage. To this drive, Freudian theories provided a rationale: Sex was a necessity of life that ruled human development. But Freudians also argued that the real sexual gratification for women lay in motherhood, and they incorrectly advised that proper orgasms were vaginal, not clitoral. The message of marriage manuals was that men were to play the dominant role and women were to be submissive.[11] Child-care experts such as Benjamin Spock told women that they must stay at home to raise their children. More than at any time since the Victorian era, pressures were placed on women to become domestic beings.

## Feminism in the 1950s

In response to the arguments of Freudians and traditionalists, the feminist rebuttal was weak. True, bold statements appeared from time to time. French author Simone de Beauvoir's *The Second Sex,* the first major feminist treatise to appear since the early twentieth century, was published in the United States in 1952. More typical of the feminism of the 1950s was Mirra Komarovsky's stated purpose for writing *Women in the Modern World*: To steer a course between feminism and antifeminism.[12] In studying feminism during the 1950s, sociologists Arnold Green and Eleanor Molnick encountered few radicals. Those they did meet felt that it was futile to issue manifestoes or to organize because the majority of Americans had become conservative in opinion and life-style. Militant feminism in the American past had often coincided with times of general reform sentiment, as in the appearance of the woman's rights movement of the mid-nineteenth century as a partial outgrowth of the temperance and abolitionist movements. But such was not the climate in the 1950s.

Old-line women's organizations continued their activities, but many had declined in strength, and disagreement over the ERA

*Helen Wilkins Claytor, second from the left, marches with other delegates of the 26th National Convention of the YWCA of the U.S.A. This march gave "visible silent witness of their concern . . . for Native Americans in this country."*

hampered united efforts. The Women's Joint Congressional Committee, for example, came to serve as an information clearinghouse for liberal organizations by the 1950s. The Consumers' League was rarely heard from; the Women's Trade Union League disbanded in 1947. Even the Lucy Stone League, founded in 1921 to encourage women to use their maiden names after marriage, had little impact in the 1950s. "The present young generation is not interested," wrote an early leader of the organization.[13]

The Woman's Party and the National Federation of Women's Clubs supported the ERA, but the League of Women Voters, the Women's Bureau of the Department of Labor, and women in the labor movement still considered it against the interests of working women. In 1950 and again in 1953, the Senate passed the ERA. But in both years, a coalition of 43 national organizations, known as the Committee to Defeat the Unequal Rights Amendment, successfully lobbied to attach to the bill riders that exempted state protective laws for working women.

Yet despite their differences, the major women's organizations were instrumental in the passage of equal-pay legislation in many states. Although the Fair Labor Standards Act of 1938 had established the principle of equal pay, the government and the courts had been unwilling to apply it with any consistency. At the same time, women's organizations pressed for a broader federal law.

During this time period, the YWCA moved in impressive directions to create interracial coalitions. In 1946, YWCA community associations had a membership of over 450,000, and by the 1950s, they had achieved a significant degree of racial integration in their organization. Through speakers and educational forums, they supported the civil rights movement and attempted to combat racism. In 1940, three-fourths of all colleges and universities had YWCA chapters. Campus YWCAs encouraged student activists, both black and white. In 1967, Helen Wilkins Claytor became the first African-American woman president of the YWCA. By 1990, women of color filled nearly half of the seats on the YWCA's 75-member National Board and held many of its top offices.

### The Reemergence of Domestic Feminism

Given the climate of the 1950s, it is not surprising that the domestic feminist argument, in evidence throughout the century, became more vocal. Even the conservative analysts of woman's role were aware that many women were discontented at home, that they were frustrated over working at a demanding job for which they received no salary and little public recognition. But the solution of the traditionalists was not that women rearrange their lives to combine work with family, but rather that women should be educated to find satisfaction in domesticity. "Many a girl marries unprepared either intellectually or psychologically for the lifetime job she is undertaking," wrote a supporter of professional training programs for future wives.[14] In a variation on the theme, journalist Agnes Meyer revived the idea of women's superior morality and chided women for not organizing on their own behalf. But Meyer was not interested in community concerns; she wanted women to organize behind the goal of raising the status of the housewife.[15]

The aim of these "domestic feminists" on one level was admirable; one can hardly deny that homemakers ought to enjoy greater recognition. But these publicists of domesticity, like those before them, had limited impact on popular attitudes. They were successful in expanding training in home economics and in introducing new courses on marriage and the family in high schools and colleges. These successes, however, did not modify the American belief that husbands' occupations defined wives' status, rather than women's own achievements as homemakers.

The feminists of the 1950s did not envision a vastly altered future. They believed that women could achieve equality with modifications in the existing social structure. Many believed that biological differences between men and women had to be respected. Writing in 1947, Margaret Bruton, identified as a housewife and part-time historian, outlined the moderate position:

> Former generations smothered a girl's intellectual capacities; the feminists and most of her teachers today ignore her emotional needs . . . . Each woman must still learn for herself and often too late the necessity for managing somehow to find outlets for her dual needs with the limitations imposed on her by society and by her biological function.[16]

By 1964, Alice Rossi, sociologist and feminist, found that the overt antifeminism of the immediate postwar years had ended but that at the same time "there was practically no feminist spark left among American women."[17] Her judgment was harsh but probably accurate. The situation with regard to feminism, however, was shortly to undergo a reversal.

## EVIDENCE TO THE CONTRARY

### New Economic, Demographic, and Medical Factors

At the same time that militant feminism was in decline and traditional attitudes were prevalent among Americans, more and more women were entering the work force. Throughout the twentieth century, the expanding American economy had absorbed increasing numbers of women workers, largely into low-paying work. In addition, by the 1950s, changing patterns in the lives of American women had made work outside the home increasingly possible. In 1900, the average woman married at 22 and had her last child at 32. With a life expectancy of 51 years, it was probable that child rearing would take up most of her adult life. By 1950, however, the average woman married at 20, bore her last child at 26, and had a life expectancy of 65 years. Even if she remained at home until her children were grown, she still had at least 20 years of life at home without children. For many women, the alternative was to go to work, and the employment figures of married women increasingly reflected this demographic situation. The proportion of married women employed outside the home was about 15 percent in 1940, about 30 percent in 1960, and over 50 percent in 1968.

Medical science, too, was helping women gain more control over their lives. By 1960, with the marketing of oral contraceptives for women, birth-control technology made an epic advance. A relatively inexpensive and almost foolproof method of contraception was now available to women, and sizable numbers began to use it. Women who chose to use the pill finally seemed to be free to have sexual intercourse without fear of pregnancy, to plan their children around their lives and not their lives around their children. (On the other hand, later studies demonstrated a potential danger from cancer in the use of this early pill, composed heavily of the hormone estrogen.)

During the 1950s, it was evident that the experience of the Depression and war had eroded older notions that work for married women violated their role as wives and mothers. Marriage rates among professional women also began to rise substantially. In 1940, 26 percent of all professional women were married; in 1960, among a sample of approximately 50,000 professional women, 45 percent were married. Significant was the increasing percentage of working mothers with dependent children. In the mid-1950s, 25 percent of women with young children had jobs; by 1969, this statistic had risen to 40 percent. Moreover, between 1960 and 1969, the category of workers that increased most rapidly was that of mothers with preschool children. By 1969, 33 percent of these women were employed outside the home.

In her survey of 489 nonfiction articles in eight popular magazines, Joanne Meyerowitz found that the domestic ideal existed along with an ideal of individual achievement for women which celebrated public activity and work. In these articles, individual women were often celebrated, like Dorothy McCulloch Lee, mayor of Portland, Oregon, who successfully crusaded against organized gambling and prostitution in her city. Over one-third of the articles on individual women featured unmarried women, divorced women, or women of unmentioned marital status. And, these articles consistently defended remunerative employment outside the home for women, although there seemed to be a consensus that women with infants or children in school should not be in the work force.

*Sharing the housework—more than "playing the part of a volunteer aide"?*

### The New Trends—Revolutionary or Not?

To what extent this movement of women into the work force was a revolutionary force is debatable. The old discriminations against women were still in evidence. Women did not move into higher-paying, skilled-labor or professional jobs after the war years. Rather, as during much of the century, clerical labor offered women their largest field of employment. Reflecting the labor shortages of the war years, the proportion of women in most professions increased somewhat between 1940 and 1950. But, by and large, these gains were not retained during the 1950s. Moreover, the postwar years spawned a new consumerism, and inflationary cycles created instabilities in husbands' salaries and increased the costs of items such as cars and college educations for children. As they had during the 1930s, many women worked to improve family finances. They did not regard themselves as full-fledged members of the labor force, and they did not readily join unions. They accepted part-time work; as late as 1980, only about 40 percent of working women were employed in full-time, year-round jobs.

It is also difficult to determine to what extent employment produced a change in family roles. Some sociologists argued that a major realignment took place. Indeed, news programs carried stories about husbands who washed dishes and diapered babies. Other analysts contended that the old masculine-feminine models remained dominant. "Wives still have the main responsibility for the home," wrote sociologist David Reisman, "the husband playing the part of a volunteer aide, and . . . the women have made a tacit bargain with their husbands not to compete with them professionally or in career terms."[18] Yet as early as 1957, before the birth-control pill was marketed, the birth rate had begun to decline—an indication of the waning of 1950s traditionalism and of a new upsurge in the reassertion of individual identity among women.

Moreover, a 1962 Gallup poll showed that only 10 percent of the women surveyed wanted their daughters to have the same lives they had had. This statistic seems to show a dissatisfaction with traditional life-styles that could become fertile ground for a feminist movement. "The problem that has no name," Betty Friedan called women's discontent. But until the advent of the second wave feminism of the 1960s, there was little outspoken protest. It would take the agitation of a group of determined women to alert the nation to the unseen inequality in its midst.

## THE SHIFT TO MILITANCY

In the face of the virulent antifeminism of American society in the immediate postwar years and the appeal of domesticity in the 1950s, the rise of a militant feminism in the 1960s is surprising. Given the long-standing ambivalence of most women about feminism, why were so many willing to embrace a radical ideology?

### A New Reform Climate

Most significant in the emergence of the new feminism was the appearance of a new reform mentality. In the late 1950s and early

*Rosa Parks, the black woman who refused to give up her seat to a white man, rides in the front of a city bus in Montgomery, Alabama.*

1960s, studies showing the growth of crime, poverty, juvenile delinquency, and drug abuse appeared in abundance, and these problems became public issues. By the mid-1950s domestic tensions created by the Cold War eased after Stalin died in 1953 and more moderate leaders took over in the Soviet Union. In 1954, the Senate censured Joseph McCarthy, casting a cloud over the excesses of anticommunism. The decline in domestic repression set the scene for the emergence of civil rights protest. And, this movement was itself partly a product of the international situation; namely, the divergence between the United States' domestic racism and its self-proclaimed mission during and after World War II as the world savior of democracy.

The militant civil rights movement emerged following the 1954 *Brown v. Board of Education* Supreme Court decision, which outlawed racial segregation in public schools, and the Montgomery, Alabama, bus boycott of 1955–56. The bus boycott began when an African-American woman, Rosa Parks, refused to give up her seat to a white man. Following this incident, black leaders in Montgomery

*Betty Friedan: her message "spread like a nuclear chain reaction."*

called for a boycott of white businesses in the city to protest racial segregation in general and the policy of segregation in public transportation in particular. They were led by Jo Ann Robinson, a professor of English at Alabama State College, and her Women's Political Council, the most active African-American group in Montgomery. Martin Luther King, Jr., emerged as a major black spokesperson during this boycott.

In 1960, African-American youth in the South began to spearhead the movement, as college sit-ins swept the South to secure the desegregation of lunch counters in drug and variety stores. Marches, protests, and "freedom rides" to dramatize the segregation in transportation followed, culminating in the Civil Rights Act of 1964 and the Freedom Summer of 1964. During the latter, hundreds of Northern college students came to Mississippi to work with African Americans in a voter registration drive among blacks.

*Eleanor Roosevelt, with John F. Kennedy, who appointed her to chair the Commission of the Status of Women, which he created in 1960.*

Participation in this movement was one component in a general radicalizing of youth. New kinds of raucous music, like rock-'n'roll, implicitly critiqued '50s complacency, and new cultural heroes like the Beat poets, dating from the 1950s, critiqued the middle-class style of life. Increasing dissatisfaction with the United States' involvement in the Vietnam War by the mid-1960s would produce mass protest demonstrations on college and university campuses.

These new trends made Americans receptive to reform in many areas. Thus, within several years of its 1963 publication, Betty Friedan's *The Feminine Mystique* captured a mass audience. Friedan's prose was powerful, and her argument gave no quarter to the defenders of women's traditional role. In Friedan's view, women were discontented not because they were untrained to be housewives, but because homemaking was boring. She refused to give any credit to the Freudians. Rather, she launched the kind of attack against Freud for confusing socialization with biology that became standard in feminist writings of the 1960s.

The new interest in social reform led to gains for women during the administration of John F. Kennedy, elected to the presidency in 1960. Kennedy was no feminist, but he was willing to listen to the suggestion made by women both inside and outside his administration that he appoint a commission to study the position of women. The concept of such a commission had been discussed since the 1940s, when it appeared that Congress might pass the ERA out of gratitude for women's war efforts. But Women's Bureau directors during the 1950s were opposed to the idea, and Presidents Harry Truman and Dwight Eisenhower went no further than tokenism when it came to women, through a few appointments to federal office. By the end of the 1950s, however, personnel shortages were occurring in feminized professions such as nursing and teaching. Some analysts called for government attention to make this work more attractive to women through, for example, equal-pay legislation and federal funds for child-care facilities.

Esther Peterson, President Kennedy's appointee to head the Women's Bureau, was responsive to these needs. More than anyone else, she put successful pressure on Kennedy to assemble a commission. Eleanor Roosevelt's influence was not absent. She was shocked that only nine women were included among Kennedy's first 240 appointees to office, and she sent him a long list of women she considered qualified for government service. Kennedy, desiring support from the Adlai Stevenson wing of the Democratic Party, which Eleanor Roosevelt led, appointed her to head the Commission on the Status of Women which he created in 1960. The commission's report, issued in 1963, was not a radical document. It supported the nuclear family and recommended that women be trained for marriage and motherhood. It withheld support for the Equal Rights Amendment on the grounds that the Fifth and Thirteenth Amendments provided sufficient constitutional guarantees for woman's rights. But among other recommendations, the report called for equal job opportunity and equal pay for women, for an end to laws discriminating against women, and for the expansion of public child-care facilities. Its debates and its recommendations stimulated some important action on behalf of women. In 1963, Congress passed the Equal Pay Act. After 1963, the states began to appoint commissions similar to the national one. Most important, Title VII of the 1964 Civil Rights Act prohibited discrimination on the basis of sex as well as of race. Women in Congress had lobbied for this measure, but a conservative Southern congressman introduced Title VII, not out of feminist sentiment, but as a strategy to block passage of the entire bill. The plan backfired, and the amendment passed together with the bill.

The pressure of old-line women activists was instrumental in persuading Kennedy to establish the presidential commission and the subsequent committees. The composition of the Committee on Civil and Political Rights under the 1960 commission offers an example of their involvement. Members of the committee included presidents of the League of Women Voters, the General Federation of Women's Clubs, the National Federation of Business and Professional Women's Clubs, and a vice president of the International Ladies' Garment Workers' Union. Over the years, these national women's organizations had taken an increasingly feminist stance. Such action, however, did not imply increased radicalism. The League of Women Voters, for example, did not endorse the ERA until 1972. The National Federation of Business and Professional Women's Clubs refused to take a strong leadership role in the 1960s women's movement because the organization did not want public identification as "feminist"—a stance it considered too radical.[19]

## New Faces and the Formation of NOW

In addition to old-line activists, a second group of women, more militant in style and demands, emerged in the mid-1960s. Generally young, these women often turned to radical feminism as a result of their disillusioning experiences in the civil rights and student movements, where they found that male leaders relegated them to housekeeping and clerical chores and often demanded sexual favors of them. Black leader Stokely Carmichael's renowned statement that the proper position of women in the movement was "prone" expressed this sexism. And, like many nineteenth-century feminists who turned from reform to feminism, they began to identify with the disadvantaged for whom they worked and to ask if they, too, were not objects of discrimination. At the same time, young women activists found powerful role models among local black women in the South. "In every southwest Georgia county," wrote one activist, "there is always a 'Mama.' She is usually a militant woman in her community, willing to catch hell, having already caught her share."[20]

The feminist issue was first raised in the civil rights movement during the summer of 1964, when whites and blacks worked together to help disfranchised African Americans register to vote in Mississippi. It surfaced in the student antiwar movement that fall at the University of California at Berkeley. As student activists began organizing communities in ghetto areas in Northern cities that same year, they encountered the same combination of sexism from male coworkers and the example of powerful local women that they had experienced in their civil rights work in the South. Again, the experience drew them in the direction of feminism.

Old-style feminists worked through existing women's organizations and through the government commissions dealing with women. New-style feminists moved in a different direction. They formed their own groups, deemphasized leadership, and stressed equality; they issued manifestoes and, like the left in general, published their own newspapers. They conducted "consciousness-raising" meetings, where they spoke out about their own oppression to heighten individual sensitivity.

The actions of both conservative and radical feminists came to national attention in 1966, when the Third National Conference of the State Commissions on Women met in Washington, DC. The

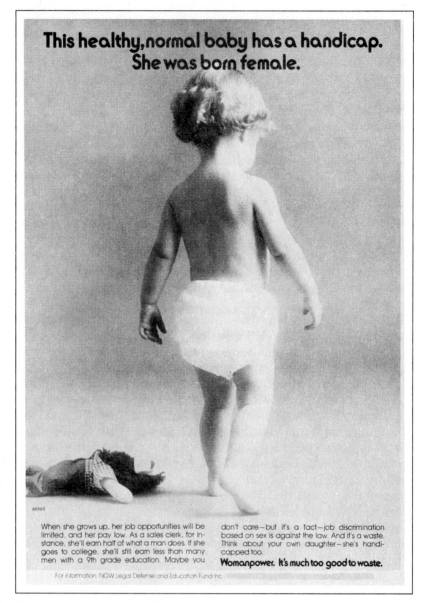

*An advertisement sponsored by the Legal Defense/Education Fund of the National Organization for Women (NOW).*

mood among the delegates was angry.[21] Most felt that the government was not meeting its obligation to implement the recommendations of the Commission on the Status of Women or to enforce existing laws. Meanwhile, women who served on federal agencies concerned with women had communicated the government's failings to, among others, Betty Friedan, who was present at the meeting and whose book, *The Feminine Mystique*, had gained her national prominence as a feminist spokeswoman. The consensus was that there was need for an organization to pressure the government on behalf of women in the same way that the civil rights organizations functioned for African Americans. These forces came to a head in Friedan's hotel room, where plans were formulated for the National Organization for Women (NOW). Events seemed to bear out Friedan's judgment that "the absolute necessity for a civil rights movement for women had reached such a point of subterranean explosive urgency by 1966 that it took only a few of us to get together to unite the spark—and it spread like a nuclear chain reaction."[22]

With the formation of NOW, the new feminism had its official, national birth. Other organizations soon followed. In 1968, academic and professional women formed the Women's Equity Action League (WEAL) for the purpose of ending sex discrimination in employment and education. The National Abortion Rights Action League (NARAL) dated from 1969. The Women's Political Caucus was organized in 1971 as a bipartisan group aimed at pressuring political parties to consider women's concerns and to elect women to office. Job placement and counseling agencies for women, like Catalyst in New York City, began to appear. Courses on women in history and in other fields were introduced in colleges throughout the nation. By the spring of 1972, over 600 were being offered. Women's studies programs soon were formed.

Meanwhile, during the late 1960s, increasing militancy in the civil rights movement prompted a number of African-American organizations to expel white members. More and more, the antiwar protest focused on an antidraft movement, and the draft issue only secondarily affected women because they were not subject to conscription. With the outbreak of riots in the black ghettos, the increasing violence of the Vietnam War, and the official repression of radicalism, male radicals began to resemble African-American militants in their adoption of violent rhetoric and a

*Germaine Greer, author of The Female Eunuch (1971).*

style of male "machismo" hostile to women. Moreover, part of the radicalism of the 1960s had always included the search for individual fulfillment—through sex, drugs, communal living, and Eastern, mystical religions. By the late 1960s, these strains began to influence radical politics: "Look to your own oppression" became a common slogan. All of these developments led to an increase in feminist commitment.

Women began to express their discontent and to translate it into action. Throughout the nation, women marched for the repeal of antiabortion legislation and established day-care centers. In New York City they picketed the *Ladies' Home Journal* offices and in Atlantic City, New Jersey, the Miss America Pageant, for perpetuating an idealized and unreal image of beauty which few women could meet. State and national equal-opportunity commissions pressed sex-discrimination suits filed by women; by 1971, the courts had awarded $30 million in back pay to women as a result of these suits. In 1970, the Women's Equity Action League brought class-action suits against 100 universities under an executive order that required federal contractors to file affirmative-action programs with federal investigators, committing themselves to schedules for ending sex discrimination. The Education Act of 1972 specifically prohibited sex discrimination in colleges and universities. Under

*Supporters of the Equal Rights Amendment of Solidarity Day—an attempt to bring together Feminists, Unionists, and others behind a New Left coalition.*

pressure from women's organizations, especially NARAL, many states repealed legislation prohibiting abortion. In 1973, the Supreme Court declared abortion to be a private decision between doctor and patient, thereby substantially liberalizing its availability to women (*Roe v. Wade*).

From 1970 onward, feminist exposés poured from the presses. Kate Millett's *Sexual Politics* (1969) became a national best-seller. It was followed by, among other books, Shulamith Firestone's *The Dialectic of Sex* (1970), Robin Morgan's *Sisterhood is Powerful* (1970), and Germaine Greer's *The Female Eunuch* (1971). Feminist writers also penned poetry and novels; some analysts traced the beginnings of the trend to Marge Piercy's *Small Changes* (1972) and Erica Jong's *Fear of Flying* (1973). In 1972, three scholarly journals devoted to women's studies appeared. That same year marked the publication of *Ms.*, the first militant feminist magazine in the history of the nation to attract a sizable readership.

Finally, in the spring of 1973, both the Senate and the House of Representatives passed the Equal Rights Amendment. In 1967, Alice Paul—still head of the Woman's Party and still dedicated to the ERA—had persuaded NOW to give the amendment special endorsement. This support, in addition to adroit maneuvering by political supporters, especially Michigan Democratic congresswoman Martha Griffiths, secured its passage 50 years after its introduction into Congress. By 1975, 32 of the required 38 states had also passed the amendment. The future looked bright for women's advance.

## Minority Protest

The civil rights and student protest movements of the 1960s encouraged militancy among other minority groups, especially among Japanese Americans, Native Americans, Latin Americans, and gays and lesbians. Women as well as men were involved in these minority protests. Indicative of the awakening anger over oppression were the Japanese-American demands for reparations for the forced incarceration of Japanese Americans during World War II. Native Americans, in protest against a century of oppression, staged, among other demonstrations, the occupation of Alcatraz in 1969 and a "Trail of Broken Treaties" March on Washington in 1972. Also indicative of the growth of

*Three Japanese women survey their new home: an evacuee colony for Japanese-Americans during World War II.*

minority self-consciousness was the formation in 1962 of the Mexican-American United Farm Workers.

In 1942, FDR signed an executive order which authorized the removal of 110,000 Japanese Americans, including women and children, to internment camps in remote locations in Arkansas, Arizona, and other parts of the West, presumably because of the danger that they might aid Japan, a U.S. enemy in World War II. This action constituted one of the most egregious violations of civil rights in the history of the nation. Of the individuals seized, 70,000 were Nisei, or native-born citizens of the United States. Their alleged crime, disloyalty to the United States, was not against the law. Living conditions in the camps, fenced by barbed wire, were miserable. Families lived in wooden barracks in single rooms, with communal bathrooms and dining rooms. The property of these people, valued at $500 million, was seized

*Delores Huerta (right) marched with Cesar Chavez and some 4,000 field workers protesting the refusal by local growers to renew the workers' contracts.*

and sold. In 1988, after years of Japanese protest, Congress voted to award $20,000 dollars and a public apology to each of the surviving 60,000 internees.

With regard to Native Americans, New Deal policy had modified the 1887 Dawes Severalty Act, based on the concept of forced Americanization, to allow more communal ownership of land and the preservation of Indian cultures. But final decision-making power over the many Indian tribal groups still rested in the hands of the federal government. During the 1960s, a sizable number of young Indians moved to the cities, where they intermingled with other Native Americans from a variety of tribal backgrounds. Meeting individuals of similar ethnicity sparked their radicalization around a pan-Indian sensitivity. This sense of united Indian purpose had often been lacking on individual

*Elizabeth Dole being sworn in as Secretary of Transportation by Supreme Court Associate Justice Sandra Day O'Connor, with President Ronald Reagan, Senator Robert Dole, and Mrs. Dole's mother in attendance.*

reservations rooted in separate tribal "ethnicities." As among other minority groups in the 1960s, these younger Native Americans threw off the caution of their elders. They demanded total Indian sovereignty over their land and an acknowledgment of their Indian values of ecology, spirituality, and community, values in keeping with the radical ethos of the 1960s.

Japanese-American protest was moderate, mostly involving lobbying before legislatures. But Native Americans, borrowing techniques from the African-American and student protest movements, occupied land, staged marches, and established a number of protest organizations. Writing about her involvement in the movement, Mary Crow Dog related it to traditions of powerful women within Indian legend and belief. And she was impressed by the participation of "old grandmothers" in the movement. These included, according to Crow Dog, Lizzy Fast Horse, a great-grandmother who climbed to the top of Mount Rushmore, located in what had once been Indian territory, to reclaim it.[23]

Mexican Americans also organized during this period. The United Farm Workers, led by Cesar Chavez, gained major attention for strikes against lettuce and grape growers in California and for national consumer boycotts. Margaret Rose, historian of the United Farm Workers, calls it "the most successful agricultural union in the United States."[24] Of equal importance to Chavez within the union leadership were Delores Huerta, a divorced mother of seven children, and Helen Chavez, wife of Cesar and mother of their eight children. Huerta, who founded the union along with Chavez and served as its first vice president, defied traditional gender norms to act as an independent agitator and organizer, and in the process challenged male control of the union. Helen Chavez integrated family, work, and unionism, often working in the fields to help support her family. Some historians call this extension of family responsibilities into the arena of work and organization "political familism." Both Huerta and Helen Chavez drew on family networks for child care.

Not since the 1930s and the CIO cannery and garment workers organizing campaigns had so many Latin-American women become active in militant protest. Delores Huerta and Helen Chavez illustrate the two patterns of involvement this activity could take. Where Huerta, in the tradition of Louisa Morena, was outspoken and welcomed media attention, Helen Chavez shunned publicity. Within the union she did not enter into the male-dominated decision-making process. But, like many other women agricultural workers and wives of workers, she did take on union organizing and strike support activity. It was simply that, in traditional fashion, she saw her home and children as especially her responsibility.

### Women of Color Organize

In addition to protesting within their ethnic groups, women of color began to organize as women—both in terms of specific national backgrounds and in terms of ethnicities. In the National Association of Black Women and the National Council of Negro Women, black women had already organized. They were now joined by organizations of other women of color.

In 1974, for example, Mexican-American women formed the Mexican-American National Association (MANA). By 1990, MANA had chapters in 16 states and members in 36 states.

MANA's leaders testified before Congress, planned strategy, and campaigned for issues ranging from the ERA to family leave. American women of Asian and Pacific Islands descent also began to form organizations. Among them was the Organization of Pan Asian Women, formed in 1976. Native-American women were less likely than other women of color to form groups separately from men, partly because Indian women had long been leaders in many Indian tribes. Among Native-American women, La Donna Harris, wife of Senator Fred Harris and Comanche by descent, was well-known for her participation in civil rights and feminist organizations, such as the Women's Political Caucus. In the early 1970s, she founded the Americans for Indian Opportunity (AIO), which worked for administrative changes in the federal agencies that handled Indian affairs.

### Lesbians, Gays, and the Stonewall Riot

Lesbians and gays also began to organize in this era of militant activism on the part of many oppressed groups. Their period of open protest was triggered by a specific event which occurred in New York City in 1969: the "Stonewall riot."

World War II had resulted in a significant expansion of lesbian and gay communities, as young men and women mingled separately with their genders in the armed forces and relocated to cities to work in war production industries. Even though the highly regarded Kinsey studies of human sexuality, issued in 1948 and 1953, found considerable numbers of both men and women admitting an attraction to members of the same gender, the popular attitude was that homosexuality was unnatural and perverted. The McCarthy-era prosecutions of the early 1950s singled out lesbians and gays for persecution, especially with legislation denying them jobs in the federal civil service and through harassment by the FBI and the post office—even when there was no suspicion of a communist affiliation. In the 1950s, laws were still on the books in many states making sexual activity aside from genital heterosexual intercourse illegal.

In response, five gays who were former members of the Communist Party founded the Mattachine Society in Los Angeles in 1950. In 1955 the lesbian Daughters of Bilitis was formed in San Francisco. The Mattachine Society took its name from a medieval mendicant order; Bilitis came from a poem by Pierre Louys in which Bilitis is a lesbian poet who lived in ancient Greece with Sappho on the island of Lesbos. In the prevailing climate of oppression, these groups remained small. Then, on June 28, 1969, the New York City police raided a gay bar in Greenwich Village called the Stonewall Inn. But unlike previous incidents, this time the patrons, including drag queens and a handful of butch lesbians, fought back. Rioting continued for two nights, with Puerto Rican transvestites and young street people leading charges against rows of police.

The Stonewall riot created a symbol both of the oppression of gays and of their potential for power. It established the beginnings of what would be a major "gay pride" movement, capable of drawing national attention, as is evident in the attention recently focused on the AIDS epidemic. As among many male immigrant groups, bars were a central feature of gay culture, a culture that at this point was often promiscuous in sexual practice. Lesbian bars also existed in major cities, and at many of them stereotypical masculine "butch" and feminine "femme" roles emerged. But lesbians more than gays were prone to monogamous, familial relationships. Yet lesbians were not absent from the Stonewall agitation, and they would play a major and highly visible role in the emerging women's movement, especially during its formative years.

## NOTES

[1] Harrison Smith, "Must Women Work?" *Independent Woman* (Dec. 1947): 34.

[2] Alva Myrdal and Viola Klein, *Women's Two Roles: Home and Work* (London: Routledge & Kegan Paul, 1956), p. 134.

[3] Benjamin Spock, *Baby and Child Care* (1946; reprint ed., New York: Dell, 1957), p. 570.

[4] Mirra Komarovsky, *Women in the Modern World: Their Education and Their Dilemmas* (Boston: Little, Brown, 1953), pp. 297–98.

[5] Ella Taylor, *Prime Time: Television Culture in Postwar America* (Berkeley: University of California Press, 1989), p. 20.

[6] *Ibid.*, p. 94.

[7] Betty Friedan, *The Feminine Mystique* (1963; reprint ed., New York: Dell, 1970), pp. 29–63.

[8] Kate Hevner Mueller, "The Cultural Pressures on Women," in Opal P. David (ed.), *The Education of Women: Signs for the Future* (Washington, DC: American Council on Education, 1957), pp. 50–51.

[9] Abraham Myerson, "Woman, the Authorities' Scapegoat," in Elizabeth

Bragdon (ed.), *Women Today: Their Conflicts, Their Frustrations, and Their Fulfillments* (New York: Bobbs-Merrill, 1953), p. 305.

[10] Elaine Tyler May, *Homeward Bound: American Families in the Cold War Era* (New York: Basic Books, 1988), p. 24.

[11] Michael Gordon and Penelope J. Shankweiler, "Different Equals Less: Female Sexuality in Recent Marriage Manuals," *Journal of Marriage and the Family*, XXIII (Aug. 1979): 459–66.

[12] Komarovsky, *Woman in the Modern World*, viii.

[13] Doris E. Fleischman, "Notes of a Retiring Feminist," *American Mercury*, LXVIII (Feb. 1949): 161–68.

[14] Helen Sherman and Marjorie Coe, *The Challenge of Being a Woman: Understanding Ourselves and Our Children* (New York: Harper & Row, 1955), p. 17.

[15] Agnes Meyer, "Women Aren't Men," *The Atlantic Monthly*, CLXXXVI (Aug. 1950): 33.

[16] Margaret Bruton, "Present-Day Thinking on the Woman Question," *Annals of the American Academy of Political and Social Science*, CCLI (May 1947): 14.

[17] Alice Rossi, "Equality Between the Sexes," in Robert Jay Lifton (ed.), *The Woman in America* (Boston: Houghton Mifflin, 1965), p. 99.

[18] David Reisman, "Two Generations," in Lifton (ed.), *The Woman in America*, p. 72–97.

[19] Judith Hole and Ellen Levine, *Rebirth of Feminism* (New York: Quadrangle, 1971), p. 81.

[20] Sara Evans, *Personal Politics: The Roots of Women's Liberation in the Civil Rights Movement and the New Left* (New York: Alfred A. Knopf, 1979), p. 51.

21 Kate Stimpson (ed.), *Women and the "Equal Rights" Amendment: Senate Subcommittee Hearings on the Constitutional Amendment, 91st Congress* (New York: R. R. Bowker, 1972), pp. 38–39.

[22] Hole and Levine, *Rebirth of Feminism*, p. 81.

[23] Mary Crow Dog, *Lakota Woman* (New York: Grove, Weidenfeld, 1990).

[24] Margaret Eleanor Rose, "Women in the United Farm Workers: A Study of Chicana and Mexicana Participation in a Labor Union, 1950–1980," Ph.D. Diss., UCLA, 1988.

## BIBLIOGRAPHY

The best introduction to the history of women in the 1950s is Betty Friedan's *The Feminine Mystique* (New York: Norton, 1963). (Later editions contain interesting forwards and afterwards by Friedan updating her point of view.) Younger scholars find women's position in the 1950s more complex than did Friedan. At present, the major reinterpretations include Eugenia Kaledin, *Mothers and More: American Women in the 1950s* (Boston: Twayne, 1984); Elaine Tyler May, *Homeward Bound: American Families in* the *Cold War Era* (New York: Basic Books, 1988); and Joanne Meyerowitz, "Beyond the Feminine Mystique: A Reassessment of Postwar Mass Culture, 1946–1958," *Journal of American History*, 79 (March 1933): 1455–82. See also Brett Harvey, *The Fifties: A Woman's Oral History* (New York: HarperCollins, 1993). Wini Breines, *Young, White, and Miserable: Growing Up Female in the Fifties* (Boston: Beacon, 1992), makes a case for control and resistance for the high-school culture of the decade.

Douglas T. Miller and Marion Nowak, *The Fifties: The Way We Really Were* (Garden City, NY: Doubleday, 1977), provide a good sense of the troubled nature of the decade. In *Center Stage: A Biography of Helen Gahagan Douglass, 1900–1980* (New York: Oxford University Press, 1991), Ingrid Scobie documents the life of the first major Hollywood actor to enter politics and shows how anticommunism was used against a woman in politics, particularly by Richard Nixon in his 1980 California Senatorial campaign against Gahagan Douglass. For a moving account of the life of a woman caught in the communist witchhunts of the 1950s, see Ilene Philipson, *Ethel Rosenberg: Beyond the Myths* (New Brunswick: Rutgers University Press, 1993). Rosenberg was only the second woman in U.S. history to be executed at the hands of the federal government.

The major statement of the Freudian position on women is Helene Deutsch, *The Psychology of Women: A Psychoanalytic Interpretation* (New York: Grune and Stratton, 1944–45). On child rearing, see Nancy P. Weiss, "Mother, the Invention of Necessity: Dr. Benjamin Spock's Baby and Child Care," *American Quarterly*, 29 (Winter 1977): 519–46. On the family, see Elaine Tyler May, above; Stephanie Coontz, *The Way We Never Were: American Families and the Nostalgia Trap* (New York: Basic Books, 1992); and Arlene Skolnick, *Embattled Paradise: The American Family in an Age of Uncertainty* (New York: Basic Books, 1991). James Gilbert details the fear about juvenile delinquency in *A Cycle of Outrage: America's Reaction to the Juvenile Delinquent in the 1950s* (New York: Oxford University Press, 1986). On violence against women, see Elizabeth Pleck, *Domestic Tyranny: The Making of Social Policy Against Family Violence from Colonial Times to the Present* (New York: Oxford University Press, 1987). Paul Robinson, *The Modernization of Sex* (New York: Harper & Row, 1977), provides an analysis of the changing ideas of sex experts, and Vance Packard, *The Sexual Wilderness: The Contemporary Upheaval in Male-Female Relations* (New York: David McKay, 1968), explores the sexual revolution of the 1960s. In *Madwives: Schizophrenic Women in the 1950s* (New Brunswick, NJ: Rutgers University Press, 1987), Carol A. B. Warren analyzes how roles in the traditional family structure of the 1950s, together with psychiatric law and practice, could cause a woman's experience of emotional difficulties to be perceived as schizophrenic and as requiring hospitalization.

In a provocative argument, Barbara Ehrenreich contends that the real issue for these years was not women but rather men, who developed an ethic of pleasure, signaled by the publication of *Playboy*, beginning in 1963, and the avoidance of supporting women and families. See her *The Hearts of Men: American Dreams and the Flight From Commitment* (New York:

Doubleday, 1983). Other scholars assert that the real concern about men was that the growth in corporate culture was feminizing them.

In *Mirror, Mirror: Images of Women Reflected in Popular Culture* (Garden City, NY: Anchor Books, 1977), Kathryn Weibel provides a useful introduction to women and popular culture. On movies in the 1940s and 1950s, see Jackie Byars, *All That Hollywood Allows: Re-Reading Gender in 1950s Melodrama* (Chapel Hill: University of North Carolina Press, 1991); Brandon French, *On the Verge of Revolt* (New York: Frederick Ungar, 1968); and Andrea S. Walsh, *Women's Film and Female Experience, 1940–1950* (New York: Praeger, 1984). On television, see Lynn Spigel, *Make Room for TV: Television and the American Family* (Chicago: University of Chicago Press, 1992), and Ella Taylor, *Prime Time: TV Culture in Postwar America* (Berkeley: University of California Press, 1987).

On policy toward unwed mothers, including the fear that they threatened the patriarchal family, see Rickie Solinger, *Wake Up Little Susie: Single Pregnancy and Race Before Roe v. Wade* (New York: Routledge, 1992). A general background to the subject is also provided by Regina G. Kunzel, *Fallen Women, Problem Girls: Unmarried Mothers and the Professionalization of Social Work, 1890–1945* (New Haven, CT: Yale University Press, 1993), and Marian J. Morton, *And Sin No More: Social Policy and Unwed Mothers in Cleveland, 1885–1990* (Columbus: Ohio State University Press, 1993).

An insightful contemporary assessment of the feminism of the 1950s is Arnold W. Green and Eleanor Melnick, "What Has Happened to the Feminist Movement," in Alvin W. Gouldner (ed.), *Studies in Leadership: Leadership and Democratic Action* (New York: Russell & Russell, 1950), pp. 277–302. Recent assessments include Cynthia Harrison, *On Account of Sex: The Politics of Women's Issues, 1945–1968* (Berkeley: University of California Press, 1988); Susan Lynn, *Progressive Women in Conservative Times: Racial Justice, Peace, and Feminism, 1945 to the 1960s* (New Brunswick, NJ: Rutgers University Press, 1992); and Leila J. Rupp and Verta Taylor, *Survival in the Doldrums: The American Women's Rights Movement, 1945 to the 1960s* (New York: Oxford University Press, 1987). For a study of pacifism in the 1960s, see Amy Swerdlow, *Women Strike for Peace: Traditional Motherhood and Radical Politics in the1960s* (Boston, Beacon Press, 1993). Some contemporary statements of various feminist positions can be found in Elizabeth Bragdon (ed.), *Women Today: Their Conflicts, Their Frustrations, and Their Fulfillments* (New York: Bobbs-Merrill, 1953); Beverly Cassara (ed.), *American Women: The Changing Image* (Boston: Beacon Press, 1962); Viola Klein, *The Feminine Character: History of an Ideology* (Urbana: University of Illinois Press, 1946); Helen Sherman and Marjorie Coe, *The Challenge of Being a Woman: Understanding Ourselves and Our Children* (New York: Harper & Row, 1955); and the May, 1947, issue of *Annals of the American Academy of Political and Social Science*.

Much writing has appeared on the leadership of African-American women in the civil rights movement. See, in particular, Daisy Bates, *The Long Shadow of Little Rock: A Memoir* (New York: David McKay, 1962); Vicki L. Crawford, Jacqueline Anne Rouse, and Barbara Woods (eds.), *Women in* the Civil Rights Movement: Trailblazers and Torchbearers, 1941–1965 (Bloomington: University of Indiana Press, 1993); Kay Mills, This Little Light of Mine: The Life of Fannie Lou Hamer (New York: Dutton, 1993); Anne Moody, Coming of Age in Mississippi (New York: Dial Press, 1968); Pauli Murray, Song in a Weary Throat: An American Pilgrimage (New York: Harper & Row, 1987); and Jo Ann Robinson, The Montgomery Bus Boycott and the Women Who Started It (Knoxville: University of Tennessee Press, 1987).

A large literature exists on the emergence of second wave feminism. See especially Alice Echols, Daring to be Bad: Radical Feminism in America, 1967–1975 (Minneapolis: University of Minnesota Press, 1989); Sara Evans, Personal Politics: The Roots of Women's Liberation in the Civil Rights Movement and the New Left (New York: Alfred A. Knopf, 1979); and Flora Davis, Moving the Mountain: The Women's Movement in America Since 1960 (New York: Simon & Schuster, 1992). An excellent film, Some American Feminists, produced in 1976 under the auspices of the National Film Board of Canada and featuring interviews with New York City leaders Ti-Grace Atkinson, Kate Millett, Lila Karp, Margo Jefferson, Betty Friedan, and Rita Mae Brown is available from Lila Karp, Program for the Study of Women and Men in Society, University of Southern California, Los Angeles, CA 90089-0036.

On the events of the 1960s, contemporary documents and surveys are also useful. The 1963 report of the President's Commission on the Status of Women was published in Margaret Mead and Frances Bagley Kaplan (eds.), American Women: Report of the President's Commission on the Status of Women and Other Publications of the Commission (New York: Scribner's, 1965). Another useful compilation is Kate Stimpson (ed.), Women and the "Equal Rights" Amendment: Senate Subcommittee Hearings of the Constitutional Amendment, 91st Congress (New York: R. R. Bowker, 1972).

In Feminism in the Labor Movement: Women and the United Auto Workers, 1935–1975 (Ithaca, NY: Cornell University Press, 1990), Nancy Gabin provides an interesting study of a union with feminist inclinations. The UAW's Women's Department was the first of its kind, and two UAW leaders were among the founders of NOW.

In 1953, in the midst of McCarthy conservatism and anticommunism, a group of leftist filmmakers braved repression to make the movie Salt of the Earth, chronicling a strike in 1950 on the part of New Mexico copper miners. Feminist in approach, the film documents women's daily lives and their leadership in the strike and offers a vision of growing power through sisterhood. See Michael Wilson, Salt of the Earth, with commentary by Deborah Silverton Resenfelt (Old Westbury, NY: Feminist Press, 1978). The movie is available from Films, Inc., 5625 Hollywood Blvd., Hollywood, CA 90028.

On Japanese internment during World War II, see Deborah Gesensway and Mindy Roseman, Beyond Words: Images from America's Concentration Camps (Ithaca, NY: Cornell University Press, 1987), and Valerie Matsumoto, "Japanese American Women During World War II," in Ellen Carol DuBois and Vicki L. Ruiz, Unequal Sisters: A Multicultural Reader in U.S. Women's History (New York: Routledge, 1990), pp. 373–86. Matsumoto analyzes the ways in which life in the internment camps both broke families apart and helped individual women develop a sense of independence and an awareness of personal ability in contrast to the traditional Japanese value of female subservience.

On Delores Huerta, Helen Chavez, and the United Farm Workers, see Margaret Eleanor Rose, "Women in the United Farm Workers: A Study of Chicana and Mexicana Participation in a Labor Union, 1950 to 1980," Ph.D. Diss., UCLA, 1988. On Indian and Chicana militancy in these years, see the bibliography to Chapter II and the insightful memoir by Mary Crow Dog, *Lakota Woman* (New York: Grove, Weidenfeld, 1990). On the Stonewall riot, see John D'Emilio, *Sexual Politics, Sexual Communities: The Making of a Homosexual Minority in the United States, 1940–1970* (Chicago: University of Chicago Press, 1983), and Martin Duberman, *Stonewall* (New York: Dutton, 1993). For an interesting discussion of the development of a lesbian community in Buffalo, New York, see Elizabeth Lapovsky Kennedy and Medeline D. Davis, *Boots of Leather, Slippers of Gold: The History of a Lesbian Community* (New York: Routledge, 1993). For definitions of lesbianism in this era, see Donna Penn, "The Meanings of Lesbianism in Postwar America," *Gender & History* , 3 (Summer 1991): 190–203.

# 7

# PROGRESS AND BACKLASH: 1970–1993

BETWEEN THE ADVENT OF SECOND Wave feminism and the decade of the 1990s, the feminist movement scored many successes. Yet at the same time, a resurgent antifeminism appeared. This antifeminism was spearheaded by a conservative "new right," rooted in religious fundamentalism. The situation resembled the 1920s, when feminist success at gaining the vote for women stimulated resistance to further change. In addition, a generation of young women in the 1980s resembled the generation of young women in the 1920s. This so-called "post-feminist" generation of the 1980s, like that of the 1920s, was suspicious of the militant goals of older women and intent on personal self-fulfillment.

But in contrast to the 1920s, high rates of work-force participation for women continued from the 1960s to the 1990s. This participation was stimulated by continued desires for affluence, periodic economic downturns, and family destabilization. By the 1980s, only one in four Americans lived in the traditional nuclear family, with a father at work and a mother as homemaker. And, a massive new immigration, especially from Mexico, Latin America, and Asia, provided new challenges—both to feminism and to the nation.

## THE FEMINIST POSITION IN THE 1970S

The spokeswomen of Second Wave feminism made it their job to disprove the contentions of the moderates of the past: first, that women had made substantial progress in achieving equality with men; and second, that women had special responsibilities to their families due to biological predispositions.

Feminist scholars scoured the available statistical evidence to demonstrate that women had made only superficial gains over the previous decades. They found impressive data to support their arguments. They turned to government reports and census figures, and they conducted their own research. Much of this material had long been in the public domain. In effect, feminists forced Americans to pay attention to a deep strain of unattended discrimination against women.

They could demonstrate, for example, that between 1920 and 1970, only 10 women had served in the Senate and only 65 women in the House of Representatives and that most of these women were widows of former senators and congressmen. Since 1920, two women had served in the cabinet: Frances Perkins, FDR's Secretary of Labor, and Oveta Culp Hobby, Eisenhower's Secretary of Health, Education and Welfare from 1953 to 1955. Neither John Kennedy nor Lyndon Johnson appointed a woman to his cabinet. Between 1920 and 1970, three women had been governors; one woman had served as a state attorney general, and three women had served as lieutenant governors. Not until feminist researchers reached the level of local library and school boards did they find women represented in the political sphere in any significant numbers. In 1968, 3 percent of the nation's judges were women. In the area of employment, feminists found similar evidence of inequality. In 1940, women held 45 percent of the professional positions in the nation. (This figure included the large proportion of women professionals who were schoolteachers.) In 1967, women held 37 percent of professional positions. The percentage of workers in domestic service did decrease, creating a crisis for employed mothers, but it was clerical work into which these women moved. All indexes showed that women earned less than men and that the percentage difference was rising. In 1959, women's earnings were 66 percent that of men; by 1968, this statistic had dropped to 58 percent. Statistics for 1970 showed that the average woman college graduate could expect a smaller annual income than the average white male who had graduated from elementary school.

As for their economic status, poverty among women was on the increase. In 1959, women constituted 26 percent of the total poor; in 1968, the figure stood at 41 percent. African-American women in particular bore the brunt of poverty, but the situation was critical for white women as well. In 1965, the average income of black women was 70 percent that of white women, 50 percent that of black men, and 40 percent that of white men. In 1969, unemployment among African-American women seeking work stood at 6 percent. Among white women, the figure was 3.4 percent; among black men, 3.7 percent; and among white men, 1.9 percent. Experts estimated that among families headed by African-American women, 50 percent had an income below the poverty line, compared with 25 percent of families headed by white women, less than 25 percent of families headed by African-American men, and about 7 percent of families headed by white men. Finally, studies showed that most alimony payments were small and in many cases, not paid, that in 1970 the median payment for child support was $12 per week, that most banks would not lend money to women, and that women were discriminated against in pension plans, insurance policies, and Social Security payments.

In education, a corresponding pattern of inequity was apparent. The proportion of women to men in college dropped from 47 percent in 1920 to 35 percent in 1958. In 1930, two out of every five B.A.s and M.A.s and one out of every seven Ph.D.s were awarded to women. By 1962, these figures had dropped to one in three and one in ten, respectively. Textbooks in all fields customarily did not mention women; in children's stories and readers, women were depicted in dependent roles, usually as wives or mothers. Powerful women were generally evil; in contrast, men were adventurous and strong professionals, explorers, and inventors. "Sex-stereotyping" was the term feminists coined to characterize the thrust of this literature.

In law, feminists found hundreds of state laws still on the books that variously forbade women to sit on juries, limited their rights to make contracts and to hold property, and held them in minor status longer than men. Prostitution, after a half-century of desultory attacks, was still thriving in many cities. Rape laws in many states made it nearly impossible for the rapist to be convicted. The statistics on violence against women were chilling. An American woman stood one chance in three of being sexually abused before the age of 18—usually by a male relative or a male friend of the family. When she reached college age, the chances were one in five she'd be raped on a date. Nine female employees out of ten had been sexually harassed on the job, and wife battering was endemic.

So universal has been women's subordination and the privileging of men in the historical past as well as the present that some feminists argued these elements constituted a system of hierarchy and domination they called "patriarchy," especially galling in the area of the sexual objectification and victimization of women. Rape, prostitution, the double standard, pornography, Freud's counsels about women's sexuality, and male gynecologists' insensitivity to their women patients were not isolated occurrences, feminists argued, but rather constituted a network of oppression designed to keep women in their place. Women in the movement began to disclose their negative experiences. Even women active in the civil rights and student movements expressed distress over their sexual exploitation in these presumably egalitarian groups. "The personal is political" became the rallying cry, as feminists demanded not only economic and legal equality but also the right to control their own bodies.

Once major organizations like NOW and the Women's Political Caucus were formed by the early 1970s, the major expansion of the feminist movement took place in terms of special interest groups. These included ones devoted to women's health issues or shelters for battered wives, or ones organized within the professions, like academic women's caucuses in sociology and in history. At the same time, militant groups like Redstockings in New York dissipated. Their leadership experienced burnout, and their ranks were thinned by factionalism. In the early years of Second Wave feminism, freelance writers and journalists such as Kate Millett and Gloria Steinem had articulated theory. Academic women now took over this task, as the field of women's studies grew to major proportions and generated innumerable books and academic journals.

### Marriage and the Family: "Equality" versus "Difference" Feminists

By the mid-1970s, feminists had begun to divide into a liberal wing, focusing on changes in laws; a Marxist wing, arguing for an end to the class system; a radical wing, focusing on the physical oppression of women; and a socialist wing, which attempted to reconcile radicals and Marxists. On questions of marriage and the family, additional divisions emerged. Radicals like Kate Millett argue that women can be free only when communal arrangements replace traditional patterns of marriage and family life. Socialist feminists insist that liberation can be won only with the fall of the capitalist economy. Others have been hostile to men and have espoused lesbianism and/or separatism as the most honest form of female behavior.

More moderate members of the movement share some, but not all, of these sentiments. The moderates are not antagonistic toward men.

They are opposed neither to marriage nor to communal living arrangements; they advocate individual choice in these matters. They do, however, support abortion as well as the establishment of day care centers. A distaste for domesticity, seen as confining, pervades their rhetoric, and the professional woman is their ideal. On the other hand, a theme in feminist writing has focused on motherhood—both as a problem and an enriching experience. Much has been written about the difficulties of combining careers and motherhood (as in Betty Friedan's *The Second Stage*, 1981). Adrienne Rich in *Of Woman Born* (1976) presents motherhood as a potentially revolutionary force; Dorothy Dinnerstein, in *The Mermaid and the Minotaur* (1976), and Nancy Chodorow, in *The Reproduction of Mothering* (1978), turn Freudian theory on its head to argue that the early developmental years of intense involvement between mother and child create warped adult personalities and that both men and women must be involved in raising children to maintain a healthy society.

To uphold their view that women should not be bound to homemaking and child rearing, feminists contend that the mother-child relationship easily may develop into a neurotic dependency. Or, pressured by financial or other difficulties, the mother may give her offspring insufficient attention. Some feminists argue that children are too valuable a national resource to be entrusted solely to parents who have little expertise in the care and education of children. On the question of domesticity, other authorities argue that this role is learned, not innate, and that working women are in fact much more content than housewives. In opposition to many postwar analysts, sociologist Jessie Bernard has contended that the majority of past and present studies show that nonworking married women are more prone to anxiety, depression, and mental breakdowns than married men, married working women, or single women.

Feminist writings celebrating motherhood have led to a split in the movement between "equality" feminists, who see no difference between men and women, and "difference" feminists, who have recast old arguments about women's moral superiority into a new compendium under which women and men are once again seen as different. One can see this controversy in evidence, for example, in the recent feminist debate over pornography. With regard to women who pose for pornography, equality feminists insist that these women are adults and that they must take

*The plight of the physically abused woman was brought to the attention of Americans during the 1980s.*

responsibility for whatever negative consequences ensue from their action. On the other hand, difference feminists argue that some women are perennial victims and that they need protection because they have been programmed by their upbringing and perhaps by sexual abuse in childhood to act in self-destructive ways.

Yet no matter the appeal of the latter argument, the difference position can create as many problems as the equality argument, which often privileges masculine behavior patterns. For example, faced with the prevalence of rape and battering, some difference feminists have equated violence with maleness. Yet lesbians, like straight women, are occasionally battered by their partners. Such circumstances lead to the conclusion that violence is not inherently male but rather one way a person gains power over another. Yet American society tolerates violence in men much more than in women and, given the violence of movies and television, it even, up to a point, encourages it.

*Coretta Scott King surrounded by other delegates to the National Women's Congress in Houston, 1977.*

## FEMINIST ACHIEVEMENTS AND THE HOUSTON NATIONAL WOMEN'S CONFERENCE

Evidences of women's advance and of feminist successes continued to surface on a variety of fronts. They were evident not only in new laws passed by legislatures and decisions rendered by the courts but also in published material and in general cultural change. In addition to feminist novels, essays, and journals, strong-willed female characters began to appear in general literature, even in books written for mass consumption by male authors like Irving Wallace. Women formed feminist theater troupes and rock groups and made feminist movies. Women joggers ran the 26-mile Boston and New York City marathons and petitioned the Olympic Committee to rescind its stand that long-distance running was too arduous for women and to open an Olympic women's marathon event. Advertising firms designed campaigns directed toward working women. In 1978, the first women were admitted to

*Patricia Ireland, president of NOW.*

the astronaut program—a bastion of the traditional male endeavors of exploring frontier space, taming technology, and defying nature by piloting airplanes. In 1983, astronaut Sally Ride became the first woman crew member of a space flight. The holder of a Ph.D. in physics from Stanford, Ride credited the women's movement with providing an impetus for her career.

Passage of the ERA by Congress marked one milestone for women in the 1970s. Another was the 1977 Houston National Woman's Conference. Composed of 1,800 delegates elected by 56 states and territorial public meetings, it was funded by the government under an act mandating the conference "to identify the final barriers that prevent women from participating fully and freely in all aspects of national life." Women of color comprised one-third of the conference delegates.

The National Plan of Action adopted by the conference was fully feminist. It called for state ratification of the ERA; free choice in abortion; extension of Social Security aging benefits to housewives; elimination of all discrimination against lesbians; federal- and state-funded programs for victims of child abuse and for education in rape prevention; and state-supported shelters for wives physically abused by husbands.

With this level of feminist attainment, why did the ERA fail to achieve ratification at the state level? At the time some analysts blamed the women's movement itself, arguing that organization at the state level was weak, that early successes made feminists complacent, and that once women did begin to organize voting drives and to lobby legislatures, their political skills were limited. Yet it was not clear until the closing moments of the campaign that the amendment was lost. Whatever political naiveté feminists demonstrated in the 1970s was rectified a decade later. During the last several years of the ERA drive, NOW assembled one of the most sophisticated fund-raising and public-awareness campaigns in recent history.

Between 1977 and 1982, NOW membership rose from 65,000 to 230,000; between January and June of 1982, NOW raised $6 million and brought in more money each month than the Democratic National Committee. In April, 1982, pollster Louis Harris reported soaring national support for the ERA; 63 percent of all respondents to his poll indicated their support for the amendment—a 13 percent increase over the 50 percent of the previous year. Thus, in the end, the defeat of the ERA cannot be traced to weaknesses in the women's movement. Rather, other areas must be examined.

## BACKLASH

In 1991, in her best-selling book, *Backlash*, journalist Susan Faludi used the term "backlash" to describe what she called "the undeclared war against American woman." Her term is now widely used to describe currents of antifeminism from the 1970s to the present. Many would agree with Faludi that "the last decade has seen a powerful counterassault on women's rights," in an attempt to retract the "hard-won victories that the feminist movement did manage to win for women."[1] In fact, Faludi argues with effect that backlash against women, especially during periods of women's advance, has been a constant in American history. And, in the modern period, American culture has never been wanting for ideologies and leaders, both male and female, who view maleness

*Backlash by Susan Faludi became a national bestseller in 1991.*

and femaleness as opposites and who desire to return women to the home. Given the success of Second Wave feminism, it is not surprising that a powerful antifeminism would arise in the contemporary era.

## The New Right

Powerful forces were united in opposition to the ERA—just as similar forces had opposed the earlier woman suffrage amendment. The traditionalist Catholic and Mormon churches, both dedicated to domesticity as women's primary role and opposed to birth control and abortion, were influential opponents. The insurance industry, which profits from differential women's rates and is regulated by state legislatures, quietly lobbied against the amendment.

But more than anything else, the ERA encountered head-on the resurgent fundamentalist conservatism of the 1970s and became its primary target for defeat. Led by Illinois lawyer Phyllis Schlafly and her National Committee of Endorsers Against ERA, right-wing groups contended that the ERA would enforce the military draft on women, invalidate laws protecting the rights of women at home

*One of the leading opponents to the ERA movement, Illinois attorney Phyllis Schlafly and her National Committee of Endorsers Against ERA fight to preserve the family.*

and in divorce, make separate toilets for men and women illegal, and ultimately undermine American morality and destroy the family. Drawing on the financial resources of powerful right-wing groups and on the fanaticism of their members, who perceived the nation's basic institutions to be under attack, members of Schlafly's coalition proved to be highly effective lobbyists before state legislatures, overwhelmingly dominated by males. Schlafly herself is a Harvard-educated lawyer, the author of nine books, and a two-time congressional candidate, but these achievements do not seem to influence her conservative stance on women.

Yet the new right, like the antisuffragists of early century and the Ku Klux Klan of the 1920s, has not been unilaterally opposed to feminism. One interview study of Evangelical women, for example, found that close to half of the informants were in favor of the ERA.[2] The new right constituted a minority of Americans. Yet its coalition of forces seemed to speak powerfully to a nation reeling from the changes wrought by the radicalism of the 1960s, the movement of women into the work force, the ongoing Cold War, a sizable new immigration, and a restructuring of the economy around computer technology and a service orientation that seemed to bode the elimination of many skilled and unskilled labor positions. The romanticization of a "golden age" of supposed cohesive family and religious values harked back to the ideology of the 1950s and afforded the same security. Within the new right leadership, economically conservative politicians appealed to the narcissism of the well-to-do and the fears of the downwardly mobile. They were joined by evangelical Christians and conservative think tanks such as the Hoover Institute and magazines such as the *National Review*. The power of this coalition was evident in the election of three conservative presidents between 1972 and 1992, beginning with Richard Nixon in 1972 and extending to Ronald Reagan in 1980 and 1984 and George Bush in 1988.

### Prolife and Prochoice

Women's right to abortion became the major issue for the new right. Coining the term "prolife" for their position, they captured the heart of the debate, arguing that there should be no medical intervention against a fertilized egg from the moment of conception. In response, feminists crafted a "prochoice" position, contending that the state had no right to dictate a woman's use of her own body. With links to the conservative presidents, with a large bloc in Congress and in many state legislatures, and with a Supreme Court increasingly composed of conservative appointments, the conservatives were able to whittle away the right to abortion granted in *Roe v. Wade*.

The 1976 Hyde Amendment, passed by Congress, cut off most Medicaid funds for abortion. Subsequently, hundreds of prohibitive rules were passed in more than 30 states, including laws in 34 states requiring parental notification or consent for minor women. The militant wing of the antiabortion forces in 1984 began to bomb and blockade birth control clinics and to threaten clinic doctors' lives. The Supreme Court decision in *Webster v. Reproductive Health Services* in 1989 upheld a Missouri statute banning the use of public funds or facilities in abortion except to save a woman's life. It also validated the restrictive state laws. The 1991 "gag rule" prohibited federally funded clinic counselors from even speaking about abortion when advising pregnant women. Meanwhile, the antiabortion movement also was successful in attaining massive cutbacks in public funding for family planning services besides abortion.

*Prolife and prochoice demonstrators angrily confront each other as the debate over abortion rights continues in America.*

For the last hundred years, women in the United States have been terminating as many as one in five pregnancies. The difference made by *Roe v. Wade* was that it legalized formerly illegal—and very dangerous—abortion practices. This high rate of abortion in the United States in contrast with most Western nations has to do with consistently poor access to new contraceptive techniques and the lack of programs of sex education. Before the Clinton presidency, the new right prevented the marketing, for example, of the drug RU-486, widely used in France. When combined with a prostaglandin, RU-486 is 95 percent successful in the first three months of pregnancy in inducing abortion.

Moreover, pregnant women in the United States can expect little help from either the government or the private sector if they decide to bear the child they are carrying. In Western Europe, in contrast, government social programs pay for most prenatal and child care. Yet the reality remains: Are women liberated if they do not have the ability to decide when and whether to bear children?

*Woman protester symbolically throwing her bra away at the 1968 Miss America Pageant.*

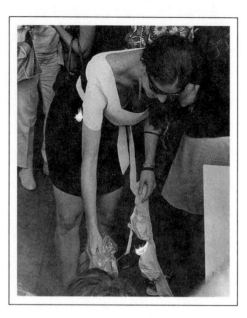

## Backlash in the Media, in Appearance, in the Movies

In addition to the new right attack against Second Wave feminism, the media created the widespread notion that feminists were ugly, man-hating, "bra-burning" radicals. At the same time, they were able to disassociate the gains for women since the 1960s from the feminist leaders who had been responsible for women's advance. By this new vilification, feminism was not only no longer necessary but it had never been necessary. Many women, while espousing a position for women's liberation, refused to call themselves feminist. Self-styled "feminist" writers attacked both mainstream and leftist feminists for causing the very problems they were supposedly solving. Thus Sylvia Ann Hewlitt, in *A Lesser Life: The Myth of Women's Liberation in America* (1985), contended that the feminist movement had ignored the issue of motherhood, even though in the early 1970s feminists had repeatedly lobbied Congress to pass a day-care bill.

The "bra-burning" charge against the feminists was especially outlandish, since, during the 1968 Miss America pageant protest, when the term was coined, no bras had been burned. In a demon-

*The slender fashion model Twiggy became the ideal body figure for women in the 1960s—a disturbing trend that continues today.*

stration of what was called "guerrilla theater," feminist protesters at the 1968 event had thrown bras, garter belts, makeup, and other symbols of women's physical oppression into a trash can. But the charge resounded to new attempts to enforce rigid standards of physical appearance on American women, standards that focused on reshaping the actual shape and contours of the body. As early as the 1960s, a cult of extreme thinness for women emerged, and this obsession has continued to the present. It has produced a multi-million dollar dieting industry as well as the life-threatening illnesses of anorexia nervosa and bulimia among American women, wherein the body's starvation response takes over with extreme

The "Cathy" cartoon pokes fun at the angst many modern American women suffer in their strides for physical perfection.

dieting and the individual becomes psychologically incapable of eating. A growing emphasis on large breasts produced another lucrative business in surgical breast implants, until the Federal Drug Administration issued warnings about the dangers of cancer from silicon-filled implants.

Plastic surgeons developed ever more esoteric techniques to remove wrinkles, to reshape eyes and noses, and to inject substances in lips to produce a fuller look. In addition, the technique of liposuction involves the surgical removal of fat cells through a vacuum suction method to reduce fatty deposits around stomachs and hips. With the increased life expectancy of the last 20 years and the consequent aging of the population, a huge and lucrative market exists among aging women for these beauty techniques, since most are designed to produce a more youthful look.

Backlash has also been apparent in the movies of the 1980s and 1990s. In movies of the 1970s such as *An Unmarried Woman* or *Alice Doesn't Live Here Anymore*, housewives left their homes to follow independent lives. But the prototypical women's films of the 1980s were *Fatal Attraction*, in which a maniacal career woman terrorizes the man who rejected her after a brief affair, and *Pretty Woman*, which glamorizes the violent, brutalizing life of streetwalking by having a handsome multimillionaire fall in love with a Hollywood Boulevard hooker. And in the 1980s, pronatal films abounded: In *Three Men and a Baby*, a single woman with career ambitions dumps her baby on the doorstep of three bachelors, who cope with raising the child. Finally, there were—and are—the macho action films of Clint Eastwood, Sylvester Stallone, and Arnold Schwarzenegger, in which the traditional lone male hero of the cowboy and detective sagas now takes on scores of villains and even the latest technology, amid a bloodbath of violence.

The National Coalition on Television Violence estimates that horror, slasher, and violent science fiction films rose from 6 percent of box office receipts in 1970 to 30 percent in 1985. One TV executive wrote in *The New York Times* that male heroes were turning violent because audiences were sick of "wimps" and "heroes who wore their sensitivity on their shirtsleeves."

### The Men's Movement

The 1980s also witnessed the birth of a self-conscious men's movement. Within this movement there are three separate groups. The first group, centered around the National Conference on Men and Masculinity, is profeminist and antisexist and is focused on changing behavior among men to create a just gender society. Its 1985 draft statement of principles calls for changes in such male traits as "excessive involvement with work, isolation from our children, discomfort in expressing emotions, lack of close friendships, excessive competitiveness and aggressiveness." It also supports women's struggle for equality and "the creation of a gay-affirmative society."[3]

The second wing of the men's movement denies the existence of any difference in power between men and women and any oppression of women. These men often sound antifeminist and sometimes antifemale. Many of these men are divorced, and many have participated in the National Congress for Men, organized in 1981. The main goal of this organization is divorce reform directed toward decreasing both alimony awards and the giving of custody of children to mothers. These men ignore statistics showing that the courts award alimony to only 14 percent of divorced women, and that only 46 percent of them collect it regularly. Similarly, child support is awarded to only 44 percent of divorced mothers, and only 47 percent of these collect it regularly.

The third wing of the men's movement is centered around Robert Bly, a renowned poet who was a peace activist during the

*Women sitting in at Seneca Falls nuclear power plant.*

1960s. In 1988, Bly began holding workshops for men directed toward regaining a masculine sense of self through primitive ritual. In these workshops, often held in wilderness retreats, men dress in masks and wild-animal costumes. They beat drums and rediscover "the beast within." Bly's theories are contained in his book, *Iron John*, which dominated best-seller lists during 1990. In this book, Bly contends that he is not antifeminist. But he critiques the "soft" male produced by 1960s feminism and recommends the Greek god Zeus as a symbol of action for men (even though Zeus regularly raped women). He sees men's major problem as the need to reunite with their fathers, and he contends that the ancient practice of male initiation is encoded in the male genetic structure.

### Robert Bly in the Context of Feminist Spirituality

Bly's "mythopoetic" stance was influenced by the theories of Carl Jung, Freud's associate early in the century who viewed ancient myth as key to understanding human behavior. As well, Bly drew from feminist spirituality, a branch of the women's movement which had discovered evidence of the existence of early societies in which the worship of a female goddess, often triune in character, had preceded that of male gods. Feminist spiritualists, some of them Jungians, draw from goddesses as models of freedom and empowerment.

In the separate work of Riane Eisler and Starhawk, feminist spirituality looks toward comity between women and men. In her writing, Eisler calls for a partnership model of society, based on egalitarian relationships, to replace a dominator model, which imposes power by force. Starhawk, leader of the Wicca, or witchcraft, movement, has written that all individuals are both male and female and that early religions always included both male shamans and female priestesses. Gathered into small covens, or bands, feminist witches celebrate the earth and work for pacific, spiritual ends. They wove a web of string around the Pentagon to protest the making of war, and they established protest encampments at nuclear power facilities and testing areas. In their 1992 best-seller, *Megatrends for Women*, Patricia Aburdene and John Naisbitt see the goddess movement as a "megatrend" for women, as well as a metaphor for women's reawakening power, which they interpret as the main trend in the present history of women.

# THE FEMINIST MOVEMENT: UNITED AND DIVIDED

## Lesbians

In the 1970s, lesbians emerged as a vanguard within the feminist movement. Many feminists were drawn to the position that men's power was based on individual heterosexual relations, in which women were inevitably nurturing and subordinate. Thus women could achieve liberation only when the heterosexual couple, the basic building block of patriarchy, no longer existed. Extending the logic of this position into their own personal lives, some feminists committed themselves to lesbianism as a way of life. Even though Betty Friedan worried about alienating the

*Lesbian and gay members of ACT-UP are confronted by the police.*

mainstream through identification with a controversial fringe group, calling lesbians a "lavender menace," in 1971, NOW voted to acknowledge the inherent feminism of lesbianism.

As the 1970s progressed, gains were won. The Stonewall riot brought a new dynamism to lesbians as well as gays, and the general successes of liberation movements in the 1960s furthered this momentum. Although the Supreme Court eventually upheld the constitutionality of laws against sodomy, many cities passed gay rights bills. At the same time, however, factionalism appeared within the lesbian movement—as it had within the mainstream feminist movement. The major division among lesbians was between essentialist lesbians, who believed that they were gay because of their biology, and feminist lesbians, who believed that they had chosen a sexual orientation toward women. In addition, there were divisions between those who wanted equality in relationships and those who wanted to retain the older butch/femme distinctions in the appearance and behavior of couples, with butch lesbians assuming dominant male behavior and dress and femme lesbians feminine models. Further divisions existed between older lesbians who were accustomed to hiding their lesbianism and those who wanted complete disclosure; finally, between sexual radicals who wanted to explore pornography and sadomasochism and feminists who saw these practices as male and patriarchal.

The conservatism of the 1980s, in addition to the factor of aging among outspoken lesbians, produced a more moderate lesbian community. Younger lesbians made fun of the seriousness of the politics of gender of the 1970s and reintroduced makeup and sexy clothing, calling themselves "lipstick lesbians." Yet by the late 1980s, some young lesbians began to demand more intensity in personal style and politics. They joined with gays in anger against the government's slow response to AIDS to form groups such as ACT-UP and Queer Nation. These groups used direct protest and "guerrilla theater" tactics to make the case for gay rights and power for homosexual people.

### Women of Color

Liberation movements provide rich soil for the nurturing of individual talent. Thus the women's movement produced novelists and poets as well as philosophers and polemicists. And, women of color have added powerful voices to the chorus, as writers such as Toni Morrison, Alice Walker, Amy Tan, and Maxine Hong Kingston won literary prizes and garnered huge sales. Critic bell hooks explains their success partially as an outgrowth of their living in a marginalized position:

> Living as we did—on the edge—we developed a particular way of seeing reality. We looked both from the outside in and from the inside out. We focused our attention on the center as well as on the margin. We understood both. This mode of seeing reminded us of the existence of a whole universe, a main body made up of margin and center.[4]

Before the 1960s, whether by inadvertence or design, racism had been an unacknowledged problem within the women's movement. And, even though Second Wave feminists opened their organizations to women of color and upon occasion welcomed them into their meetings, minority women were not especially drawn to organizations such as NOW or the Women's Political Caucus. The consciously egalitarian thrust of the YWCA has not been characteristic of other women's organizations. Yet

*Nobel Prize for Literature recipient Toni Morrison.*

the problems that women of color discerned were manifold, and for a long time they simmered under the surface.

Black women, for example, had a legacy of resentment against white women for their treatment of African-American women as domestic servants. Moreover, rape was a conflicted issue for black women, who were not so willing to condemn men as perpetrators. White men had raped African-American women over the centuries with impunity while black men, unjustly accused of raping white women, had been lynched. For many black women, sterilization abuse was a more significant issue than the right to abortion, and they charged that indigent women using public hospitals for childbirth or gynecological surgery in many locales were sterilized without their knowledge. Moreover, like most women of color, black women were not so willing to critique the nuclear family as were white women. In their culture, "familial politics," or the participation of the family unit in political organization and struggle, has been primary, just as family and kin have been key to survival in cultures of poverty. They were outraged by what they perceived as attacks on the African-American family as "matriarchal" and dysfunctional, stemming from the famed Moynihan report, *The Negro Family: The Case for National Action*, an agenda paper drafted by presidential staffer Daniel Moynihan for Lyndon Johnson.

At the 1977 Houston Conference, one-third of the delegates were women of color. The "minority women" plank they drafted as part of the final document expressed their concerns. Their priority issues concerned economic survival rather than the professional or personal advancement important to middle-class Anglo feminists. Thus, they called for an end to racism, sterilization abuse, high infant and maternal mortality, ghettoized housing, and health services that made no provision for those who can't speak English.

The attacks on white women for racial insensitivity were both extensive and telling. By speaking as if all women were white and middle class, white feminists made women of color feel invisible. The concept of "patriarchy" seemed problematic to them, since men of color often seemed to be more victimized by poverty and racism than white women by sexism. In an open letter to renowned feminist theologian Mary Daly, black writer and poet Audre Lorde charged that Daly had distorted black women's heritage in her major writings by ignoring African goddesses and by including African-American women only as victims of genital mutilation. (In some African societies, young girls are subjected to the excision of the clitoris as a cultural requirement for marriage. The operation is performed by older women.)

Many women of color demanded the right to set their own priorities. Novelist Alice Walker, for example, made a case for calling united African-American women "womanist" rather than "feminist."[5] At the same time, in her novel *Possessing the Secret of Joy* (1992), Walker severely criticized the African practice of genital mutilation. Drawing criticism from non-Western women on the grounds of cultural imperialism, Walker countered that organizations of African women had formed to end the practice and that as many as 10,000 daughters of African migrants to England and the United States faced having to undergo the operation. These girls were under the legal jurisdiction of their new country of settlement.

Members of other ethnic groups added their voices to the litany of complaints. In *This Bridge Called My Back: Writings by Radical Women of Color*, Cherrié Moraga wrote of her body as being thrown over a river of history to bridge the gap between women of color and white women, who refused to acknowledge their complicity as oppressors. And a movement arose to abandon the term "minority women," with its pejorative connotation of second-class status, and to substitute for it the term "women of color."

At the same time, minority groups demanded that they be accorded new names. For blacks the new term was African American. For individuals of Latin American heritage, it was Latino or Latina (to refer to women). For Mexican Americans, especially those with a more radical orientation, it was Chicano or Chicana (to refer to women). For Asians, the preference was a breakdown along national lines; as in Japanese American, Korean American, and Filipino American. For Indians the new term was Native American. In response, opponents charged that the new multiculturalism, with its drive toward mandating the recognition of precise ethnic distinctions as well as toward celebrating ethnic heritages and condemning mainstream culture, was stifling dissent. Conservatives coined a new, pejorative term—"political correctness"—and they went so far as to contend that the multicultural point of view was violating the First Amendment right to free speech.

## RECENT IMMIGRATION

The Immigration Act of 1965 abolished discriminatory quotas based on national origins which had existed since the 1920s and which had favored the immigration of Northwestern Europeans. Instead, the 1965 act established a system based on family preference. Although under its terms only 170,000 immigrants were permitted to enter the United States each year from the Eastern hemisphere and 120,000 from the Western hemisphere, close relatives of individuals already in the United States were exempt from these quotas.

Other special immigration acts granted political asylum to individuals whose lives were threatened under authoritarian regimes and allowed special access, for example, to Vietnamese allies after the end of the Vietnam War. During the 1970s, scores of people of color emigrated to the United States, constituting a period of "new" immigration as sizable as that of the early twentieth century.

These "new" immigrants came from, among other countries and regions, Indochina, Mexico, Central and South America, Korea, Taiwan, India, and the Dominican Republic. And many migrants from Mexico and South America, fleeing poverty and political persecution entered the United States illegally through its southern borders.

In contrast to the immigration of the early twentieth century, in which many single men had migrated to the United States, this was a migration of families: two-thirds of these immigrants were women and children. Among them were numerous professionals: for example, 13,000 Korean medical specialists came to the United States in 1965, and a majority of these immigrants were nurses. Still, issues of poverty and acculturation were constant. Even among Asian Americans, considered to be a "model minority" because of their high rates of education and professional advancement, many women worked on electronic assembly lines and in garment factories. The priorities for these women were access to health insurance and employment training. And the Organization of Pan Asian Women was especially concerned about the issue of mail-order brides being brought in from the Philippines and other Asian countries. These women had no support system in the United States; they spoke little English, and they lived with the threat of being deported if they displeased their husbands.

## THE RECENT SITUATION

Indications of increasing equality for women are strong. Growing numbers of women, for example, are moving into the professions. In 1970, 8.9 percent of all doctors were women; by 1990, the percentage had risen to 19.3. More women, too, are winning political office. Although the number of women in Congress is small, negative reaction to the all-male Senate Judiciary Committee and its treatment of University of Oklahoma law professor Anita Hill during her testimony on her charges of sexual harassment against Supreme Court appointee Clarence Thomas were strong. These reactions seemed a deciding factor in the election of two women senators from California, Dianne Feinstein and Barbara Boxer, and an African-American woman senator from Illinois, Carol Moseley-Braun. Whether or not Hill's charges were correct, women

*Carol Moseley-Braun won her 1992 campaign bid for the U.S. Senate.*

across the nation were galvanized in anger against her treatment by the Judiciary Committee.

Within his first year in office, President Bill Clinton took the unprecedented step of appointing a second woman, feminist Ruth Bader Ginsburg, to join moderate Sandra Day O'Connor on the Supreme Court, even as he appointed numbers of women to his cabinet and other administrative positions. Moreover, his wife, Hillary Rodham Clinton, before his election a well-paid corporate lawyer, defined a new activist style for first ladies, especially with her appointment as head of the president's task force to devise a national health care policy. At first reviled by the media and the public, she quickly rose in public estimation.

Growing numbers of women are being elected to local and state offices. In 1969, there were 301 women state legislators nation-wide; in 1981, there were 908. In 1991, almost one out of every five statewide elected officials and state legislators was female. In 1971, 1 percent of all elected mayors were female, but in 1991, women comprised 17 percent of all elected mayors. With regard to African-

*Principal Chief of the Cherokee Nation, Wilma Mankiller, in a 1988 meeting with President Ronald Reagan and Interior Secretary Donald P. Hodel.*

American women, nearly 11 percent of the approximately 1,300 women state legislators are black, and about 55 percent of Democratic Party state officials are African American. On the other hand, only about 17 Asian-American women currently serve as state legislators, only about 14 Chicana women, and in 1990, only 5 Native-American women. The predominance of African-American women in politics in comparison to other women of color is probably the result of their longer experience as community and church leaders.

The figures showing women's increasing election to political office are a reflection of women's increased sophistication about how to win electoral office. Fund-raising through organizations such as the Women's Political Caucus and the Democrat's EMILY'S List, with the proceeds targeted to support promising women candidates, has brought in unprecedented sums. (EMILY'S List stands for Early Money is Like Yeast—it Makes the Dough Rise; in other words, injecting money early into a campaign will bring in more money to a candidate.) Women politicians nationwide share successful strategies

*Anita Hill's testimony against Judge Clarence Thomas at his Supreme Court confirmation hearings forced many Americans to examine the overlooked problem of sexual harassment in the workplace.*

through the Center for the Study of Women and Politics on the Douglass Campus of Rutgers University.

This issue of women in politics is important, for most studies show that the women in elected office, whether Republican or Democrat, are more likely than men to support liberal or feminist issues. The reason seems to be that women are more likely to have been care givers and to have seen first hand the economic and health care problems of the aged and the need for child care. And the "gender gap" in politics, or differential voting between women and men, has consistently surfaced since at least the Eisenhower administration, with women placing family issues as a priority.

Moreover, issues of rape and wife beating have gained national attention; stronger laws against rapists have been passed in many states, and federal money has been made available for "battered wives" centers. Sexual harassment has emerged as a national issue, with women consistently winning cases against male employers and coworkers. Within the labor movement, women have formed a Committee of Labor Union Women (CLUW) and have begun to work toward the greater unionization of women and even of the vast group of nonunionized white-collar workers. Women are now 41 percent of the membership of the nation's unions. In 1986, four national unions had women presidents: the National Education Association; the Association of Flight Attendants; Actors Equity Association; and the Screen Actors' Guild. In 1988 CLUW had 75 chapters and a membership of 18,000.

Gains also have been registered by African-American women, who have moved into employment areas traditionally dominated by white women. In 1965, 24 percent of all employed black women were white-collar workers, compared with 62 percent of all employed white women. By 1981, these figures were 46 percent for black women and 66 percent for white women. And African-American women increasingly abandoned the category of domestic service, with which they had been identified for a century. In 1965, 30 percent of all employed African-American women were domestic workers; by 1977, the figure had dropped to 9 percent. In many instances, immigrants from Mexico and Latin America replaced them.

Yet major evidences of discrimination against women remain. The work force is still, for the most part, segregated by sex. Such sex segregation still underlies wage discrimination. In 1982, women still made about 57 cents of every dollar men made, and although this figure recently has moved to 70 cents, the advance is partly based on a drop in men's wages. The majority of college undergraduates are women, but the vast majority of faculty members are male. More than one-third of all candidates for the masters degree in business administration in business schools are women, but only 5 percent of the executives in the top 50 American companies are women. Reference is now made to a "glass ceiling" holding back women's promotions in business and other professions.

Over the last decade the greater incidence of poverty among women has increased precipitously. Bureaucrats and scholars now routinely discuss the "feminization of poverty"; 81 percent of all welfare recipients are women. Programs such as Social Security and Medicaid have reduced poverty among older Americans, but the estimate now is that one in four children live in poverty.

*The "sandwich" generation.*

## WOMEN AND AGING IN CONTEMPORARY TIMES

One of the major trends in the recent history of women in modern America is the aging of the population. In 1982 individuals under 20 years of age constituted 31 percent of the population, while 12 percent were over 65. If the current low levels of fertility and mortality are maintained, it is estimated that in the year 2050, individuals under 20 will comprise 18 percent of the population and those over 65 will comprise 29 percent.

These figures represent both possibilities and problems for women. As among the general population of women, a "feminization of poverty" has occurred among the elderly, with women constituting about 59 percent of the elderly and about 72 percent of the elderly poor. Women generally live longer than men—about seven years on the average—and this disparity has created demographic imbalances that dictate that many heterosexual aging women will not be able to find a mate. The problem of caring for aging, unwell parents has created significant issues for middle-aged daughters, since women invariably are the caretakers for elderly relatives in a situation in which the vast majority are still cared for at home. Analysts now refer to a "sandwich generation" of women who care not only for their own children but also for aging parents and, given increased life span, sometimes even grandparents.

Still, aging itself is undergoing changes in definition, as gerontologists conclude that proper diet and exercise can eliminate many of the physical problems associated with growing old. And, older patterns of cohort behavior have become increasingly flexible in the last decade or so. Previously, women moved almost lockstep through the life cycle: They spent their early years gaining an education before marrying in their late teens or early 20s, then raising their children, and working until retirement in their early 60s. Today, however, both men and women marry later. They move in and out of the work force and educational institutions. And there is a striking trend on the part of women to bear children at older ages. Moreover, divorce at any point during the life span can propel individuals into unexpected behavior. Actress Elizabeth Taylor in 1987 articulated the impact of the new trends, under which she found herself dating at 55: "I feel strange to be dating at my age. When I grew up women in their fifties were generally grandmothers who stayed at home with their husbands and were visited by their children and grandchildren."[6]

## THE PRESENT—REVOLUTIONARY OR NOT?

It cannot be denied that the broad social changes affecting women's lives throughout America's modern age have recently taken a revolutionary direction, prompting some analysts to predict that the traditional ways in which Americans have lived will cease to exist. Census data reveals that the birth rate is producing near-zero population growth; the age of first marriage is high; more and more individuals are living alone; the divorce rate is high; and women, especially married women and women with preschool children, are increasingly entering the work force. In 1965, about 39 percent of all American women were employed for remuneration outside the home. In 1982, the rate stood at 53 percent, and it is expected to rise to 65 percent by 1995. Surveys reveal that only 19 percent of Americans continue to live in the legendary American family, in which the husband works and the wife stays at home with the children.

As we move into a postindustrial economy and technology changes our lives more radically than ever before, women may be eliminated from vast sectors of the work force, as clerical labor is taken over by sophisticated office machines that perform filing and typing chores with only a minimal need for operators. Or, with the advent of computers and the decline in factory routinization, more and more work may be done at home, thereby returning economic and social functions to a family setting. And, some analysts speak of a "feminization" of the work force, as cheaper female workers are hired to replace more expensive male workers.

Social indicators are never easy to interpret. The reported new interest on the part of young women in traditional marriages and the rise in sales of diamond engagement rings may indicate the resurgence of a new conservatism among the younger generation— or these trends may reflect a psychological need to adjust to new forces by reaffirming traditional rituals without a need for the substance behind them. The seeming decline in open sexuality may be a reaction against 1960s radicalism, but it may also be a reaction to the new, virulent strain of the herpes virus, which is transmitted sexually and for which there is no cure, and to the AIDS virus, which is becoming a major killer of Americans.

How do we interpret the increased incidence of rape in recent years? Or the popularity of sadomasochistic pornography centered around the victimization of women? The lyrics of rock'n'roll and, more recently, rap music have been filled with images of violence against women. How do we explain the motivation of the writers and performers of this music and of the audiences (both male and female) that respond to it? Entertainment superstar Madonna, in her music and her stage acts and videos, manipulates traditional images of women's victimization to create what she contends is a female persona of independence and power. Recently she has gone so far as to become the central figure in a photographic album of pornography. How do we interpret her career? Does she represent a continuation of feminism or a reaction against it?

On the one hand, Americans seem overwhelmed by the new social trends, by the incidence of divorce and the breakdown of the family, by the danger of nuclear war and the seeming inability of government administrators to solve the nation's economic difficulties, by women's new threat to traditional definitions of masculinity. On the other hand, many Americans seem willing to explore new sexual and social roles and increasingly to applaud the extension of equality to women. And, as evidences of women's advance continue, the reaction becomes increasingly shrill, with writers like Camille Paglia enunciating a conservative line under which menstruation is redefined as an illness, not an experience; rape as the responsibility of the victim, not the perpetrator; and women's manipulation of her sexuality, through dress and adornment, a positive means to achieving power. This latter stance suggests that female vamps and sirens—perhaps even prostitutes—are the ultimate feminists, the ultimate independent women.

Meanwhile, new feminist authors emerge, as do new generational divides, with the central issues remaining how to interpret gender trends and what direction feminism—in terms of both individuals and of organizations—ought to take. In her 1991 *The Beauty Myth*, Naomi Wolf give little quarter in castigating backlash forces for focusing on the perverse control of women's bodies. Yet in her 1993 *Fire With Fire*, she contends that the Anita Hill confrontation and the election of Bill Clinton as president constituted a "genderquake" of massive proportions. Even though little evidence exists of any decrease in women's extreme dieting and their use of cosmetic body reconstruction, she now calls for women to abjure what she calls "victim" feminism and to adopt "power" feminism, acknowledging their supposed electoral, financial, and professional authority. One wonders what her position will be if the radical right regains political power and once again places a priority on re-establishing the nuclear, patriarchal family.

What the future holds is difficult to predict. Once before in the history of modern America, with the attainment of suffrage and the movement of women into the work force, equality for women seemed in sight, only to dissipate in the face of a depression and a war. But the feminist revolution of the last 30 years has so permeated the national consciousness that it is difficult to visualize its demise. The recent feminist dissension in many ways is a sign of strength; although individuals may disagree over what direction to take, feminist organizational vitality remains strong. And, with its emphasis on flexibility in gender definitions and its sensitivity to race and class, ultimately feminism holds out a different and more humane way of life for men as well as women—for all Americans.

## NOTES

[1] Susan Faludi, *Backlash: The Undeclared War Against American Women* (New York: Crown, 1991), xviii.

[2] Carol Virginia Pohli, "Church Closets and Back Doors: A Feminist View of Moral Majority Women," *Feminist Studies*, IX (Fall 1983): 549–50.

[3] Anthony Astrachan, *How Men Feel: Their Response to Women's Demands for Equality and Power* (Garden City, NY: Doubleday, 1986), p. 295.

[4] bell hooks, *From Margin to Center* (Boston: South End Press, 1984), Preface.

[5] Audre Lorde, *Sister/Outsider: Essays and Speeches* (Trumansburg, NY: Crossing Press, 1984); and Alice Walker, *In Search of Our Mother's Gardens: Womanist Prose* (New York: Harcourt Brace Jovanovich, 1983), xi–xii.

[6] Elizabeth Taylor, *Elizabeth Takes Off* (New York: Putnam, 1987), p. 104.

## BIBLIOGRAPHY

On developments from the 1970s onward, I have used, in particular, Flora Davis, *Moving the Mountain: The Women's Movement in America Since 1960* (New York: Simon & Schuster, 1991); Rochelle Gatlin, *American Women Since 1945* (Jackson, MS: University Press of Mississippi, 1987); Paula Ries and Anne J. Stone (eds.), *The American Woman, 1992–93: A Status Report (Women and Politics)* (New York: W. W. Norton, 1987); Sara E. Rix (ed.), *The American Woman, 1987–88: A Report in Depth* (New York: W. W. Norton, 1987); and Winifred Wandersee, *On the Move: American Women in the 1970s* (Boston: Twayne, 1988). For representative studies from the early years of second wave feminism exploring unseen discrimination, see Kirsten Amundsen, *The Silenced Majority: Women and American Democracy* (Englewood Cliffs, NJ: Prentice-Hall, 1971); Caroline Bird, *Born Female: The High Cost of Keeping Women Down* (New York: David McKay, 1968); and Cynthia Fuchs Epstein, *Woman's Place: Options and Limits in Professional Careers* (Berkeley: University of California Press, 1970).

On the new feminism as an intellectual movement, the outpouring of literature speaks for itself. In addition to Shulamith Firestone, *The Dialectic of Sex* (New York: William Morrow, 1974); Germaine Greer, *The Female Eunuch* (New York: McGraw Hill, 1970); and Kate Millett, *Sexual Politics* (Garden City, NY: Doubleday, 1970), also consult Susan Brownmiller, *Against Our Will: Men, Women, and Rape* (New York: Simon & Schuster, 1975); Vivian Gornick and Barbara K. Moran (eds.), *Women in Sexist Society: Studies in Power and Powerlessness* (New York: Basic Books, 1971); Robert

Jay Lifton (ed.), *The Woman in America* (Boston: Houghton Mifflin, 1961); and Robin Morgan, *Sisterhood is Powerful: An Anthology of Writings from the Women's Liberation Movement* (New York: Random House, 1970). Betty Friedan's more recent writings include *It Changed My Life: Writings on the Women's Movement* (New York: Random House, 1976), and *The Second Stage* (New York: Summit Books, 1981).

Representative novels from the early years of the new feminism include Marilyn French, *The Women's Room* (1980); Erica Jong, *Fear of Flying* (1973); Marge Piercy, *Small Changes* (1972); and Alix Kates Shulman, *Memoirs of an Ex-Prom Queen* (1972).

Feminist theory since the 1970s is reviewed in two major works: Alison M. Jaggar and Paula S. Rothenberg, *Feminist Frameworks*, 3rd. ed. (New York: McGraw Hill, 1993), and Rosemarie Tong, *Feminist Thought: A Comprehensive Introduction* (Boulder, CO: Westview Press, 1989). The major work in the "difference" versus "similarity" debate is Carol Gilligan, *In a Different Voice: Psychological Theory and Women's Development* (Cambridge, MA: Harvard University Press, 1982). One might also consult Nancy Chodorow, *The Reproduction of Mothering: Psychoanalysis and the Sociology of Gender* (Berkeley: University of California Press, 1978); Josephine Donovan, *Feminist Theory: The Intellectual Traditions of American Feminism* (New York: Frederick Ungar, 1985); Ellen Carol DuBois et al., *Feminist Scholarship: Kindling in the Groves of Academe* (Urbana: University of Illinois Press, 1987); Marianne Hirsh and Evelyn Fox Keller, *Conflicts in Feminism* (New York: Routledge, 1990); Nannerl O. Keohane, et al., *Feminist Theory: A Critique of Ideology* (Chicago: University of Chicago Press, 1982); Juliet Mitchell and Ann Oakley, *What is Feminism? A Re-Examination* (New York: Pantheon, 1986); Adrienne Rich, *Of Woman Born: Motherhood as Institution and Experience* (New York: W. W. Norton, 1976); and Carol S. Vance, *Pleasure and Danger: Exploring Female Sexuality* (Boston: Routledge & Kegan Paul, 1984).

Recent academic feminist writings include Michèle Barrett and Anne Phillips, *Destabilizing Theory: Contemporary Feminist Debates* (Stanford, CA: Stanford University Press, 1993); Judith Butler, *Bodies that Matter: On the Discursive Limits of "Sex"* (New York: Routledge, 1993); Sue Fisher and Kathy Davis (eds.), *Negotiating at the Margins: The Gender Discourses of Power and Resistance* (New Brunswick, NJ: Rutgers University Press, 1993); Judith Grant, *Fundamental Feminism: Contesting the Core Concepts of Feminist Theory* (New York: Routledge, 1993); Marianne Hirsch and Evelyn Fox Keller, *Conflicts in Feminism* (New York: Routledge, 1990); Linda S. Kaufman (ed.), *American Feminist Thought at Century's End* (New York: Blackwell, 1993); Donna Landry and Gerald MacLean, *Materialist Feminisms* (New York: Blackwell, 1993); Judith Mitchell and Ann Oakley (eds.), *What is Feminism?* (New York: Pantheon Books, 1986); and Marilyn Pearsall, *Women and Values: Readings in Recent Feminist Philosophy*, 2nd. ed. (Belmont, CA: Wadsworth, 1993).

On the new feminist theory written by African Americans and other women of color, see Asian Women United of California, *Making Waves: An*

*Anthology of Writings By and About Asian Women* (Boston: Beacon Press, 1989); Patricia Hill Collins, *Black Feminist Thought: Knowledge, Consciousness, and the Politics of Empowerment* (New York: Routledge, 1990); Alice M. Garcia, "The Development of Chicana Feminist Discourse, 1970–1980," in Ellen Carol DuBois and Vicki L. Ruiz, eds., *Unequal Sisters: A Multicultural Reader in U.S. Women's History* (New York: Routledge, 1990); bell hooks, *Thinking Feminist, Thinking Black* (Boston: South End Press, 1988); Patricia Spelman, *Inessential Woman: Problems of Exclusion in Feminist Thought* (Boston: Beacon Press, 1988); and Patricia J. Williams, *The Alchemy of Race and Rights* (Cambridge, MA: Harvard University Press, 1991).

Among the most interesting of the autobiographies and novels by women of color are Maya Angelou, *I Know Why the Caged Bird Sings* (1969); Sandra Cisneros, *The House on Mango Street* (1985); Maxine Hong Kingston, *The Woman Warrior: Memoirs of a Girlhood Among Ghosts* (1976); Toni Morrison, *Song of Solomon* (1977) and *Tar Baby* (1987); Amy Tan, *The Joy Luck Club* (1989); Alice Walker, *The Color Purple* (1982), *The Temple of My Familiar* (1989), and *Possessing the Secret of Joy* (1992). Recent literature by African-American women is analyzed in Karla F. C. Holloway, *Moorings & Metaphors: Figures of Culture and Gender in Black Women's Literature* (New Brunswick, NJ: Rutgers University Press, 1992). An interesting lesbian "coming-of-age" novel is Rita Mae Brown, *Rubyfruit Jungle* (1973).

The struggle for the ERA and its failure are examined in Mary Frances Berry, *Why the ERA Failed: Politics, Women's Rights, and the Amending Process of the Constitution* (Bloomington: Indiana University Press, 1986), and Donald G. Mathews and Jane S. DeHart, *Sex, Gender and the Politics of the ERA* (Chapel Hill: University of North Carolina Press, 1990). On the New Right, see in particular, Andrea Dworkin, *Right-Wing Women* (New York: G. P. Putnam's Sons, 1968), and Judith Stacey, *Brave New Families: Stories of Domestic Upheaval in Late Twentieth-Century America* (New York: Basic Books, 1990). On Phyllis Schlafly, see Carol Felsenthal, *The Sweetheart of the Silent Majority: The Biography of Phyllis Schlafly* (Garden City, NY: Doubleday, 1981). Sonia Johnson has documented her difficulties as a feminist in the Mormon Church in *From Housewife to Heretic* (Garden City, NY: Doubleday, 1981). On women in politics, see Linda Witt et al., *Running As a Woman: Gender and Power in American Politics* (New York: Free Press, 1993).

On the abortion debate, see Kristin Luker, *Abortion and the Politics of Motherhood* (Berkeley: University of California Press, 1984); Rosalind P. Petchesky, *Abortion and Women's Rights: The State, Sexuality, and Reproductive Freedom* (Boston: Northeastern University Press, 1985); and Lawrence Tribe, *Abortion: The Clash of Absolutes* (New York: W. W. Norton, 1990). Patricia G. Miller, *The Worst of Times* (New York: HarperCollins, 1993) documents the horrors of illegal abortions in the era before *Roe v. Wade*. The two major recent works on "backlash" are Susan Faludi, *Backlash: The Undeclared War Against American Women* (New York: Crown, 1991), and Naomi Wolf, *The Beauty Myth: How Beauty Images are Used*

*Against Women* (New York: William Morrow, 1991). An interesting academic account of backlash, drawing on theoretical perspectives now current in scholarly writing, is Susan Jeffords, *The Remasculinization of America: Gender and the Vietnam War* (Bloomington: Indiana University Press, 1989).

On the men's movement, see especially Anthony Astrachan, *How Men Feel: Their Response to Women's Demands for Equality and Power* (Garden City, NY: Doubleday, 1986). On men's studies in the university, see Harry Brod (ed.), *The Making of Masculinities: The New Men's Studies* (Boston: Allen & Unwin, 1987). On feminist spirituality the bibliography is large. Good introductions include Monica Sjöö and Barbara Mor, *The Great Cosmic Mother: Rediscovering the Religion of the Earth* (San Francisco: Harper & Row, 1987), and Charlene Spretnak, (ed.), *The Politics of Women's Spirituality: Essays on the Rise of Spiritual Power Within the Feminist Movement* (Garden City, NY: Doubleday, 1982). The major academic scholar on goddess religions is Marija Gimbutas. See Gimbutas, *The Language of the Goddess* (New York: Harper & Row, 1989). See also Riane Eisler, *The Chalice & the Blade: Our History, Our Future* (New York: Harper & Row, 1987); Gloria Feman Orenstein, *The Reflowering of the Goddess* (New York: Pergamon Press, 1990), and Starhawk, *The Spiral Dance: A Rebirth of the Ancient Religion of the Great Goddess* (New York: Harper & Row, 1979). Patricia Aburdene and John Naisbitt refer to the growing importance of goddess belief in *Megatrends for Women* (New York: Villard Books, 1992).

On women and the economy, see Teresa Amott, *Caught in the Crisis: Women and the U.S. Economy Today* (New York: Monthly Review Press, 1993). For interesting case studies of women and labor activism in recent eras see Cynthia G. Costello, *We're Worth It! Women and Collective Action in the Insurance Workplace* (Urbana: University of Illinois Press, 1991), an analysis of four strikes in Wisconsin in the 1970s and 1980s; Laurie Coyle, Gail Hershatter, and Emily Honig, "Women at Farah: An Unfinished Story," in *Mexican Women in the United States: Struggles Past and Present* (Los Angeles: University of California, Chicano Studies Research Center, 1980), on a garment workers' strike in El Paso, Texas; and Karen Brodkin Sacks, *Caring by the Hour: Women, Work, and Organizing at Duke Medical Center* (Urbana: University of Illinois Press, 1988). On the complexities of work for women in ethnic communities, see Nazli Kibria, *Family Tightrope: The Changing Lives of Vietnamese Americans* (Princeton, NJ: Princeton University Press, 1993); Louise Lamphère et al. (eds.), *Sunbelt Mothers: Reconciling Home and Work* (Ithaca, NY: Cornell University Press, 1993); and Patricia Zavella, *Women's Work and Chicano Families: Cannery Workers of the Santa Clara Valley* (Ithaca, NY: Cornell University Press, 1987). On the gendered nature of the use of technology, see Lana Rakow, *Gender on the Line: Women, the Telephone, and Community Life* (Urbana: University of Illinois Press, 1991). On women and poverty, see Linda Gordon (ed.), *Women, the State, and Welfare* (Madison: University of Wisconsin Press, 1990), and Ruth Sidel, *Women & Children Last: The Plight of Poor Women in Affluent America* (NY: Viking Penguin, 1986). On mythologies about motherhood, especially as they pertain to African Americans, see Mary Frances Berry, *Politics, Childcare, and the Myth of the Good Mother* (New York: Viking, 1993).

On issues of the family and violence against women, see in particular Susan Estrich, *Real Rape* (Cambridge, MA: Harvard University Press, 1987); Emily Martin, *The Woman in the Body: A Cultural Analysis of Reproduction* (Boston: Beacon Press, 1987); Barrie Thorne and Marilyn Yalom (eds.), *Rethinking the Family: Some Feminist Questions*, 2nd. ed. (Boston: Northeastern University Press, 1992); and Lenore E. Walker, *The Battered Woman* (New York: Harper & Row, 1979).

On working-class women, see Kathy Kahn, *Hillbilly Women* (Garden City, NY: Doubleday, 1973); Mirra Komarovsky, *Blue-Collar Marriage* (New York: Random House 1964); Lee Rainwater, Richard P. Coleman, and Gerald Hendel, *Workingman's Wife: Her Personality, World, and Life Style* (New York: Institute of Social Research, 1959); Lillian Breslow Rubin, *Worlds of Pain: Life in the Working-Class Family* (New York: Basic Books, 1977); and Nancy Seifer, *Nobody Speaks for Me! Self-Portraits of American Working-Class Women* (New York: Simon & Schuster, 1976). An interesting exploration of the world of women service workers is contained in Louise Kapp Howe, *Pink Collar Workers: Inside the World of Women's Work* (New York: G. P. Putnam's Sons, 1977).

Camille Paglia's major work is *Sexual Personae: Art and Decadence from Nefertiti to Emily Dickinson* (New Haven, CT: Yale University Press, 1990). Naomi Wolf's most recent work is *Fire with Fire: The New Female Power and How It Will Change the 21st Century* (New York: Random House, 1993).

# PHOTO CREDITS

# INDEX

Abbott, Grace, 99, 183
Abortion
  Comstock Law and, 12, 13
  as demand of Houston National
    Women's Conference, 264
  nineteenth-century attitudes toward,
    16–17
  and Margaret Sanger, 69
  and NOW, 264
  right-wing opposition to, 268–69
ACT-UP, 277
Addams, Jane, 15, 33, 99, 109, 117,
  120, 142, 158, 172, 175, 177
*Adkins v. Children's Hospital,* 158
Advertising, and women, 140, 149,
  222, 263
African-American women
  as blues singers, 203–05
  and Chicago Columbian
    Exposition, 17–18
  and Communism, 1930s, 192
  excluded from AFL, 67
  on farms, 51
  as "mammies" and temptresses, 61
  in movies, 204
  and New Deal, 177, 180–81
  in 1930s, 187–89
  recent period, 277–80
  and settlement houses, 134
  as workers and professionals, 60–62
  and World War II, 209
Aging
  African Americans, rural, South, 71
  Hispanics, Southwest, 71
  employment, 1930s, 185
  menopause, 219
  recent period, 286
  turn-of-the-century, 15
Airline hostesses, 160–61
Allen, Florence, 130, 178
Allen, Paula Gunn, 73
Amalgamated Clothing Workers of
  America, 182
American Association of University
  Women, 17, 134. *See also*
  Association of Collegiate
  Alumnae

American Federation of Labor, 67–69,
  190–91
American Home Economics
  Association, 110
American Medical Association, 136–42
Americanization Campaigns, among
  Mexican Americans, 155
Ames, Jessie Daniel, 174
Anarchism, 102, 107
Anderson, Margaret, 107, 172
Anderson, Marian, 177
Anderson, Mary, 69, 132
Andrews, Regina, 152
Anorexia nervosa, 271
Anthony, Susan B., 2, 23, 25, 26, 27,
  34, 90
Antiabortion movements, 13, 242
Anticommunism, 1950s, 226
Antifeminism
  Freudian theory and, 218–20, 233
  in 1920s, 138–42
  post-World War II, 217–20, 233
  recent period, 257, 265–73
Antilynching crusaders, 173
Antilynching laws, 97, 174
Antioch College, 5
Antisuffrage movement, 87–88
Antiwar movement, student, 1950s,
  237, 239, 244, 260
Arden, Elizabeth, 150
Arts, women in, 151–53
Association of Collegiate Alumnae, 17,
  90, 94. *See also* American
  Association of University Women
Association of Southern Women for
  the Prevention of Lynching,
  172–74
Athletics, and women. *See* Sports
Aunt Jemima, as symbol, 17–18
Austin, Mary, 14, 34
Automobile strike, Flint, Michigan
  (1937), 203
Aviation, and women, 161

*Baby and Child Care* (Spock), 219
"Baby Doll" look, 1950s, 221
"Backlash," 267–73

*Backlash* (Faludi), 265–66
Back-to-the-home movement, 222–26
Bacon, Albion Fellows, 95–96
Ball, Lucille, 222
Bara, Theda, 163
Barnard College, 27, 104, 159
Beat poets, 237
*Beauty Myth, The* (Wolf), 289
Beauty parlors, appearance of, 76
Beauty techniques, recent, 271–72
Beauvoir, Simone de, 227
Beecher, Catharine, 31
Behaviorism, 140, 218
Bennett, Joan, 202
Berdache, 73
Bernard, Jessie, 261
Bethune, Mary McCleod, 180–81
Bicycling, 22–24
Bird, Caroline, 196
Birth control
  Comstock Law and, 12
  and Margaret Sanger, 69, 108
  movements to attain
    in 1920s, 132
    in 1930s, 196
  and "the pill," 231, 233
Birthing practices, 13, 223
Blackwell, Elizabeth, 28
Black women. *See* African-American
  women
Blatch, Harriot Stanton, 90, 117
*Blondie and Dagwood*, 197
Bloomer, Amelia, 21–23
Bloomer dress, 21–23
*Blue Angel, The*, 214
Blues, and African-American women
  singers, 218
Bly, Nellie (Elizabeth Seaman), 28, 30
Bly, Robert, 273
Boston marriages, 36
Bow, Clara, 157
BPW. *See* National Federation of
  Business and Professional Women's
  Clubs
Breadwinner ethic, 147
Breckinridge, Sophonisba, 100
Brico, Antonia, 153
Brides, picture. *See* mail-order brides
*Bridge Called My Back, This* (Moraga),
  279
Bromley, Dorothy Dunbar, 139
Bryn Mawr College, 5, 31, 32, 90
Buck, Pearl, 197
Bulimia, 271
Business, women as executives and
  entrepreneurs, 149–50, 186, 285

Canneries, 192, 248
Carmichael, Stokeley, 239
Cather, Willa, 151
Catholic Church
  against ERA, 266
  against woman suffrage, 95
  and immigrant women, 78–79
  and Mexican-Americans, 98–99
Catt, Carrie Chapman, 48, 118, 119,
  120, 121, 133
Censorship, movies, 201–02
Chafe, William, 209
Chase, Mary Ellen, 149
Chavez, Cesar, 248
Chavez, Helen, 248
Chicanas, 280. *See also* Hispanic-
  American women, Latin-American
  women, Latinas, Mexican-
  American women.
Childcare, 156, 208, 219, 227, 237
Child Labor Amendment, 130, 134, 136
Child labor laws, 92, 147
Child-rearing, 140, 205, 231–33, 239,
  259–60
Children's Bureau, 99, 101, 132, 134,
  180, 183
Chinatowns, 52, 57
Chinese immigrants, 57–58
Chodorow, Nancy, 261
Cinema, women and. *See* film actresses
Civil Rights Act (1964), 235, 238
Civil rights movement, 234–37, 239,
  241, 244, 260
Clarke, Edward H., 11
Claytor, Helen Wills, 229
Clerical labor
  and BPW, 133
  entry of women, 10
  male dominance in, 10
  and 1930s, 185, 186, 188, 191
  and 1950s, 232
  in recent period, 258
Clothing styles. *See* fashion
Colbert, Claudette, 203
Cold War, 225, 234, 267
Columbian Exposition, Chicago, 17–18,
  23–24, 35, 197
*Come Back, Little Sheba*, 222
Commission on Interracial
  Cooperation, 185
Commission on the Status of Women,
  238
Committee for Industrial Organization,
  190–91
Committee of Labor Union Women,
  285

Communism
  charges against feminists in 1920s,
    152–53
  in 1930s, 192
  in 1950s, 239
  and unions in 1920s, 157
Community Chests, 134
Comstock, Anthony, 12
Comstock Law, 12
Congress of Industrial Organizations
    (CIO), 190–92, 210
Congressional Union, 119, 120
Consumers' League, 68, 96, 100, 109,
    157, 158, 176, 178, 181, 184
Cooper, Julia, 17
Cooperative housing
  and women reformers, 94
Cosmetics, 140, 150, 163
Cott, Nancy, 129
Council for Interracial Cooperation,
    173–74
*Country Girl, The*, 222
Crawford, Joan, 203
Croly, Jane, 92–93
*Curanderas*, 71

Dancing
  dance craze, 1912, 76
  and dance halls, 76
  modern dance, 151
  new styles of, 78
  in 1920s, 144
Dandridge, Dorothy, 205
Daughters of the American Revolution
    (DAR), 17, 94, 142, 177, 190
Daughters of Bilitis, 249
Davis, Bette, 201, 203
Davis, Katherine Bement, 96, 141, 195
Dawes Severalty Act (1887), 72
Day, Doris, 222
Daycare centers, 156, 208, 242
Demographic transition, 13
Dentists, women as, 149
Depression, 1930s
  family response to, 193–96
  marriage as security in, 193–96
  unemployment in, 185–87
Deutsch, Helene, 219
Dewson, Mary, 179
*Dialectic of Sex, The* (Firestone), 244
Dickinson, Emily, 151
Dietrich, Marlene, 163, 201
Dinnerstein, Dorothy, 261
Dior, Christian, 221
Divorce, 45, 46, 50, 71, 146, 194, 222,
    273, 287

Doctors, women as, 9, 281
Dole, Elizabeth, 266
*Doll's House, A* (Ibsen), 110
Domestic science movement, 31, 110
Domestic service
  and African-American women, 60,
    156, 278
  Latinas and Asian Americans, 156
  and middle-class women's discon-
    tent, 46–47
  and rural women, 50
  and unions, 1930s, 191
Domesticity, and 1950s, 220–27
Dorr, Rheta Childe, 11, 32, 90, 107,
    113, 117, 133
Dress reform, of 1890s, 23–24
Dress styles. *See* fashion
Duncan, Isadora, 151
Duniway, Abigail Scott, 88

Earhart, Amelia, 147, 158–61
Eastman, Crystal, 132
Ederle, Gertrude, 138
Education
  arguments for, 3–6
  of 1960s, 259
  women's entry into higher, 26–27
Education Act (1972), 242
Eisenhower, Dwight D., 237
EMILY'S List, 283
Employment
  of immigrant women, 53–57
  in 1890s, 5–10, 26
  in 1920s, 148–58
  in 1930s, 185–89
  in 1950s and 1960s, 230–33
  in World War I, 121
  in World War II, 205–10
  recent period, 285. *See also* factory
    work, professions
Engle, Lavinia, 130
Equal Pay Act (1963), 238
Equal-pay legislation, 228, 237
Equal Rights Amendment, 108, 131–32,
    171–72, 182, 210, 228, 237, 238,
    244, 249
  Eye makeup, 163

Fair Labor Standards Act (1938),
    182–83
Faludi, Susan, 265, 266
"Familial politics," 248, 278
Family
  African American, South, 71
  Asian, 57–60
  courses, in high school, 229

Hispanic, Southwest, 71
Native American, 73
in 1930s, 193–96
Family wage, as concept, 67
Farnham, Marynia, 217, 218
Fashion
and dress reform, 23–24
and New Woman, 19–20
of 1920s and 1930s, 199–200
of 1950s, 221–22
Victorian models, 24
versus uniform clothing, radicals, 102
*Fatal Attraction*, 272
*Father Knows Best*, 222
Fauset, Jessie, 152
*Fear of Flying* (Jong), 244
Federal Art Project, 181
Federal civil service, women in, 26, 172
Federal Council of Negro Affairs, 180
Federal Music Project, 181
Federal Theatre Project, 177, 181
Federal Writers Project, 181–82
Federation of Child Study, 47
*Female Eunuch, The* (Greer), 244
*Feminine Mystique, The* (Friedan), 224, 237, 241
Feminism, 91–115, 138–42, 171–72, 217, 227–30, 277–80
Feminist Alliance, 106, 132, 142
Feminization, sociologists' definition of, 9
*Femme couverte*, 1
*Femme fatale*, 162–63
*Femme sole*, 1
Ferber, Edna, 24
*Fire With Fire* (Wolf), 289
Firestone, Shulamith, 244
First World War and women, 120–22
Fitzgerald, Ella, 205
"Flaming youth" image, 143–48, 196–97
Flappers, 144, 145, 163
Flexner, Eleanor, 120
Florodora girls, 162
Flynn, Elizabeth Gurley, 64, 106, 107, 121, 122, 192
Food, Drug, and Cosmetic Act (1936), 171
*Fool There Was, A*, 163
Freudian theories, 113. 140, 218–20, 221, 227, 237, 259
Friedan, Betty, 224, 233, 235, 237, 241, 261, 275
Friendly visitors, 95. *See also* social workers

Functionalism, 219
Garbo, Greta, 163, 201
Garment industry, and women, 7–8, 63, 64, 157, 248
Gays, 249–50
*Generation of Vipers* (Wylie), 217
General Federation of Women's Clubs, 16, 69, 90, 93, 117, 133, 134, 171, 238
Genital mutilation, 279
Gibson, Charles Dana, 19
Gibson Girl, 19–20
Gilman, Charlotte Perkins, 102, 103, 105, 107, 113, 114, 141
Ginsburg, Ruth Bader, 282
Glass ceiling, 285
Going steady, as courtship ritual, 224
Goldman, Emma, 102, 107, 114, 142
*Gone With the Wind*, 198, 204
González, Rosalinda, 155
Graham, Martha, 151
Grant, Jane, 138
*Grapes of Wrath*, 195
Greer, Germaine, 242, 244
Griffiths, Martha, 244
*Group, The*, 196

Hadassah, founding of, 97
Hale, Ruth, 138
Hamilton, Alice, 96, 149
Hamilton, Cicely, 102
Harlem Renaissance, 152
Harlow, Jean, 201
Harper, Ida Husted, 1
Harriman, Florence Jaffray, 178
Held, John, Jr., 144, 145
Hellman, Lillian, 143
Henrotin, Ellen, 69
Henry Street Settlement, 96, 99
Hepburn, Katharine, 203
Heterodoxy, 107, 115, 141, 145
Hewitt, Nancy, 101
Hewlitt, Sylvia Ann, 270
Hill, Anita, 281
Hispanic Americans, 51, 52, 71, 73. *See also* Latinas, Mexican Americans
Hobby, Oveta Culp, 258
Home economics, 31, 110, 229
Homemaker image, of 1950s, 230, 237
Homestead Act, 1865, and women, 51
hooks, bell, 277
Horne, Lena, 205
Housekeeping, and technology, 35, 109–10
Houston National Women's Conference, 264

Huerta, Delores, 248
Hull House, 99–100
Hunt, Harriot, 28
Hurston, Zora Neale, 152–53

Ibsen, Henrik, 103
Illegitimacy, 1950s, 226
*I Love Lucy*, 222
Immigrants
  1890s, 53–67
  1920s, 153–56
  recent, 280–81
Immigration Act of 1965, 280
Incest, 219, 259
Indians. *See* Native-American women
Industrial Workers of the World (IWW), 68
International Council of Women, 2
International Ladies' Garment Workers' Union (ILGWU), 65–68, 157, 189, 192, 238
*Iron John* (Bly), 274
*It Happened One Night*, 203
Italian women
  family structure, 57
  as immigrants, 53
  overseen by fathers and brothers, 54
  patterns of work, 54

Japanese Americans
  and picture brides, 59
  and protest, 1960s, 59
  internment camps, 244–48
Jazz, and African-American women singers, 203–05
Jewish women
  in garment industry, 53
  as immigrants, 53
  radicalism among, 68
  and social service organizations, 97
  as street vendors, New York City, 56
  work force patterns, 53
Johnson, Lyndon, 258
Jones, Jacqueline, 52, 71
Jones, Mary "Mother", 64
Jong, Erica, 244
Journalism, women in, 28, 30

Kael, Pauline, 196
Keene, Carolyn, 197
Kelley, Florence, 100, 142
Kennedy, John F., 237, 258
Kerr, Louise, 188
Key, Ellen, 102, 114, 115
Keyes, Frances Parkinson, 11–12, 48
Kindergartens, 92–93, 101, 117
Kingston, Maxine Hong, 277
Kinsey studies of human sexuality, 249

Knights of Labor, 16, 67–68, 92
Komarovsky, Mirra, 219, 224, 227
Korean immigration, 59–60
Kraditor, Aileen, 90
Ku Klux Klan, 142, 267

Labor movement
  in 1900s, 64–69
  in 1920s, 156–68
  in 1930s, 189–92
  in recent period, 285. *See also* AFL, CIO, ILGWU, union activities
Ladies' garment industry, factory women in, 9, 63–69
*Ladies' Home Journal*, 24, 47, 49, 112, 242
*Lady in the Dark*, 203
*Lady, The* (Putnam), 104
LaFollette, Suzanne, 138
La Leche League, 223
Lamaze natural childbirth method, 223
Lange, Dorothea, 181, 207
Langtry, Lily, 6, 15
Larson, Nella, 152
Lathrop, Julia, 99, 134
Latinas (Latin Americans), 187–89, 244–48. *See also* Hispanic Americans, Mexican Americans
Lawrence, Mass., textile mills, 65
Lawyers, women as, 6, 9, 29–30, 32, 149, 208
League of Women Voters, 129, 130, 131, 134, 137, 171, 172, 176, 181, 238
Lemons, Stanley, 136–37
Lesbianism, 36, 141, 244, 249–50, 262
LeSeuer, Meridel, 182
*Lesser Life: The Myth of Women's Liberation in America* (Hewlitt), 270
Librarians, women as, 10, 133, 186
Lindbergh, Anne Morrow, 146
Lindsey, Ben, 145
Lorde, Audre, 279
Lowell mills, 26
Lucy Stone League, 138, 228
Luhan, Mabel Dodge, 113, 141
Lundberg, Ferdinand, 217, 218
Lynching, 172–74

McCarthy, Mary, 145–46, 196
McCormick, Ruth Hanna, 130–31
McDaniel, Hattie, 204
McDowall, Mary, 100
Madonna, 288
*Magnificent Obsession*, 122
Mail-order brides, 59, 281
*Male and Female* (Mead), 220

*Man and Superman* (Shaw), 103
Mansfield, Arabella, 29
Marriage
    companionate, 46, 148
    courses, in high school, 229
    middle-class wife and, 46–48
    in 1920s, 146–48
    in 1930s, 193–96
    in 1950s, 230–31
    in recent feminist thought, 260–61
    rural women, 48–50
    as "sex parasitism", 103
    working-class women and, 69–71
Marriage manuals, 11, 140, 227
Married women
    work prohibitions during New Deal,
        183
    increase in numbers working,
        147–48, 193
Martineau, Harriet, 6
Mattachine Society, 249
Maximum-hour laws, 101, 108, 182
May, Elaine, 226
Mead, Margaret, 153, 158, 220
Medicine
    admission of medical schools, 149
    female sexuality and, 14–17
    opportunities, during World War II,
        208
    women in, 11, 28–29. 149
Memorial Day Massacre (1937), 191
Menopause, 219
*Mermaid and the Minotaur, The*
    (Dinnerstein), 261
Methodist Women's Missionary
    Council, 175
Mexican American National
    Association (MANA), 248
Mexican Americans
    and Catholic Church, 98
    family structure, 57
    migration through Texas, 53
    and organizations, 98, 192
    and unions, 191–92, 248
    radicalized by Mexican War for
        Independence, 99
    and Sheppard-Towner clinics, 135
    in Southwest, 52
    and work, 53–56, 153–56
Meyerowitz, Joanne, 231
Middle-class women, 45–48
*Middletown* (Lynd and Lynd), 35, 46,
    195–96, 203
Milholland, Inez, 111, 113, 114
Millay, Edna St. Vincent, 151
Millett, Kate, 244, 260

Minimum-wage laws, 97, 101, 108,
    109, 158, 182
*Minor v. Happersett*, 1
Miss America Pageant, 162–63, 242,
    270
Mitchell, Margaret, 198
*Modern Woman: The Lost Sex* (Farnham
    and Lundberg), 217
Modernization, impact on families, 45
Monroe, Marilyn, 222
Montague, Ashley, 220
Montgomery Bus Boycott, 234
Moraga, Cherrié, 279
Moreno, Louisa, 192, 248
Morgan, Robin, 244
Morrison, Toni, 277–78
Moseley-Braun, Carol, 281–82
Motherhood
    and behaviorism, 140
    career versus, 48
    and Freudianism, 140, 227
    glorifying of, 48, 114, 123, 220, 224
    illegitimacy and, 116
    and pacifist rhetoric, 133
Mother's Day, 47
Mount Holyoke, seminary and college,
    5, 27
Movie actresses
    in 1920s, 161–63
    in 1930s, 199–203
    in 1950s, 222
    in 1970s and 1980s, 272
Moynihan, Daniel Patrick, 279
*Ms.* magazine, 244
Muckraking journals, feminist exposés
    in, 91
*Muller v. Oregon*, 109
Muncy, Robyn, 101, 185
Myrdal, Alva, 219

National American Woman Suffrage
    Association (NAWSA), 17, 32, 56,
    93, 118, 119, 120, 130
Nancy Drew (fictional heroine), 197
Nathan, Maude, 35, 158
National Association for the
    Advancement of Colored People
    (NAACP), 97, 98, 173, 177
National Association of Colored
    Women, 97, 173, 180, 248
National Association Opposed to the
    Further Extension of Suffrage for
    Women, 87
National Child Labor Committee,
    96–97
National College Equal Suffrage
    League, 90

National Conference on Men and Masculinity, 273
National Conference on the Cause and Cure of War, 133
National Congress for Men, 273
National Congress of Parents and Teachers, 129, 134
National Congress of Spanish-Speaking People, 192
National Council of Jewish Women, 97, 134
National Council of Negro Women, 180, 248
National Council of Women, 17
National Federation of Business and Professional Women's Clubs (BPW), 129, 133, 134, 184, 238
National Industrial Recovery Act (NRA), 182–83, 188, 189
National Labor Relations Board, 208
National Organization for Women (NOW), 105, 239–41, 244, 260, 265, 276, 277
National Parent-Teachers Association, 17, 129
National War Labor Board, 208
National Youth Administration, 181
Native-American women (Indians), 71–73, 135, 244–48
Natural childbirth, 223
*Natural Superiority of Women, The* (Montague), 220
*Negro Family: The Case for National Action, The* (Moynihan), 279
Nevelson, Louise, 181
New Deal, 174–85
"New Look", 221
New Right, 257, 266–68
"New Woman" image, 19–20
Nineteenth Amendment, passage of, 120
Nobel Peace Prize (Jane Addams), 172
Nurses, women as, 11, 96, 133, 134–36, 237

Oberlin College, 5
O'Connor, Sandra Day, 282
*Of Woman Born* (Rich), 261
O'Keeffe, Georgia, 153
Organization of Pan Asian Women, 249, 281
Owen, Ruth Bryan, 178

Pacifism, and women, 92, 129, 132, 133, 142
Paglia, Camille, 289
Parker, Dorothy, 151

Parks, Rosa, 234
Patriarchy, as feminist terminology, 259, 279
Paul, Alice, 118, 119, 120, 131, 143, 244
Pecan-shelling industry, 188, 192
*Perils of Pauline*, 163
Perkins, Frances, 179, 184–85, 258
"The personal is political", 260
Peterson, Esther, 237–38
Philippines, immigration, 60
Pickford, Mary, 158, 161–62
Picture brides. *See* mail-order brides
Piercy, Marge, 244
Pimps, prostitutes and, 75–76
"Pin-money theory", 63
Pornography, 261–62
*Possessing the Secret of Joy* (Walker), 279
Post-feminist generation, 257
Poverty, feminization of, 285
*Pretty Woman*, 272
Prochoice (abortion), 268–69
Professional associations, rise of, 133
Professions
    and marriage, 147
    in 1890s, 7, 11
    in 1920s, 129, 148–53
    in 1950s, 231–232
    in recent period, 281
    World War II, 208. *See also* doctors, lawyers
Professors, 149, 186, 259, 285
Progressive movement
    feminism and, 91–102, 115
    1920s and, 138–43
    1930s and, 175
    and New Deal, 184–85
Prohibition Amendment, 121
Prolife (abortion), 268–69
Prostitution, 73–76, 101
    and African-American blues singers, 205
    in recent period, 259
    and tramps, 1930s, 186
Protective legislation, 210–228. *See also* maximum-hour laws, minimum-wage laws
Pruette, Lorine, 147
*Psychological Care of Infant and Child* (Watson), 140
*Psychology of Women* (Deutsch), 219
*Public Enemy, The*, 202
Puerperal fever, 14
Puerto Ricans, 155, 188
Pure Food and Drug Act (1906), 92
Putnam, Emily, 104
Putnam-Jacobi, Mary, 29, 32

Queer Nation, 277

Radcliffe College, 32
Radicalism
  of 1900s, 102–08
  of 1920s, 136–37, 142
  of 1930s, 192
  of 1960s, 247, 251–56
Rainey, Ma, 205
Rape, 259, 262, 278, 284, 288
Red light districts, 79
Red Scare, 137
Redstockings, 260
Reisman, David, 233
*Reproduction of Mothering* (Chodorow),
  261
Reynolds, Debbie, 222
Rich, Adrienne, 261
Richards, Ellen, 110
Ride, Sally, 264
Robins, Margaret Dreier, 69
Robinson, JoAnn, 235
Rock'n'roll, 237, 288
Rodman, Henrietta, 106, 132
*Roe v. Wade*, 244, 268, 269
Rogers, Ginger, 203
Roosevelt, Eleanor, 137, 174–78, 237–38
Roosevelt, Franklin, 130, 174–77, 185
Rose, Margaret, 248
"Rosie the Riveter", 206, 207, 220
Rossi, Alice, 230, 242
Rubinstein, Helena, 150, 163
Rural women, 48–52, 121
Russell, Lillian, 6, 15, 161
Russell, Rosalind, 202–03

*Saint Joan* (Shaw), 103
Saleswomen, 7, 62–63, 158
Sandwich generation, 286–87
Sanger, Margaret, 69, 70, 102, 107, 113,
  142, 209
Scarlett O'Hara (*Gone With the Wind*),
  198
Scharf, Lois, 172
Schlafly, Phyllis, 266–67
Schneiderman, Rose, 184, 191
Schreiner, Olive, 102
Scientists, women, in 1930s, 186
Scott, Anne Firor, 17, 96
Scudder, Vida, 138
Sealander, Judith, 132
Seaman, Elizabeth (Nellie Bly), 28, 30
*Second Sex, The* (de Beauvoir), 227
*Second Stage, The* (Friedan), 261
Second Wave feminism, 257–65,
  275–86

Second World War, and women,
  205–10
Seelye, L. Clark, 31
Servants, women as, 46–47, 50, 60, 156,
  191, 278. *See also* domestic service
Settlement houses, 99–102, 114,
  133–34, 159, 161
*Seventh Heaven*, 201
*Sex in Education* (Clarke), 11
Sex manuals, 11, 140, 227
"Sex parasitism", marriage as, 103
Sex-stereotyping, 259
Sex-story magazines, 141
Sexual harassment, 259
Sexual revolution, 1920s, 146
Sexuality
  in 1920s, 143–47
  in 1950s, 227
  post-Victorian views on, 10–13
  recent, 288
  and working class, 69–71. *See also*
    marriage, prostitution
*Sexual Politics* (Millett), 244
Sharecropping, 51
Shaw, Anna Howard, 32, 89, 121, 129
Shaw, George Bernard, 103
Sheppard-Towner Act (1921), 129, 134,
  136, 181
Sheppard-Towner clinics, 129, 135–36
Shirtwaist blouse, 19, 24, 64
Shirtwaist workers' strike, 64, 66
Siren, 19
*Sisterhood is Powerful* (Morgan), 244
Sit-down strikes, 1930s, 191
Skocpol, Theda, 101, 102
Slavic women, 53, 56
*Small Changes* (Piercy), 244
Smith, Bessie, 205
Smith College, 26, 138, 146, 149
Social purity campaigns, 12, 75
Social Security Act (1936), 130, 171,
  180, 181, 183, 259, 264
Socialism
  in 1920s, 148
  in 1930s, 192
  and suffrage, 115–17
  and unions, 68
  and Women's Trade Union League,
    69
Social workers, 156, 178, 186. *See also*
  friendly visitors
Sollinger, Rickie, 226
Sorosis, 92
Special legislation for working women,
  101, 108, 109, 114, 172. *See also*
  maximum-hour laws, minimum-
  wage laws

SPARS (Coast Guard), 208
Spock, Benjamin, 219
Sports
  and Gibson Girl, 20
  in nineteenth century, 22, 24
  in 1920s, 138
  and recent period, 263
Spousal abuse, 106, 259
St. Denis, Ruth, 151
Stanton, Elizabeth Cady, 2, 23, 25, 90
Starhawk, 275
Stein, Gertrude, 152
Sterilization abuse, 278, 279
Stewardesses, 161
Stone, Lucy, 27, 34, 90, 96, 138
Stonewall riot, 249, 276
Stowe, Harriet Beecher, 31, 151
*Strike!* (Vorse), 182
Strikes, 64–69, 190–92
Suburban housewife, role of, 225
Suffrage, 87–91, 110, 115–22, 129, 130
Sugar beet industry, 155, 192
Swanson, Gloria, 163
Sweatshops, 63, 192

*Take A Letter, Darling*, 202
Tan, Amy, 277
Teachers
  entry into profession, 5, 9–10, 32
  feminization in, 50
  in 1920s, 149
  in 1930s, 186
  in 1970s, 269
  in ruralities, 50
  shortage, 1950s, 237
  in World War II, 208
Technology
  and housekeeping, turn-of-century,
    35
  and recent period, 288
Teenagers, 145, 224
Television, female image in, 222
Temple, Shirley, 161
Textile industry, 190–91
Textile workers' strike, Lawrence, Mass.
  (1912), 65
*Their Eyes Were Watching God* (Hurston),
  153
Third National Conference of State
  Commissions on Women, 239
Thomas, M. Carey, 31, 90
*Three Men and a Baby*, 272
Triangle Fire, 66
Triangle Shirtwaist Company, 66
*True Confessions* magazine, 141
Truman, Harry S, 237

Unemployment, women, in 1930s,
  185–87
*An Unmarried Woman*, 272
Union activities
  and Mexican Americans, 248
  in 1900s, 64–69
  in 1920s, 156–58
  in 1930s, 183, 189–93
  in 1950s, 232
  in recent era, 285
  and Women's Trade Union League,
    108
  and World War II, 210. *See also* AFL,
    CIO, ILGWU, labor movement
United Cannery, Agricultural, Packing,
  and Allied Workers of America
  (UCAPAWA), 191–92
United Farm Workers, 248
Urban League, 97–98

Vamps, 19, 158, 161–63, 201
Vassar College, 4, 5, 26, 32, 96, 138
Victorian culture, rebellion against, 144
Visiting nurses, 100
Vorse, Mary Heaton, 182

WACS (Women's Auxiliary Army
  Corps), 203–08
Waitresses, 78–79
Wald, Lillian, 15, 96, 99
Ware, Susan, 179
Washington, Booker T., 103
Waters, Ethel, 205
Watson, John B., 140
WAVES (Navy), 208
*Wedding Present*, 202
Wells-Barnett, Ida, 98
Wellesley College, 5
West, Mae, 202
Wharton, Edith, 151
White, Pearl, 163
White House Conference on the
  Emergency Needs of Women, 181
White-slave hysteria, 76
Wicca, 275
Wife-beating. *See* spousal abuse
Willard, Frances, 22, 26, 36, 92
Williams, Fannie Barrier, 17
Wills, Helen, 138
Wolf, Naomi, 289
Woman's Christian Temperance Union
  (WCTU), 12, 16, 22, 36, 50, 92, 113,
  121, 134
Woman's Party, 120, 131, 132, 244
*Women in the Modern World: Their
  Education and Their Dilemmas*

(Komarovsky), 219, 227
Women Marines, 208
Women's Bureau, 69, 129, 132, 149,
    180, 187, 208–09, 237
Women's clubs
    in 1890s and 1900s, 92–94, 97–98
    in 1920s, 129, 132–33
    in 1930s, 191–92
    in 1950s, 228
Women's colleges, founding and mis--
    sion of, 26–27. See also Barnard,
    Bryn Mawr, Mount Holyoke,
    Smith, Vassar, Wellesley
Women's Committee of the Council for
    National Defense, 121
Women's Division, Democratic Party,
    179
Women's Equity Action League
    (WEAL), 242
Women's International League for
    Peace and Freedom (WILPF), 133,
    172
Women's Joint Congressional
    Committee (WJCC), 129, 228
Women's Medical College, 32
"Women's Network", New Deal, 179–80
Women's organizations
    in 1890s and 1900s, 15–18, 87–102,
    106–08
    in 1920s, 129–36
    in 1930s, 171–74
    in 1950s, 227–29, 238–44, 246–49
    in recent period, 277, 283–84
Women's Political Caucus, 241, 260,
    283
Women's studies, as movement, 241
Women's Trade Union League (WTUL),
    63, 68–69, 108, 129, 132, 138, 157,
    158, 176, 178, 181, 182, 184, 191,
    228
Woodward, Ellen, 179
Working-class women
    1900–1920, 53, 80
    and New Deal, 185–87
    and work, in 1920s, 156–58
Workmen's compensation, 97
Works Progress Administration (WPA),
    181, 183
World's Fair (1939), 197
World War I, and women, 120
World War II, and women, 205–210
Wylie, Philip, 217

Young Women's Christian Association
    (YWCA), 12, 17, 94, 101, 129, 133,
    188, 229, 277